Cornerstone on Social

For Yasmin, my BB.

Cornerstone on Social Housing Fraud

Andrew Lane LLB (Hons)
Barrister, Cornerstone Barristers

Bloomsbury Professional

Bloomsbury Professional

An imprint of Bloomsbury Publishing Plc

Bloomsbury Professional Ltd	Bloomsbury Publishing Plc
41–43 Boltro Road	50 Bedford Square
Haywards Heath	London
RH16 1BJ	WC1B 3DP
UK	UK

www.bloomsbury.com

**BLOOMSBURY and the Diana logo are trademarks of
Bloomsbury Publishing Plc**

British Library Cataloguing-in-Publication Data

A catalogue record for this book is available from the British Library.

ISBN:	PB:	978 1 52650203 2
	ePDF:	978 1 52650204 9
	ePub:	978 1 52650205 6

Typeset by Phoenix Photosetting Ltd, Chatham, Kent
Printed and bound by CPI Group (UK) Ltd, Croydon, CR0 4YY

To find out more about our authors and books visit
www.bloomsburyprofessional.com. Here you will find extracts, author information, details of forthcoming events and the option to sign up for our newsletters.

Foreword

Be under no illusion that tenancy fraud is the single biggest threat to social housing provision for decades. With fewer social housing properties being built to provide homes for an unprecedented demand, social landlords must take effective and organised action to tackle tenancy fraud; failure to do so could be regarded as a governance failure.

The lack of secure and permanent accommodation has a detrimental effect on the health and education of children, in creating settled communities and in improving lives. If you truly believe in creating great opportunities for social tenants, then combatting tenancy fraud should be at the top of your list.

Those who perpetrate tenancy fraud can make tens of thousands of pounds profit or obtain the tenancy of a home that they would not otherwise be entitled to. There are a number of legal remedies available to assist social landlords in the identification, investigation and repossession of social homes as well as criminal offences to deter offenders.

I am delighted that Andrew Lane has written this quite brilliant book which will be your constant source of reference in what will surely be your successful fight against tenancy fraud.

Katrina Robinson MBE
Solicitor and Chair of the Tenancy Fraud Forum

Preface

When an opportunity arose to pitch for ideas for the next book in the 'Cornerstone series' I had no hesitation in suggesting the theme of social housing fraud. I was motivated by two primary factors – firstly, it seemed to be a topic that has long merited special attention and treatment in the legal writing field. Secondly, it represented an area that I have most enjoyed in my social housing practice.

That proved, though, to be the easy bit and I cannot pretend that, despite the tremendous support, guidance and tolerance of my family, colleagues, clerks, chief executive and editors, it has been anything other than difficult. I am not a natural writer as my teachers from Northampton School for Boys would no doubt testify if they could ever remember me (it was only seven years).

But it is published now, despite my procrastinations, re-writes and re-re-writes. It is trite to say, but true nonetheless, that despite the fantastic input of my friends, colleagues and sub-editors – Dean Underwood, Kuljit Bhogal, Richard Hanstock, Ryan Kohli and Tara O'Leary – all mistakes (and references to Manchester United players past and present) are very much mine.

I am indebted to those sub-editors, as I am to the wonderful resources of Westlaw, Lawtel and brilliant blogs such as Civil Litigation Brief and Nearly Legal. The many solicitors, local authority and housing association officers and even some of the defendants (no names), I know or have come across during my practice and before have also provided me with tremendous insight, understanding and assistance.

I have never read so many cases nor considered so many statutes, regulations, guidance and other documents.

Finally (-ish), I want to pay special tribute to my family. I have been blessed with wonderful parents, siblings, grandparents, children, nephews and nieces and have always failed to repay them properly for all the love and support they have shown me. Most of all, I have been so lucky to have found a special, kind and beautiful wife in my best friend, Yasmin. This book is very much for her.

To finish on a less sloppy note (and I exercised admirable restraint in not citing some lyrics from the always inspiring Half Man Half Biscuit at this point), I hope you enjoy the book and provide ideas as to how it can be improved. As I said at the start, this is an important area and the foreword by Katrina Robinson MBE, for which I am so grateful, emphasises this point.

Andrew Lane
November 2017

About the Author

Andy was called to the Bar in 1999 and has practised since that time in the social housing field. Before coming to the Bar he worked in advice work in both the statutory and voluntary sector and was for four years, in the early 1990s, a local councillor on Oxford City Council, including a period as Chair of the Housing Committee. He is married with two children, and has an unhealthy obsession with Manchester United.

Contents

Table of cases

L

M

N

P

R

Table of statutes

Table of statutory instruments and other guidance

*[All references are to paragraph numbers. Paragraph numbers in **bold** indicate where material is set out in part or in full]*

CHAPTER 1

Fraud in the Social Housing Sector

'It is, of course, a fundamental and reasonable principle of law that a person cannot take advantage of his own fraud and profit from his own wrong.'[1]

INTRODUCTION

1.1   Social housing fraud has long been a concern of local authorities, housing associations, central government and those individuals in housing need. It takes many forms. While the focus is often on the actions of tenants and would-be tenants, regrettably there are occasions when someone working for or on behalf of the landlord is also involved.

1.2   This is, of course, a serious matter, not least at a time when social housing is an increasingly scarce resource and demand for it far exceeds supply. The number of new households has exceeded the number of new homes built since 2008; at the same time, the cost of housing has increased as a proportion of average income.[2]

1.3   The continuing support and promotion for right to buy from central government (including the proposed extension to housing associations, in addition to the existing right to acquire) along with continued below-market rents, an increasing role for shared ownership and the perennially high-cost private rented sector means that the attraction of the social housing sector has never been greater. Consequently, it is more susceptible and attractive to fraud, whether that means:

- obtaining a social housing unit to which one is not entitled;

- making a profit by sub-letting the whole or part of the demised premises;

- obtaining significant benefits by exercising a right to buy or acquire when, in fact, there is no such entitlement; or

- allowing others to stay in premises no longer required or used by the tenant, without the knowledge or approval of the landlord.

1.4   The need for effective and focused action on social housing fraud is, therefore, of crucial importance now more than ever.

---

1   Lord Justice Mummery in *Islington LBC v Uckac & another* [2006] EWCA Civ 340, [2006] 1 WLR 1303 at [47].
2   See, eg, the key issues for the 2015 Parliament report. Available at: www.parliament.uk/ business/publications/research/key-issues-parliament-2015/social-protection/housing-supply/.

THE BOOK

1.5   The purpose of this book is to set out clearly the options available to local housing authorities and housing associations, primarily by reference to England, in seeking to detect and act upon housing fraud as referred to at 1.3.

1.6   It has been written with four particular questions in mind:

(1) What are the options available to a landlord or owner seeking to obtain the evidence to detect fraud?

(2) How can they, in practical terms and employing best practice, recover the property which has been 'misused' by the tenant?

(3) Can they receive financial 'compensation' from the fraudsters?

(4) What are the criminal repercussions of the fraud?

1.7   There are inevitably gaps, not least because there is so much overlap with matters of general housing law. For example, Chapter 2, in dealing with the discretionary ground for possession pertaining to a tenant who has obtained their tenancy by reason of a false statement, addresses, in an admittedly cursory fashion, questions of public law and discrimination when looking at potential defences.

1.8   Some ancillary matters, such as housing benefit, council tax reduction or council tax fraud are also left to other reference materials, though these will frequently be considered and dealt with alongside the question of possession of premises and recovery of monies. For example, if someone is found to have been sub-letting their flat whilst living elsewhere, and is still claiming housing benefit or the housing element of universal credit, then there will inevitably be an issue of overpayment and possible criminal prosecution for the same.

1.9   The focus is on good and pragmatic practice. However, such issues are, it is hoped, sufficiently 'flagged up' to demonstrate that, in certain situations, considerations outside the purview of this book must be addressed.

THE FIGURES

1.10   Housing Associations that own 1,000 or more social housing units which represent 95% of their whole stock, must provide an annual report to the Homes and Communities Agency (HCA)[3] setting out any losses they have suffered as a result of fraudulent activity.[4]

---

3   Smaller associations have the option of so doing. For the statistical data return 2015–2016, 95% of private registered providers submitted information in April and May 2016.

4   'NROSH + Fraud reporting – Guidance for Registered Providers' (London: The Stationery Office, updated March 2017).

1.11   By definition it is next to impossible to gain a completely accurate picture of the extent of the fraud impacting upon the social housing sector, although there are good indicators. In November 2012 the (now defunct) Audit Commission published its annual report *Protecting the Public Purse* (PPP). This estimated that social landlords had lost control of the allocation of nearly 98,000 properties in England.[5] The report provided the main evidential base for the Prevention of Social Housing Fraud Act 2013 (PSHF) referred to below.

1.12   The Audit Commission's final PPP Report in 2014 showed that 3,030 local authority properties had been recovered from tenancy fraudsters (an increase of 15% on the previous year). The loss to local government of housing fraud was estimated at £845 million,[6] with a further £919 million loss to housing associations.

1.13   However, it was not all doom and gloom. Between 2009/10 and 2013/14, the total number of cases of housing tenancy fraud detection increased by 92%.

1.14   More recently, the PPP Report in 2015 produced by the European Institute for Combating Corruption and Fraud (TEICCAF) warned about the implications of any extension of the 'right to buy' scheme to housing associations:

> '97. We draw to the government's attention the significant levels of fraud that councils have detected within the current RTB scheme for council housing stock. Housing associations, with a few notable exceptions, do not have either an equivalent capacity or capability to tackle RTB fraud.
>
> 98. We encourage the government to incorporate within the proposed legislative extension sufficient measures to protect housing associations against RTB fraud.'

1.15   The 2016 report identified an estimated 6.89% fall in tenancy fraud investigations and, in keeping with the previous year's report, a 448.26% rise in right to buy investigations with a total savings valuation of the two areas of £96.6 million. The report also identified the most common types of social housing fraud:[7]

Fraud type	Percentage
Abandonment	34%
Subletting	32%
Succession/Assignment	19%
Other	15%

---

5   They had estimated 50,000 units in 2011.
6   National Fraud Office Annual Fraud Indicator 2013.
7   See p 21 of the Report.

DETECTION OF FRAUD

1.16   In many instances, social housing landlords are alerted to potential tenancy fraud by matters such as:

- neighbour 'suspicion';

- activity at the property and a high number of complaints;

- persons other than tenant/household seen at property whilst tenancy audit, repair, annual gas safety inspection, etc. visit being carried out;

- lack of response to letters and calling cards;

- no contact from tenant/household (eg about repairs);

- credit on rent account or, conversely, high arrears; and

- 'right to buy' investigations.

1.17   The Audit Commission's 2014 PPP report demonstrated the clear benefits of a greater focus on social housing fraud:

> '74 In 2013, the London Borough of Camden offered an amnesty lasting two months. In this time, tenancy fraudsters could hand back the keys to properties they had unlawfully occupied or sub-let, without further action taken on cases that were not being prosecuted for other offences. Fraudsters returned seven properties (with a replacement value of over £1 million) to the Council. This represented a good return on the £25,000 spent on publicising the amnesty. LB Camden recovered 103 properties subject to tenancy fraud in total during 2013/14.
>
> 75 The publicity had wider benefits. Prior to the campaign, the Council had received just six referrals from the public to its tenancy fraud hotline. In the two months during the campaign, it received 50 calls, with many more in the months that followed. The Council launched a number of investigations as a direct result of the increased hotline referrals and has so far recovered four more properties from these referrals with a further four pending prosecution.'

1.18   The Fraud Advisory Panel's 'Tackling Fraud in the Social Housing Sector'[8] encourages, amongst other measures:

- regular tenancy audits;

- use of application forms *however* the property was allocated;

- requirement for colour photographs of tenant at sign-up;

- making the report of tenancy fraud suspicions as easy as possible; and

- use of due diligence of tenants – credit reports, shared databases, etc.

---

8   'Tackling Fraud in the Social Housing Sector: A Short Guide for Directors and Senior Managers of Housing Associations' (London: Fraud Advisory Panel, December 2015).

LEGISLATION

1.19   Recovery of social housing units obtained either by fraud and/or subject to misuse by means of abandonment, sub-letting or parting with possession is, evidence permitting, comparatively straightforward. Housing legislation, in particular the Housing Acts of 1985, 1988 and 1996, provides for such eventualities and the basis upon which to take action.

1.20   In the criminal arena, the Proceeds of Crime Act 2002 has long provided a potential avenue to the recovery of monies lost by fraud, both in criminal and civil proceedings, whilst the Fraud Act 2006 sets out a comparatively simple and comprehensive range of offences to allow for successful prosecutions against those involved in any fraud, housing-related or otherwise.

1.21   More recently, the PSHF has provided a comprehensive and focused route to criminal prosecution of those sub-letting or parting with possession of their premises, recovery of any profit gained by reason of such activities and investigation powers supplemented by regulations made under the Act.

1.22   All this is in addition to allocations and homelessness offences under sections 171 and 214 of the Housing Act 1996 and benefit fraud offences such as can be found, for example, in the Council Tax Reduction Schemes (Detection of Fraud and Enforcement Regulations) (England) Regulations 2013[9] and sections 111A and 112 of the Social Security Administration Act 1992 (offences of dishonest representations for obtaining benefit and false representation for obtaining benefit respectively).

1.23   The PSHF is most obviously focused on the social housing sector. The Explanatory Notes explain the purpose of the legislation:

> '4. The policy rationale for the new provisions is to ensure that social housing is being occupied by those to whom it was allocated, and that local authorities have access to more information in order to be able to detect fraud in the social housing stock. Whilst the current law provides that a secure tenant who has sub-let or parted with possession of the whole dwelling-house ceases to be a secure tenant and that a tenant who is not in occupation of the dwelling-house cannot be an assured tenant (which enables the landlord to gain possession of the dwelling-house more easily), this has not proved to be an adequate deterrent to sub-letting and parting with possession, as tenants only risk losing the tenancy of a property in which they do not live.'

---

9   Council Tax Reduction Schemes (Detection of Fraud and Enforcement Regulations) (England) Regulations 2013 (SI 2013/501). Summary offences of false representations for the purpose of obtaining a council tax reduction (reg 7) and failure to notify of changes of circumstances (reg 8).

CONCLUSION

1.24   The main priority of many housing practitioners is to identify the means they have at their disposal to properly investigate a potential fraud, along with enjoying a clear understanding of the point at which recovery proceedings of money and/or property can and should be instituted.

1.25   That this represents a more focused look at housing fraud is clear; indeed the Tenancy Fraud Forum was established in April 2012 to bring social landlords together to combat tenancy fraud.

1.26   Finally, it is worth re-stating why social housing fraud is such an important issue. The website of the Chartered Institute of Housing contains a quote from Eugene Sullivan, then Chief Executive of the now defunct Audit Commission:[10]

> 'Housing tenancy fraud is not a victimless crime – it reduces the quality of life for tens of thousands of families who are unable to access social housing. Tenancy fraud affects families on housing waiting lists and costs taxpayers at least £900 million per year. It is essential for social housing providers and local authorities to work together sharing best practice, knowledge and experience to tackle tenancy fraud and free up homes for those in need. In particular, they should make better use of data matching services, such as the National Fraud Initiative, and take part in the Tenancy Fraud Forum.'

10   Available at: www.tenancyfraudforum.org.uk/index.html.

CHAPTER 2

Tenancy Procured by False Statement

- Ground 5 (Housing Act 1985)
- Ground 17 (Housing Act 1988)
- Rescission

Key points

- The Housing Acts of 1985 (secure tenancies) and 1988 (assured tenancies) provide identical, discretionary grounds for possession in Schedule 2 – Grounds 5 and 17 respectively – to deal with tenants who obtain their tenancies because of a false statement.

- The grounds permit the landlord to rely on omissions as well as a false statements (eg a failure to inform the landlord of a change of circumstances).

- The statement can come from a third party, but will only be relevant in such a case if it is made at the tenant's instigation.

- If the landlord does not, in fact, rely on the false statement or omission, then the ground is not made out.

- If Ground 5 or 17 is available, the landlord cannot seek the remedy of rescission.

- For Introductory Tenancies, a landlord will simply seek (mandatory) possession in the usual way provided for at Part 5 of the Housing Act 1996 – service of a section 128 notice, section 129 review (if requested) and claim.

INTRODUCTION

2.1   In most instances in which fraudulent activity has led to someone obtaining social housing, the social landlord's primary concern is to recover possession of the premises so that it can be re-allocated to another household in accordance with its allocation scheme or nomination agreement.

2.2   This is most obviously the case when the original reason for the allocation proves to be flawed because of a misrepresentation either by or at the instigation of the tenant.

2.3 For example, if a person has only been allocated housing because they falsely represented that their family were living in overcrowded accommodation, can the landlord seek possession in reliance on such a misrepresentation?

2.4 In broad terms, and in the circumstances explored below, the answer to this question is 'yes' and by 'ordinary' possession proceedings.[1] Schedule 2 to the Housing Acts of both 1985 (secure tenancies)[2] and 1988 (assured tenancies)[3] provides a *discretionary* ground for possession for this very purpose.

2.5 Of course, if a mandatory ground for possession is also available at the time the misrepresentation is discovered,[4] which may be many years after the tenancy commenced, or the landlord is otherwise entitled to possession in domestic law,[5] it may prefer to rely on that ground or entitlement, either in addition to or instead of the discretionary ground.

2.6 This chapter focuses, however, on how a social landlord is able to recover premises occupied by a tenant under a tenancy which was procured by way of a false statement.

2.7 Before addressing the statutory ground referred to at 2.4, an analysis is first given of what may have been thought of as the more obvious and appropriate common law remedy of rescission. This would have the effect of voiding any tenancy agreement *ab initio*.

RESCISSION

2.8 Chapter 1 begins with the words of Lord Justice Mummery:[6]

> 'It is, of course, a fundamental and reasonable principle of law that a person cannot take advantage of his own fraud and profit from his own wrong.'

2.9 His judgment, though, continued to demonstrate that such an obvious principle is neither absolute nor guaranteed:

> *'The provisions of the Housing Act 1985 have produced a situation in which it is possible for a person in the assumed position of the first defendant*

---

1   See, eg, *North Hertfordshire DC v Carthy* [2003] EWCA Civ 20, in which the Carthys, who had legitimately applied to the authority as homeless, failed to advise the local authority that their home in the Philippines was, once again, habitable.
2   Ground 5.
3   Ground 17.
4   For example, Ground 8 in Sch 2 to the 1988 Act, which provides a mandatory ground in respect of rent arrears or there is a sub-letting question which might encourage use of the notice to quit 'route'.
5   For example, following the service and expiry of a notice requiring possession under s 21 of the 1988 Act, in respect of a periodic assured shorthold tenant.
6   *Islington LBC v Uckac & another* [2006] EWCA Civ 340, [2006] 1 WLR 1303 at [47].

to violate that principle. The fact that she was a party to the fraudulent representation and was not, when she stepped into her husband's shoes, a bona fide purchaser for value without notice does not prevent her from resisting an application for an order for possession of the flat under the 1985 Act. The unpalatable result is that, as a result of the assignment, she is in a stronger legal position than her husband was and that she is occupying a flat which should be available for the occupation of a homeless person making an honest application to the council for accommodation' (emphasis added).

2.10   As referred to at 2.7, it might be thought that if a tenant has procured their tenancy by means of a false representation, then the landlord would have a clear remedy at common law – namely rescission – which would avoid the need to rely on any discretionary ground for possession or to address ancillary issues such as the reasonableness of making any such order.

2.11   Rescission is an equitable and therefore, discretionary, remedy, which would seem ideal in cases of tenancies obtained by false statement (it is also available, for example, in right-to-buy frauds – see 5.33–5.38). In essence, it undoes the fraud and takes the parties back to the position they were in *before* they entered into the tenancy agreement in issue. That is not, of course, always possible; there may be instances where an agreement has been affirmed by the landlord.[7] Yet for the reasons set out in the following paragraphs, there are more fundamental bars to the use of this remedy in a false statement case.

2.12   Put bluntly, rescission is not available in respect of secure or assured tenancies procured by fraudulent misrepresentation (as indicated in the Key points section, introductory tenancies can be 'easily' ended by means of usual and mandatory possession proceedings). Instead, Parliament has provided an alternative route to repossess properties let on such tenancies and in such circumstances – statutory possession Grounds 5 and 17.[8] This has effectively ousted the common law jurisdiction.[9]

2.13   In *Islington LBC v Uckac & another*,[10] the facts of which are referred to at 2.37–2.39 below, Lord Justice Dyson explained why as follows:

'29 In my judgment, the express wording of section 82, when read with section 84, is a negative enactment in Coke's sense. It clearly shows that *Parliament intended to take away from landlords the right to bring secure tenancies to an end by rescission, whether for misrepresentation or on any other ground. Schedule 2 provides a detailed and exhaustive code of the grounds on which a landlord may bring a secure tenancy to an end and*

7   *Long v Lloyd* [1958] 1 WLR 753 – an innocent misrepresentation case.
8   That is, Housing Act 1985, Sch 2, Ground 5 (secure tenancies) and Housing Act 1988, Sch 2, Ground 17 (assured tenancies).
9   *Islington LBC v Uckac & another* [2006] EWCA Civ 340, [2006] HLR 35 paras 27–30 *per* Dyson LJ.
10   Ibid, para 12 *per* Dyson LJ.

obtain an order for possession. It is to be assumed that Parliament decided on policy grounds that a landlord should be able to bring a secure tenancy to an end and obtain an order for possession where it has been induced to grant a tenancy by a fraudulent misrepresentation, but not where it has been so induced by an innocent or negligent misrepresentation' (emphasis added).

2.14   As a postscript to this *Uckac* ruling,[11] the Court of Appeal did, in dismissing the local authority's appeal against two preliminary decisions, give them permission to re-amend their particulars of claim to plead, in the alternative, that the original grant of the tenancy to the husband had been null and void, as it depended on the local authority's decision to accept a full duty to make accommodation available to the defendants under the homelessness provisions of Part 7 of the Housing Act 1996. This decision was, it was said, itself void as it had been induced by fraud and/or was based on a fundamental mistake of fact.

2.15   In the later judgment of *Birmingham City Council v Qasim*,[12] however, the local authority had claimed seven secure tenancies were void as they had been wrongly granted by an officer of the authority outside the statutory allocation scheme. There was no evidence that the tenants granted these tenancies had made any payments for them or, unlike in *Uckac*, otherwise induced the officer to grant them a tenancy.

2.16   The Court of Appeal dismissed the local authority's appeal and held that the allocation of housing accommodation did not extend to the actual grant of a tenancy. The failure of the authority was one of allocation, which was a public law obligation.[13] There was nothing in the Housing Act 1996, which covered the allocation scheme requirements at Part 6, to suggest that the secure tenancies made as a result of an 'improper' allocation were defective.

2.17   Lord Neuberger, however, went on to consider *Uckac* and left open the remedy of rescission where dishonesty was shown on *both* parties' part:

'*42 Neither the decision in Islington [2006] 1 W.L.R. 1303 nor our conclusion on this appeal by any means necessarily imply that, in a case where both the applicant and an officer of the authority are involved in dishonestly enabling the applicant to obtain a tenancy, the authority would be precluded from setting aside the tenancy or treating it as void.* It may be arguable that ground 5 could be interpreted to cover such a case (in which case the reasoning in Islington [2006] 1 W.L.R. 1303 would appear to apply), or it may very well be that the reasoning in this judgment could be

11 Ibid, *per* Lord Justice Dyson paras 36–41.
12 [2009] EWCA Civ 1080, [2010] HLR 19.
13 In the earlier authority of *R v Port Talbot BC ex parte Jones* [1988] 2 All ER 207, the respondent authority granted a secure tenancy of a property to a member of the council. The tenancy was not allocated in accordance with the authority's waiting list and in a public law challenge the leader of the council successfully applied for judicial review, with the court quashing the decision to grant the tenancy and declaring the grant of the tenancy to be void.

distinguished where the tenant is dishonestly involved in the inappropriate allocation. These are issues which would have to be considered as and when such a case arises' (emphasis added).

2.18   That would therefore seem to leave open the argument that where a tenancy has been procured by the fraud of both the landlord officer *and* the tenant, then rescission *is* available, not least because in such cases the landlord can hardly be said to have relied on any false statement of the tenant, whereas:

(a) if the fraud is just on the part of the tenant, then the statutory ground is the appropriate, and indeed only, if security of tenure persists, means of seeking possession;[14]

(b) if the fraud is just on the part of the officer of the landlord, then subject to any *ultra vires* argument (ie it was clear that the officer did not have the authority to allocate the premises) the tenancy agreement is good and inviolable.

2.19   Conversely, as indicated at 2.5, where security of tenure has been lost, permanently or otherwise, for example because of sub-letting or the tenant's failure to occupy the property as their only or principal home, then rescission arguably remains an option because the statutory grounds of possession are not then available. In practical terms, however, proceeding in reliance on a notice to quit as further described at Chapters 3 and 4 may be the better – and legally and evidentially easier – route to recover possession of the premises in issue.

DISCRETIONARY GROUND FOR POSSESSION: PERIODIC TENANCY

2.20   As noted in 2.4 above, the Housing Acts of 1985 and 1988 provide – in Grounds 5 and Ground 17 respectively ('the Ground') – a discretionary and identically worded ground for possession, which is demonstrated where:

> The tenant is either the person or one of the persons, to whom the tenancy was granted and the landlord was induced to grant the tenancy by a false statement made knowingly or recklessly by
>
> (a) the tenant, or
>
> (b) a person acting at the tenant's instigation.

2.21   Before taking such possession action, a social landlord will not only need to serve[15] a notice seeking possession in reliance on the Ground – which can be relied upon within 12 months of the date provided for in the notice after which

---

14 See, eg, paras 32 and 35 of Lord Neuberger's judgment.

15 Unless the Court considers it just and equitable to dispense with the requirement for such a notice: Housing Act 1985, s 83(1)(b) (secure tenancies)/Housing Act 1988, s 8(1)(b) (assured tenancies).

proceedings may be issued[16] and would allow the issue of proceedings within 14 days (assured tenancies) or 28 days of service (secure tenancies)[17] – but should also pay particular regard to any relevant pre-action protocols and policies that may be relevant to the proposed action.

2.22   'The pre-action protocol for possession claims by social landlords' has no application, focusing as it does on rent arrears and mandatory possession claims, though the practice direction on pre-action conduct and protocols may assist, in particular paragraphs 3 and 6:[18]

> '3.   Before commencing proceedings, the court will expect the parties to have exchanged sufficient information to—
>
> (a) understand each other's position;
>
> (b) make decisions about how to proceed;
>
> (c) try to settle the issues without proceedings;
>
> (d) consider a form of Alternative Dispute Resolution (ADR) to assist with settlement;
>
> (e) support the efficient management of those proceedings; and
>
> (f) reduce the costs of resolving the dispute.
>
> 6.   Where there is a relevant pre-action protocol, the parties should comply with that protocol before commencing proceedings. Where there is no relevant pre-action protocol, the parties should exchange correspondence and information to comply with the objectives in paragraph 3, bearing in mind that compliance should be proportionate. The steps will usually include—
>
> (a) the claimant writing to the defendant with concise details of the claim. The letter should include the basis on which the claim is made, a summary of the facts, what the claimant wants from the defendant, and if money, how the amount is calculated;
>
> (b) the defendant responding within a reasonable time – 14 days in a straightforward case and no more than three months in a very complex one. The reply should include confirmation as to whether the claim is accepted and, if it is not accepted, the reasons why, together with an explanation as to which facts and parts of the claim are disputed and whether the defendant is making a counterclaim as well as providing details of any counterclaim; and
>
> (c) the parties disclosing key documents relevant to the issues in dispute.'

---

16 Housing Act 1985, s 83(4) (secure tenancies)/Housing Act 1988, s 8(3)(c) (assured tenancies).

17 Housing Act 1985, s 83(5) (secure tenancies)/Housing Act 1988, s 8(4B) (assured tenancies).

18 Failure to comply with the Practice Direction could impact upon any costs order made, or may lead to a sanction or a stay being applied to allow for compliance: see paras 13 to 15 of the Practice Direction.

DISCRETIONARY GROUND FOR POSSESSION: FIXED TERM/FLEXIBLE TENANCY

2.23 With regard to *fixed term* and *flexible tenancies*[19] (and indeed shared ownership agreements fall within the former definition) the Ground is also available. However, there are a number of factors that require special consideration.

2.24 For *assured tenancy*[20] fixed-term agreements, provision must be made for the tenancy to be brought to an end on the basis of the Ground, section 7(6) of the Housing Act 1988 stating:

'(6) The court shall not make an order for possession of a dwelling-house to take effect at a time when it is let on an assured fixed term tenancy unless–

(a) the ground for possession is Ground 2, Ground 7A, Ground 7B or Ground 8 in Part I of Schedule 2 to this Act or any of the grounds in Part II of that Schedule, other than Ground 9 or Ground 16; and

(b) *the terms of the tenancy make provision for it to be brought to an end on the ground in question (whether that provision takes the form of a provision for re-entry, for forfeiture, for determination by notice or otherwise)* (emphasis added).'

2.25 Assuming these two conditions are satisfied, in particular the second one in a claim relying on the Ground, the landlord can then simply serve a notice seeking possession and proceed in the same way as for a periodic tenancy (see 2.21 and 2.22).

2.26 The difficulty arises for *secure tenancies* by reason of the security of tenure provision in section 82 of the Housing Act 1985. This confirms that a secure tenancy, whether periodic or fixed term where 'subject to termination by the landlord'[21] (eg by means of a break clause) will only end where a possession order has been executed or where there has been a demotion order or section 82(3) order terminating the fixed-term tenancy in reliance on the forfeiture provision as referred to at 2.28.

2.27 If it were not for the section 82(3) provision, then, as with periodic tenancies and fixed-term assured tenancies, the landlord would simply need to serve a notice seeking possession relying on the Ground.[22]

---

19 Introduced by the Localism Act 2011 (creating secure flexible tenancies, a form of secure fixed-term tenancies) and through changes to the regulatory regime applying to registered providers of social housing, such as local housing authorities and housing associations.
20 Whether assured or assured shorthold.
21 Housing Act 1985, s 82(1)(b).
22 On 29 June 2012, Jon Holbrook wrote in the *New Law Journal* that, in his opinion and considering s 107D of the Housing Act 1985 – '(10) This section is without prejudice to any right of the landlord under a flexible tenancy to recover possession of the dwelling-house let on the tenancy in accordance with this Part,' possession could simply be sought by service of a notice seeking possession. It is worth reading that article along with the contrary view expressed by Andrew Dymond (2014) 'Flexible Tenancies and Forfeiture' 17(1) *Journal of Housing Law* 4.

2.28 *However*, section 82(3) of the Housing Act 1985 effectively provides that, absent the break notice route of terminating the fixed-term tenancy (or arguably, the provision of a termination clause absent forfeiture by reliance on the section 82(1)(b) reference noted at 2.26) a landlord, who will then be 'forced' to rely on the usual provision for re-entry or forfeiture, cannot get possession, but can get an order terminating the tenancy:

> '(3)   Where a secure tenancy is a tenancy for a term certain but with a provision for re-entry or forfeiture, the court shall not order possession of the dwelling-house in pursuance of that provision, but in a case where the court would have made such an order it shall instead make an order terminating the tenancy on a date specified in the order and section 86 (periodic tenancy arising on termination of fixed term) shall apply.'

2.29   No determination as to the breach is required from the First-tier tribunal (Property Chamber), as would normally be the case for long leases, because the flexible tenancy would, in all probability, not be for a period exceeding 21 years which is required to bring it within such a provision.[23]

2.30   A section 146[24] notice is though required as this would be a non-rent arrears breach.[25] Section 146 provides:

> (1) A right of re-entry or forfeiture under any proviso or stipulation in a lease for a breach of any covenant or condition in the lease shall not be enforceable, by action or otherwise, unless and until the lessor serves on the lessee a notice—
>
> (a) specifying the particular breach complained of; and
>
> (b) if the breach is capable of remedy, requiring the lessee to remedy the breach; and
>
> (c) in any case, requiring the lessee to make compensation in money for the breach;
>
> and the lessee fails, within a reasonable time thereafter, to remedy the breach, if it is capable of remedy, and to make reasonable compensation in money, to the satisfaction of the lessor, for the breach.

It will be immediately apparent that there does need to be a term or condition of the tenancy which has been said to have be breached (or, at present, a break clause. When in a different, though related, context complaint was made that in the absence of rescission, fixed-term secure tenancies could not be terminated by the landlord Lord Neuberger responded:[26]

> '... there is no reason why a fixed-term tenancy should not contain a provision for re-entry or forfeiture for misrepresentation. Secondly, even if the 1985 Act does not permit a landlord, before the expiry of a fixed-term

---

23 Commonhold and Leasehold Reform Act 2002, ss 76–77 and 168(4).
24 Law of Property Act 1925.
25 Landlord and Tenant Act 1925.
26 *Uckac*, para 35.

secure tenancy, to obtain possession on the grounds that the tenancy was induced by a tenant's fraudulent misrepresentation, this is an insufficient reason for failing to give effect to the plain meaning of section 82(3)(4). For the reasons already given, the statutory scheme clearly excludes the common law right of rescission.'

2.31 It follows, and section 82(4) of the 1985 Act makes this clear, that the usual forfeiture issues, waiver (such as acceptance of rent), the availability of relief applications,[27] etc, very much apply:

'(4) Section 146 of the Law of Property Act 1925 (restriction on and relief against forfeiture), except subsection (4) (vesting in under-lessee), and any other enactment or rule of law relating to forfeiture, shall apply in relation to proceedings for an order under subsection (3) of this section as if they were proceedings to enforce a right of re-entry or forfeiture.'

2.32 There is no apparent reason why a possession claim could not also then be pleaded alongside the termination claim (seeking thereby both remedies).[28] This would be a sensible approach given a periodic tenancy arises automatically at the termination of the flexible tenancy.[29] Section 83 of the 1985 Act, which deals with service of a notice seeking possession, seemingly allows for such a service and process, providing:

'(6) Where a notice under this section is served with respect to a secure tenancy for a term certain, it has effect also with respect to any periodic tenancy arising on the termination of that tenancy by virtue of section 86; and subsections (3) to (5)[30] of this section do not apply to the notice.'

2.33 Paragraphs 3.51–3.57 deal with issues surrounding fixed-term tenancies and cases where security of tenure has been lost (eg the whole of the premises have been sub-let or the tenant no longer lives there as their only or principal home).

2.34 Section 119 of the Housing and Planning Act 2016, which is not yet in force at the time of writing, seeks, somewhat unsuccessfully, to clarify and simplify matters for flexible tenancies by amending section 82 of the Housing Act 1985 for new fixed-term secure tenancies by inserting a new sub-section (amongst other amendments set out in the Act):

'(A1) A fixed-term secure tenancy of a dwelling-house in England that is granted on or after the day on which paragraph 4 of Schedule 7 to the Housing and Planning Act 2016 comes fully into force cannot be brought to an end by the landlord except by—

---

27 Law of Property Act 1925, s 146(2).
28 As prescribed by Part II of the Schedule to the Secure Tenancies (Notices) Regulations 1987 (SI 1987/755).
29 Housing Act 1985, s 86(1).
30 These provisions include the requirement to provide a date in the notice after which any possession proceedings may be begun.

    (a) obtaining—

        (i) an order of the court for the possession of the dwelling-house, and

        (ii) the execution of the order, or

    (b) obtaining a demotion order under section 82A.

(A2) A secure tenancy can be brought to an end by the landlord as mentioned in subsection (A1)(a) whether or not the tenancy contains terms for it to be brought to an end (emphasis added).'

MATTERS TO PROVE

2.35   The Ground has six primary elements:

(1) There must be a material statement (see 2.40–2.53).

(2) The statement must be false.

(3) It must be made before the tenancy is granted.

(4) It may be made by either the tenant (or one of joint tenants), or someone acting at their instigation (see 2.54–2.58).

(5) It must be made in the knowledge that it is false, or the maker must be reckless as to its accuracy (see 2.59–2.61).

(6) The statement must induce the landlord to grant the tenancy (see 2.62–2.72).

2.36   The language of the Ground also signifies that the tenancy to which it refers is *the* tenancy granted immediately following the misrepresentation. It follows, therefore, that if, for example, a tenant obtains an assured tenancy in reliance on a false statement, but later assigns the tenancy to another, then the opportunity to seek possession on this Ground is lost.

2.37   In *Uckac*,[31] a couple applied to the local authority as being homeless. The authority granted the husband a secure tenancy of a two-bedroom flat which, a year later, he otherwise validly assigned to his wife.

2.38   The authority later discovered that the information contained in the couple's original homelessness application concerning their previous addresses was false and issued a claim either to repossess the property based on Ground 5 or, alternatively, to rescind the tenancy agreement for misrepresentation.

2.39   The trial judge rejected the claims, finding, as a preliminary issue, that Ground 5 was only available in respect of the person to whom the tenancy had been granted (ie the husband). The Court of Appeal agreed (see Mummery LJ's explanation at paragraph 47 of the judgment, set out at 2.9 above).

---

31 See para 12 *per* Dyson LJ.

FALSE STATEMENT

2.40   Turning back to the substance of the Ground and the six elements that must be demonstrated, as set out in 2.35 above, although it refers exclusively to a 'statement', a material omission may also give the landlord a ground for possession. An obvious example would be an applicant's failure to notify either their would-be landlord or the person charged with nominating/allocating its accommodation of a relevant change of circumstances.

2.41   In *North Hertfordshire DC v Carthy*,[32] for example, the defendant family was placed in temporary accommodation by the local housing authority, having returned to the country after running out of money while building a property in the Philippines. The following year they were allocated accommodation.[33] By that time, however, they had obtained the funds to make the Philippines property habitable again and had done so.

2.42   At trial, the Recorder had dismissed the authority's possession claim on the premise that the omission had not induced the authority to grant the tenancy. The Court of Appeal allowed the authority's appeal and remitted the case to a different judge.[34]

2.43   The Court considered the relevance of the tenant's failure to update the landlord and the nature of any continuing representation by *omission*.

2.44   When the omission is the result of a failure to update a local housing authority or housing association about information that was accurate at the time it was first included in a housing application or similar form, the situation is usually straightforward. Most forms of this type will require the applicant to sign not only a declaration attesting to the accuracy of the content at the time of its production, but also an agreement that the applicant will inform the would-be landlord/nominator of any changes in the information provided.

2.45   Not all allocations of social housing, however, rely on application forms. Is there a general requirement to advise the authority or association of material information, absent any such agreement? Sedley LJ suggested there might be when he said in *Carthy*:

> '8. The recorder accepted that Mr Carthy was in breach of these obligations. Indeed it is arguable that even if he had not signed the material forms, he would have been guilty of making a false statement by not correcting a

---

32   [2003] EWCA Civ 20 – see footnote 1.

33   Had the change been noted prior to the grant of the tenancy, the authority would have been entitled to revisit and rescind the decision that it had an obligation to house the applicant under Housing Act 1996 s 193, if that decision had resulted from a fundamental mistake of fact: *Porteous v West Dorset DC* [2004] EWCA Civ 244, [2004] HLR 30.

34   The Recorder had not gone on to consider whether it was reasonable to make a possession order given his finding that the information should not have made any difference to the allocation of a secure tenancy.

continuing representation. *It may well be that not every relationship or situation carries such an obligation, but it is clear in my view that the information which is needed by a housing authority to process claims for temporary accommodation for the homeless, and equally that is needed to decide whether to offer secure accommodation to people on the housing list, constitutes a continuing representation by an applicant.* One has only to refer to section 196 of the Housing Act 1996[35] to see why this is so. If so, it brings with it a duty to tell the council of any change in circumstances which is capable of affecting the council's actions in response to the application' (emphasis added).

2.46   Indeed, section 214 of the Housing Act 1996, considered in more detail in Chapter 7, makes criminal offences of the following representations and omissions:

(a) making a false statement;

(b) withholding information; and

(c) failing to notify changes,

committed when false information is provided with a view to inducing the local housing authority to provide Part VII homelessness accommodation. The section states in terms:

'(2) If before an applicant receives notification of the local housing authority's decision on his application there is any change of facts material to his case, he shall notify the authority as soon as possible.'

2.47   Section 171 of the Housing Act 1996 provides for a similar criminal offence in the context of housing allocation under Part VI of the 1996 Act:

'(1) A person commits an offence if, in connection with the exercise by a local housing authority of their functions under this Part—

(a) he knowingly or recklessly makes a statement which is false in a material particular, or

(b) he knowingly withholds information which the authority have reasonably required him to give in connection with the exercise of those functions.'

Unlike section 214(2), however, it does not provide for any extended criminal offence for failing to inform the authority of a change of circumstances.

2.48   As noted in *Carthy* (and referred to in 2.44 above) most allocation forms will include a requirement that the applicant inform the would-be landlord of any

---

35 This provision deals with the duty owed by the local housing authority to those becoming threatened with homelessness intentionally. It expressly refers to the applicant doing or failing to do something the likely result of which is that they will be forced to leave their existing accommodation.

such changes. It would certainly be good practice, it is suggested, to include such a requirement in all application forms, in case the landlord later wishes to seek possession because of an alleged omission at the time of the application or at any stage before the allocation of social housing.

2.49   It follows that applicants must inform the local housing authority of any changes in circumstance in cases of Part VI allocation and homelessness applications, as well as other cases in which the applicant is informed of such a requirement. Any failure to do so can satisfy the first step in this Ground for possession.

2.50   Whether, more generally, a failure to disclose a material change of circumstances amounts, in the words of Sedley LJ in *Carthy*, to a 'continuing representation' is a moot point and is, as yet, undecided, though in *Akinbolu v Hackney LBC*,[36] a case in which the tenant had not advised the authority of his immigration status and was not asked about it either, the court held at [270]:

> 'The circumstances in which the tenant took possession prima facie created a tenancy and any argument to the contrary is fanciful. A process through the courts is required even in the case of a tenancy the grant of which was induced by a false statement under Ground 5. *This appellant was not guilty of any misrepresentation to or deception of the housing authority.* Even if the tenant condition is not satisfied so that a tenancy is not a secure tenancy, an application to the court for possession is required. We would hope that the occasional practice of this Borough to change the locks in order to regain possession of its property would be reconsidered as a matter of some urgency' (emphasis added).

MATERIALITY

2.51   If a false statement has been made, it is necessary to consider whether the statement:

(a) is material and made knowingly or recklessly;

(b) is made by the tenant, or somebody acting at the tenant's instigation; and

(c) impacts upon the decision to grant a tenancy of the property concerned.

2.52   To establish that the statement was material, the landlord will need to adduce evidence about the impact that it had on the decision to grant a tenancy, and where the tenant would have been placed in its allocation scheme or that of the nominating authority had the correct information been provided.

2.53   If, for example, the tenant gives their year of birth as 1962 rather than the real year of 1963; this is unlikely to have been material or induced any grant

---

36 (1997) 29 HLR 259. The tenant was not asked by the local authority and did not provide any information about his immigration status. The Court of Appeal allowed his appeal against a refusal to grant him an injunction to re-enter the premises and found that he was a secure tenant.

of a tenancy. Conversely, if they have failed to record that they owned or had an interest in accommodation elsewhere, this is likely to have been extremely material to the grant of the particular tenancy.

INSTIGATION

2.54   Grounds 5 and 17 were both extended by the Housing Act 1996[37] to include statements made by a third party at the tenant's instigation, in addition to those made by the tenant.

2.55   In *Merton LBC v Richards*, Pill LJ explained the meaning of 'instigate':[38]

'32 ... On any view "instigate" means more than tolerate. It means to bring about or initiate. The Latin source of the word, as mentioned in the *Concise Oxford Dictionary*, is instigare: to urge or incite. The ground refers to instigation and not merely to someone "acting on behalf of the tenant". On the judge's findings of fact, there was no instigation by the respondent in this case.'

2.56   In *Richards*, the tenant was greatly assisted by her mother, a housing officer, in arranging an exchange with an elderly tenant, Mrs Mahon. In fact, Mrs Mahon had made it clear to the tenant's mother that she had no intention of moving to the daughter's flat and was rather going to live with her family in Lowestoft.

2.57   At trial the Recorder found that the tenant had been unaware of Mrs Mahon's true intentions. Chadwick LJ said:

'39 The judge found that the respondent did not, herself, know that the statement as to Mrs Mahon's intentions was false at the time when the tenancy was granted. Nor was she reckless in that regard. Other tribunals might have reached a different conclusion on that issue. If a different conclusion had been reached, it would have been difficult, if not impossible, to attack that conclusion in this court. But the question in this court is whether there was material on which the judge could reach the conclusion which he did reach. For the reasons which Pill L.J. has set out—and with which I agree—there was sufficient material for the judge to reach the conclusion on that issue which he did.'

2.58   Simply acting on the tenant's behalf, therefore, is not necessarily the same as acting at the tenant's instigation: the latter requires the tenant actively to incite a third party to make a false statement, which then leads to the grant of the tenancy.[39]

---

37 Housing Act 1996, ss 102 and 146 – with effect from 12 February 1997 (Ground 5) and 28 February 1997 (Ground 17).
38 [2005] EWCA Civ 639, [2005] HLR 44.
39 Ibid, para 33 *per* Pill LJ.

KNOWLEDGE AND RECKLESSNESS

2.59   It follows, from the plain language of the Ground, that the tenant must not only make or instigate the statement but must also know that it is false, or be reckless about its accuracy.[40] For example, this may be the case where they claim not to own or have an interest in any other premises but:

(a) they are still aware that they are registered as a joint owner of residential accommodation with their former partner following a right to buy purchase some years before; or

(b) they thought they might be so registered but 'couldn't be bothered' to find out; though not arguably where

(c) they had been advised by their former partner that the previous premises were now in the former partner's sole name as previously agreed by both parties.

2.60   This is potentially an important distinction, not because the Ground itself distinguishes between knowledge and recklessness, but because the degree of culpability on the tenant's part could be relevant when the court considers whether it is reasonable to make a possession order, once the Ground is satisfied.[41]

2.61   The issue or reasonableness, in the context of claims brought on this Ground, is dealt with at 2.73–2.90 below.

INDUCEMENT

2.62   The last element of this Ground requires the landlord to demonstrate that the false statement played '*... a real and substantial part, though not by itself a decisive part, in inducing [it] to act*'.[42]

2.63   For example, if the tenant had completed an application form for housing and failed to refer to an existing tenancy but the landlord had paid no regard to the form (or that part of it) when granting the tenancy, then the Ground will not be satisfied.

2.64   It has been suggested that there is a presumption[43] that if the false statement is sufficiently material,[44] such as the second example referred to at 2.53, then it is a fair inference of fact that the landlord has been induced by it to grant the tenancy.[45]

---

40   Ibid, para 51 *per* May LJ.
41   *Rushcliffe BC v Watson* (1991) 24 HLR 124, CA at [127] *per* Nourse LJ. In that case it was not disputed that Ground 5 was satisfied, the trial turning solely on the question of whether it was reasonable to make a possession order.
42   *JEB Fasteners Ltd v Marks Bloom & Co* [1983] 1 All ER 583 *per* Stephenson LJ at [589 A–B].
43   *Waltham Forest LBC v Roberts* [2004] EWCA Civ 940, [2005] HLR 2, paras 42–43.
44   *Downs v Chappell* [1997] 1 WLR 426 *per* Hobhouse LJ at [433].
45   *Smith v Chadwick* (1884) 9 App Cas 187 *per* Lord Blackburn at [1961].

2.65   In *Windsor and District Housing Association v Hewitt*,[46] Ms Hewitt applied to transfer from her one-bedroom flat in part, she said, because she needed a second bedroom for her son, who was also her carer. Over two years later she was offered and accepted a tenancy of a two-bedroom, ground-floor flat. Around this time, she also spoke to somebody at the Association and said that she was likely to live at the property on her own.

2.66   The landlord brought a claim to repossess the property on Ground 5 but did not succeed at first instance because:

(a) it could not show that the false statement had been made knowingly or recklessly; and

(b) it could not prove that it had been induced to grant the tenancy by reason of the false statement, not least because of the tenant's clear representation at the time of the letting that she would be living there alone.

2.67   The Court of Appeal allowed the Association's appeal. It found that the first reason for the trial judge's decision was unsustainable, given that it was Ms Hewitt's own case (though not accepted by the trial judge) that her son did live with her after all.

2.68   As for the seemingly honest information given by her at the time of the letting, this had been given for data purposes only and was not a document relied upon when letting the property. It was not, therefore, sufficient to rebut the presumption that the false statement had induced the Association to grant her a tenancy.

2.69   It follows that false statements pertaining to material matters are likely to lead to a finding of inducement, unless it can be shown that the statement either did not form part of the landlord's reason for granting the tenancy or was not considered by the landlord in any event.

STANDARD OF PROOF

2.70   A possession claim is a civil matter and decided accordingly on the balance of probabilities. This is best explained by Lord Nicholls's statement in *In re H (Minors) (Sexual Abuse: Standard of Proof)* [1996] AC 563 at [586C–H]:

> 'The balance of probability standard means that a court is satisfied an event occurred if the court considers that, on the evidence, the occurrence of the event was more likely than not. When assessing the probabilities the court will have in mind as a factor, to whatever extent is appropriate in the particular case, that the more serious the allegation the less likely it is that the event occurred and, hence, the stronger should be the evidence

46 [2011] EWCA Civ 735, [2011] HLR 39.

before the court concludes that the allegation is established on the balance of probability ... [T]his does not mean that where a serious allegation is in issue the standard of proof required is higher. It only means that the inherent probability or improbability of an event is itself a matter to be taken into account when weighing the probabilities and deciding whether, on balance, the event occurred.'

2.71 It is often not possible to call the person who decided to grant the tenancy to give evidence that he or she was induced to do so by the tenant's representation, but this is, though to be avoided if at all possible, not necessarily fatal to the possession claim.

2.72 In *Waltham Forest LBC v Roberts*,[47] Newman J considered the concept of the 'presumption of inducement':

'37 ... The judge was strongly influenced by the absence of evidence from the actual decision maker and rejected the evidence which was before him about the Authority's policy in responding to housing applications. In so far as he is to be taken to have concluded that without evidence from the actual decision maker, the burden of proof could not be discharged, he was plainly wrong. No basis for the existence of such a strict evidential requirement has been made out. Nor could it be, for there are none save that it is to be noted that in certain circumstances, to which I shall refer later, a presumption of inducement can arise. The Authority called its rehousing manager, Mr Bourne. His evidence, which was uncontradicted, was that in accordance with its policy, the Authority would have wanted to investigate the true position. As a result, he stated it was unlikely that Mrs Roberts would have been granted a tenancy of this particular accommodation, at the date it was granted, had the Authority known of her joint ownership of 143 Westdown Road. Her ownership would have generated inquiries into who was living at the property, the type of security the owners had and the amount of equity in the property.'

REASONABLENESS

2.73 The Ground is, as noted above, a discretionary one and so even if made out and there are no issues with the landlord's notice seeking possession, the court must go on to consider whether:

(a) it is reasonable to make a possession order;[48] and

(b) if so, whether that order should be outright or its enforcement suspended on terms.[49]

---

47 [2004] EWCA Civ 940, [2005] HLR 2, para 37.
48 Housing Act 1985, s 84(2)(a); Housing Act 1988, s 7(4).
49 Housing Act 1985, s 85(2); Housing Act 1988, s 9(2).

2.74   The leading authority on the court's role in assessing reasonableness remains *Cumming v Danson*,[50] in which Lord Greene MR held that:

> 'In considering reasonableness under section 3(1), it is, in my opinion, perfectly clear that the duty of the judge is to take into account all relevant circumstances as they exist at the date of the hearing, that he must do in what I venture to call a broad, common-sense way as a man of the world, and come to his conclusion giving such weight as he thinks right to the various factors in the situation. Some factors may have little or no weight, others may be decisive, but it is quite wrong for him to exclude from his consideration matters which he ought to take into account.'

2.75   It necessarily follows that some circumstances will militate against the making of an outright order for possession, or indeed the making of any possession order.

2.76   Factors such as delay on the part of the landlord, laxity of procedures and hardship for the defendant if evicted are just three issues that, it has been suggested, are potentially relevant when considering the question of reasonableness.[51]

2.77   A Convention right defence (usually under Article 8 ECHR) is unlikely to provide a defendant with much comfort[52] any more than a defence based on a wider public law challenge.

2.78   Indeed, it could be said that such defences are better dealt with in any event under the umbrella of 'reasonableness'. In handing down the judgment of the court in *Manchester City Council v Romano; Manchester City Council v Samari*,[53] Lord Justice Brooke remarked with reference to discrimination defences to discretionary possession claims:

> '64 In our judgment, it would be preferable, in a case involving a secure tenancy or an assured tenancy, for the tenant to assert the matter on which he relies as part of his case that it would be unreasonable for the court to make a possession order, rather than to complicate the proceedings by adding a formalistic counterclaim for a declaration or an injunction.'

2.79   It is, though, worth noting when considering some of the common examples of public law or discrimination defences:

- Section 11(2) of the Children Act 2004 applies to local authorities and other designated public bodies and concerns the safeguarding and promotion of the welfare of children, but as Sharp LJ said in *Mohamoud v Kensington & Chelsea RLBC*:[54]

---

50 [1942] 2 All ER 653.
51 *Lewisham LBC v Akinsola* (2000) 32 HLR 414 at [417] *per* Sedley LJ.
52 *Thurrock BC v West* [2012] EWCA Civ 1435, [2013] HLR 5 paras 22–31.
53 [2004] EWCA Civ 834, [2005] 1 WLR 2775 – the Disability Rights Commission intervening in both cases.
54 [2015] EWCA Civ 780, [2015] HLR 38.

'67 Further, as in Collins, it is difficult to see how the s11(2) duty adds anything material to the art.8 analysis. If it does so, it seems to me, more as a matter of form, rather than substance.

…

70 If however, contrary to my view, there was a duty to conduct an assessment as the appellants assert, I do not think these facts show any basis for interfering with the possession orders that were made, as there is no link between the making of those orders and a failure to conduct such an assessment. It would follow that a failure to comply with such a duty did not give rise to a defence to the claims in any event: see *Wandsworth LBC v Winder* [1985] A.C. 461 HL at 509E–F and *London Borough of Hackney v Lambourne* (1993) 25 H.L.R. 172 at 181.'

- Equally, the public sector equality duty[55] is unlikely to add significant weight to the tenant's defence: as reasonableness is in issue, the factors to which section 149 of the Equality Act 2010 refers would, in all probability, be considered by the court in any event.

- As for discrimination,[56] the tenant would need to demonstrate, at the very least, a connection between the protected characteristic (eg disability) and the making or instigation of a false statement – a connection which is likely to be very difficult to prove.[57]

2.80 Whilst the detail of discrimination and public law defences is beyond the scope of this book, if a landlord believes it has sufficient evidence to justify a possession claim under the Ground, then when making a decision to issue such a claim, and keeping its prosecution under review, it would be prudent to not only be satisfied of the evidence but also:

(a) consider the tenant's present circumstances in full and any culpability that could be laid at the door of the landlord;

(b) address, in particular, any issues surrounding any relevant, protected characteristic,[58] such as disability, as well as any wider public law issue;

(c) consider the impact on and integrity of the allocation scheme in operation, including the interests of those awaiting allocation of social housing; and

(d) comply with any necessary pre-action protocol (see 2.22).

2.81 It has been said that the nature and degree of the tenant's untrue statements could only be considered relevant to the question of reasonableness

---

55 Equality Act 2010, s 149.
56 Under the Equality Act 2010.
57 Though see *Lewisham LBC v Malcolm* [2007] EWCA Civ 763, [2008] Ch 129 (overturned on appeal [2008] UKHL 43, [2008] 1 AC 1399).
58 Equality Act 2010, s 4 – the protected characteristics are age; disability; gender reassignment; marriage and civil partnership; pregnancy and maternity; race; religion or belief; sex; sexual orientation.

in exceptional circumstances; the attitude and response of the defendant when the fraud was exposed being a more reasonable factor to consider.[59]

2.82   That approach stands in marked contrast to the treatment of reasonableness claims brought on other grounds for possession. In *City West Housing Trust Ltd v Massey*,[60] conjoined anti-social behaviour possession cases,[61] Arden LJ observed, when considering the required cogency of evidence necessary to allow suspension of the enforcement of a possession order:

> '53 However, because each case must be considered on its own facts, the judge has to decide whether there is a sound basis for saying that the tenant changed his or her ways. There is no absolute rule that a tenant who has lied in his evidence cannot ever succeed in having a SPO made in his favour. Even though lies have been told, it may be appropriate for a district judge nonetheless to make the assessment that cogent evidence exists which provides a real hope that the terms of the tenancy agreement will be respected in future. That will require careful consideration and appropriate explanation when the district judge gives his reasons for making an SPO.'

2.83   The courts have significantly held in possession claims based on the Ground that when considering whether it is reasonable to make a possession order the judge is entitled to take into account the *public interest* in discouraging deceitful applications for housing, which result in the unjust relegation of honest applicants. Nourse LJ said in *Rushcliffe BC v Watson* in reference to the relevance of considering the 'public interest':[62]

> 'I think it desirable to emphasise that what the judge was doing was considering whether it was reasonable to make an order for possession. Mr. Westgate accepts that, in doing that, the judge was entitled, and indeed bound, to take account of the public interest. But he says that he took too narrow a view of it, in particular by not recognising the public interest in keeping a family together as a unit. The judge's view of the public interest was wrongly confined to a policy of discouraging deceitful applications which result in the unjust relegation on the housing list of applicants who are honest.
>
> Again I cannot accept this submission. I am quite certain that the judge recognised the public interest in keeping a family together as a unit. But since he thought that there was no real likelihood that this family would be split up, that was not something which affected his consideration of the public interest in this case. On the broader aspect of the public interest the judge was fully entitled to attach the importance which he evidently did to the policy to which I have referred. The statistics which he recounted demonstrate the acute shortages in the plaintiff's housing stock.'

---

59 *Shrewsbury BC v Atcham* (1998) 30 HLR 123 *per* Beldam LJ at 132.
60 [2016] EWCA Civ 704, [2017] 1 WLR 129.
61 Housing Act 1988, Sch 2, Grounds 12 and 14.
62 (1991) 24 HLR 124, CA at [130–31].

2.84   *Rushcliffe* also serves as a helpful reminder to landlords that, if they wish to rely on the Ground it makes sense to provide evidence of those affected by such deceitful applications, along with other information, such as:

(a) the number of people on the landlord's allocation list, or the local housing authority's if nominations come from them to a housing association;

(b) the average wait time for accommodation; and

(c) the likely outcome of the tenant's application if they had not misrepresented their position.

2.85   Further, in claims brought on the Ground, the court will only consider the effect on the tenant of making a possession order in exceptional circumstances. In *Shrewsbury & Atcham BC v Evans*,[63] the Court of Appeal dismissed the tenant's argument that the trial judge had failed to give proper weight to the fact that she might be found intentionally homeless if evicted and that the family might not be able to stay together if the possession order was made.

2.86   Indeed, in *Lewisham LBC v Akinsola*,[64] the Court of Appeal expressly rejected an argument that a possession order would be futile as it would – it was said – simply require the authority to secure accommodation for the errant defendant, who had lied about being homeless to obtain the accommodation in the first place. There were, in effect, still issues for the authority to decide upon any homelessness application, such as intentionality.[65]

2.87   The Court did, however, caution that, if a homelessness application would manifestly succeed or fail, this may be a relevant factor when considering the reasonableness of a possession order.[66]

2.88   Some 17 years on, however, with greater reliance by local housing authorities on the private rented sector to discharge their homelessness duties, it may properly be argued that, even if the household were likely to be owed the full housing duty, it does not necessarily follow that it would be offered social housing such that possession is still warranted.

2.89   In *Evans*, Beldam LJ in any event cautioned against 'overplaying' the potential re-housing card when he said at [132]:

---

63 (1997) 30 HLR 123, CA at [132] *per* Beldam LJ, though see *Southwark LBC v Erekin* [2003] EWHC 1765, [2003] JHL D96, in which the High Court refused to overturn a county court decision that it would not be reasonable to make a possession order under this Ground, even though the defendant had been sent to prison for fraud for obtaining the tenancy, because the defendant's children had been enjoying a stable home life in the property with the defendant's mother.

64 (2000) 32 HLR 414.

65 Note *R v Exeter City Council, ex p Glidden and Draper* [1985] 1 All ER 493 in this respect, in which it was held that it would be not reasonable to permit the tenant to continue to occupy accommodation which the landlord wishes to recover because of discovered fraud.

66 In *Shrewsbury BC v Atcham* (1998) 30 HLR 123 at [132], Belfam LJ had previously said: '... only in exceptional cases would the court consider the effect of the homelessness legislation. It is not the function of the court to decide whether or not a person is intentionally homeless. That is the function of the local authority and has been entrusted to the local authority by Parliament'.

> 'Those who are on the housing list who have an equal or even greater claim to public housing would, in my view, justly be indignant to find that the court did not think it reasonable in circumstances where someone has obtained accommodation by a deliberate and flagrant lie, to make an order for possession merely because the effect of the order would result in the occupant having to be considered by the local authority as homeless or intentionally homeless.'

and more recently, in the context of fraudulent subletting, Turner J remarked in *Poplar HARCA v Begum & Rohim*:[67]

> '… it is not compassionate to allow profiteering fraudsters indefinitely to continue to occupy premises and thereby exclude from such accommodation more needy and deserving families'.

2.90   Finally, though discretionary, the Ground is in some respects 'all or nothing'. There is, it is suggested, little merit in the landlord securing a possession order, the enforcement of which is suspended on terms, in the absence of any credible conditions of suspension (unless there are other discretionary grounds being relied on, such as regards rent arrears or anti-social conduct). In these cases, the mischief has already happened; of necessity it cannot happen again for that particular tenancy.

CONCLUSION

2.91   If a secure tenancy or assured tenancy has been procured by a false representation then possession proceedings may be available on discretionary grounds – Grounds 5 or 17. This is the usual route to repossessing the premises and, generally, the remedy of rescission will not be available.

2.92   Once there has been an assignment or ending of the tenancy, then the Ground will not be available.

2.93   Where security of tenure is lost, for example where the tenant no longer lives at the premises as their only or principal home, rescission may be a possible remedy though there could be more practical sense in acknowledging the tenancy and seeking to terminate it by the usual 'notice to quit' route, depending upon the evidence of sub-letting, parting with possession or an only or principal home case.

2.94   If the fraud is committed by *both* the officer entitled to allocate the accommodation and the recipient tenant, then again rescission may be available.

2.95   Finally, the particular hurdles that may impinge upon a flexible or fixed-term tenancy need to be appreciated and care taken both in how the agreement is drafted and how the tenancy is sought to be terminated and possession taken.

---

67   [2017] EWHC 2040 (QB), para 40.

CHAPTER 3

Misuse of Property

- Sub-letting
- Parting with possession
- Possession claims

Key points

- Sub-letting or parting with possession of the whole of the demised premises will lead to an automatic and permanent loss of security of tenure for secure and assured tenancies.

- Secure or assured status cannot be regained in such circumstances, even if the tenant resumes occupation of the premises.

- Lack of direct evidence of such activity may not be fatal to a landlord's claim for possession, as long as proper inferences can be drawn from the facts.

- For periodic tenancies, the service of a notice to quit will bring the remaining common law tenancy to an end, with effect from its expiry.

- Fixed term/flexible tenancies,[1] which necessarily includes shared ownership leases, cannot be brought to an end by means of a notice to quit. In such cases possession in reliance on an appropriately worded forfeiture provision will be required.[2]

- A secure tenant has the right to take in lodgers and sub-letting or parting with possession of part of the premises is available to such tenants with the written permission of their landlord. Failure to get such authority can lead to a ground for possession – breach of tenancy – provided for in Schedule 2 to the Housing Acts 1985 (secure tenancies – Ground 1) and 1988 (assured tenancies – Ground 12).

- It is an implied term of most periodic assured tenancies[3] that in order to sub-let or part with possession of the whole or part of the subject premises (or, indeed, assign the same) the landlord's consent is required.[4]

---

1   Housing Act 1985, s 107A states in terms that 'a flexible tenancy is a secure tenancy' and refers to fixed terms of two years or more.

2   Nearly Legal identified an interesting question with regard to 'anti-sub-letting' provisions in right-to-buy leases whilst looking at Airbnb issues on 28 March 2017 given the provision of Housing Act 1985, Sch 6, para 17(1) (which concerns right to buy) – 'A provision of the lease, or of an agreement collateral to it, is void in so far as it purports to prohibit or restrict the assignment of the lease or the subletting, wholly or in part, of the dwelling-house.'

3   Housing Act 1988, s 15(3) explains those tenancies where there is no such implied term: see 3.30.

4   Housing Act 1988, s 15(1).

- Introductory tenancies can be ended in the same way as for secure tenancies upon sub-letting or parting with possession of the whole – see 3.27. Any such action in respect of part of the premises may simply lead to a notice being served under section 128 of the Housing Act 1996, and mandatory possession proceedings thereafter being issued (subject to review).

INTRODUCTION

3.1   Chapter 2 concerns instances where the tenant should never have been allocated the social housing unit in the first place. This chapter, conversely, considers the situation where they acquired the tenancy in proper fashion but have not dealt with the premises appropriately. In short, they have allowed others to 'take over' the premises, either in whole or in part.

3.2   The question of sub-letting or parting with possession of premises by a tenant is, to varying degrees and in all practical senses, an issue of evidence, though it is important to understand some basic factors underpinning security of tenure and the impact on this caused by such activity, as well as the proper and appropriate court processes to undertake in order to secure possession of the subject premises.

3.3   As will be explained further below, it is the mere fact of statutory protection provided for by the Housing Acts of 1985 (secure tenancies) and 1988 (assured tenancies) that prevents a secure or assured periodic tenancy from being brought to an end on a mandatory ground by means of an otherwise properly served and valid notice to quit.[5] In short:

Security of Tenure

- A secure introductory or assured tenancy retains its status for as long as at least one of the tenants occupies the demised premises as their only or principal home.[6]

- Indeed, this basic premise is further extended[7] by the fact that a spouse or civil partner can occupy the said property in the absence of the tenant and security is retained for as long as the marriage or civil partnership persists (assuming the departing tenant does not serve a notice to quit).[8] This may, however, be a breach of tenancy (see bullet point below).

---

5   Housing Act 1985, s 82 (secure tenancies)/Housing Act 1988 s 5 (assured tenancies).
6   Housing Act 1985, ss 79(1) and 81 (secure tenancies)/Housing Act 1988, s 1(1)(b) (assured tenancies)/Housing Act 1996, s 125(5)(a) (introductory tenancies).
7   Family Law Act 1996, s 30(4)(b) (as amended by the Civil Partnership Act 2004).
8   See *Derwent Housing Association v Taylor* [2016] EWCA Civ 508; [2016] HLR 25, para 4 where the Court of Appeal confirmed that Family Law Act 1996, s 30 only conferred rights of occupation on the tenant's spouse/civil partner whilst the tenant remains entitled to occupy the dwelling house; once the tenancy had been terminated by notice to quit, s 30 did not apply.

- If security of tenure is lost because the whole of the property has been sub-let or the tenant has parted with possession of the same, then it cannot be 'regained',[9] save by the parties entering into a fresh tenancy.

- Conversely, if it is lost because the tenant(s) simply no longer live there as their only or principal home then this has 'merely' an ambulatory effect, such that security of tenure can be regained if the tenant (or at least one of them) returns to live at the premises before the expiry of any valid notice to quit properly served.[10] See Chapter 4 for further details.

- The tenant in that situation will, however, have undoubtedly breached either the express or implied term of their tenancy – which requires them or at least one of the joint tenants to live at the premises as their only or principal home – by not living there, such that it provides the landlord with the option and in many instances alternative to the notice to quit approach where the facts are unclear, of serving a notice seeking possession in reliance on the said breach.

- A notice to quit, and possession claim in reliance on the same, is only available, therefore where the tenancy is periodic and security of tenure is lost, which will be where:
  – the tenant has sub-let or parted with possession of the *entirety* of the premises, or
  – the tenant has moved away, and does not live there any longer as their only or principal home at the time the notice to quit expires.

3.4 This chapter is therefore primarily concerned with the question of sub-letting and parting with possession (with particular focus on periodic tenancies) and not the concept of 'only or principal home', which is dealt with in Chapter 4. Of course, it is true to say that if the tenant has sub-let or otherwise parted with possession of their premises then they are by definition not living there themselves. The phrase 'primarily concerned' is deliberately phrased in acknowledgment of the fact that it has to be addressed *to a degree* where such activity relates to only part of the premises and action. In such a situation, the tenant's residence will make a difference to questions of criminal sanction and nature of possession claim.

3.5 It is a topic which may present both a mandatory and discretionary possession ground for the social landlord. As such, they ought to be alive to the Pre-action Protocol for Possession Claims by Social Landlords:

'PART 3 MANDATORY GROUNDS FOR POSSESSION

3.1 This part applies in cases where if a social landlord proves its case, there is a restriction on the Court's discretion on making an order for possession

---

9 Housing Act 1985, s 93(2) (secure tenancies)/Housing Act 1988, s 15A(2) (assured tenancies).
10 See *Hussey v Camden LBC* (1995) 27 HLR 5 at [7–8] *per* Leggatt LJ.

and/or to which s. 89 Housing Act 1980 applies (e.g. non-secure tenancies, unlawful occupiers, succession claims, and severing of joint tenancies).

3.2 In cases where the court must grant possession if the landlord proves its case then before issuing any possession claim social landlords—

(a)   should write to occupants explaining why they currently intend to seek possession and requiring the occupants within a specified time to notify the landlord in writing of any personal circumstances or other matters which they wish to take into account. In many cases such a letter could accompany any notice to quit and so would not necessarily delay the issue of proceedings; and

(b)   should consider any representations received, and if they decide to proceed with a claim for possession give brief written reasons for doing so.

3.3 In these cases the social landlord should include in its particulars of claim, or in any witness statement filed under CPR 55.8(3), a schedule giving a summary—

(a)   of whether it has (by statutory review procedure or otherwise) invited the defendant to make representations of any personal circumstances or other matters which they wish to be taken into account before the social landlord issues proceedings;

(b)   if representations were made, that they were considered;

(c)   of brief reasons for bringing proceedings; and

(d)   copies of any relevant documents which the social landlord wishes the Court to consider in relation to the proportionality of the landlord's decision to bring proceedings.'

3.6   If a discretionary ground is pursued, 2.22 in the previous chapter explains the protocol to follow. First, however, the definitions of 'sub-letting' and 'parting with possession' must be explored.

WHAT IS SUB-LETTING?

3.7   'Sub-letting' requires the whole premises or part of the premises, to be let out to a third party or parties:[11]

●   with exclusive possession (see 3.62)

●   for a term at a rent, and

●   with an intention to create legal relations between the parties.[12]

---

11   *Street v Mountford* [1985] AC 809 at [818C–F] *per* Lord Templeman.
12   To be judged by the parties' conduct and not by their professed intentions: ibid at [821C–D; 822B–C] *per* Lord Templeman.

Normally it will be very clear whether or not a particular living situation is properly characterised as a sub-letting.

3.8   In *Brent LBC v Cronin*,[13] the defendant, a secure tenant of Brent, suffered from epilepsy and wished to stay with his sister-in-law away from his home for a short time. A friend of his suggested that a couple live in his one-bedroom flat in his absence. The defendant thereupon entered into an oral agreement with this couple under which they were to pay a deposit to him of £20, in addition to a weekly payment of £40 per week for the flat. The couple were given the keys to the flat and duly moved in. As for the defendant, he went, as planned, to stay with his sister-in-law.

3.9   The local authority landlord learned of this arrangement and began possession proceedings on the basis of alleged sub-letting of the whole of the let premises, having first served a notice to quit. At trial, the defendant was able to successfully argue that he had not, in fact, sub-let or parted with possession of his flat at all and that this was never his intention.

3.10   The trial judge did accept that the couple had:

- exclusive possession of the premises,

- for a term at a rent

but also found that the tenant's plans were confused and uncertain, and that he had only intended to be away for a short time, and further had not intended to part with possession of the flat.

3.11   There was certainly a superficial attractiveness to such arguments, because the defendant may well have fully and genuinely intended to return to the premises at some time in the future. The Court of Appeal, however, rejected such an approach and took a clear view that as all the elements for a tenancy had been created between the defendant and the couple, as set out at 3.7 above, a tenancy had, in fact, been formed.

3.12   They therefore accepted the authority's appeal, Sir Ralph Gibson summarising the rejection of the trial judge's approach as follows:[14]

> 'The judge was not, in law, in my judgment, entitled to decide the nature of the transaction by reference to the uncommunicated intention or uncertainty of Mr Cronin. This is a clear, longstanding principle of law (see *Chitty on Contract* 7th edn, para 12–040 and cases there cited). We were referred to those passages by Miss McAllister.

---

13   (1998) 30 HLR 43.
14   Ibid at [47].

The appellants were entitled to have their claim for possession determined according to law. The special needs and vulnerability of Mr Cronin are matters to be dealt with by a different agency.'[15]

3.13   The Court of Appeal rejected the relevance of subjective intention to return. To use the phrase of Lord Justice Waite, a tenancy is a tenancy, whether for a long or short period.

WHAT IS PARTING WITH POSSESSION?

3.14   'Parting with possession' is not as easily defined as 'sub-letting'.

3.15   Whilst sub-letting of the whole will encompass the 'parting with possession' definition, the latter also covers much wider forms of arrangement. For example, if a tenant purports to assign their tenancy to a third party and allows the latter into exclusive occupation in anticipation of the same, then this may constitute parting with possession, the elements for a tenancy being entirely absent to allow a finding of sub-letting. Similarly, an unauthorised tenants' 'swap' of properties would not be sub-letting, but would, in all probability, constitute a parting with possession.

3.16   Conversely, a 'caretaker' arrangement, where the tenant asks someone to look after the property in their (prolonged) absence (eg during a period of imprisonment or employment away from the area) does not, if properly constituted, fall within the parting with possession definition, nor does (usually) other occupation under a licence. Why?

3.17   The key to this distinction is the question of *exclusive possession*, the first of the elements referred to at 3.7 above. In *Stenning v Abrahams*,[16] Farwell J explained the importance of this definition:

> 'A lessee cannot be said to part with the possession of any part of the premises unless his agreement with his licensee wholly ousts him from the legal possession of that part. If there is anything in the nature of a right to concurrent user there is no parting with possession. Retention of a key may be a negative indicium, and the authorities on the whole show that nothing short of a complete exclusion of the grantor or licensor from the legal possession for all purposes amounts to a parting with possession. The fact that the agreement is in form a licence is immaterial, as the licence may give the licensee so exclusive a right to the legal possession as to amount to a parting with possession.'

---

15 It is fair to say that the relevance of subjective intentions was left open by the Court of Appeal in *Dreamgate Properties Ltd v Arnot* (1998) 76 P&CR 25 because it was able to decide the question on objective considerations alone. In *London Baggage Company v Railtrack plc* [2000] L&TR 439, Mr Justice Pumfrey said at [445] 'It is not settled whether the intention of the parties, to which regard must be had, includes their subjective and uncommunicated intentions.'

16 [1931] 1 Ch 470 at [473].

3.18   The courts have therefore settled on the 'test' of whether those in occupation have the right to exclude all others from the premises, including the tenant.[17]

SECURITY OF TENURE

Introduction

3.19   Now the definitions of sub-letting and parting with possession are, hopefully, understood, the question of how this impacts upon the tenant's security of tenure comes to the fore. The underlying factors are summarised at 3.3, which also deals with the inevitable 'nuances', such as the role and effect of having a spouse or civil partner.

Secure tenancies

3.20   A secure tenancy only remains as such, and security of tenure is therefore only retained:[18]

'… at any time when the conditions described in sections 80 and 81 as the landlord condition and the tenant condition are satisfied'.

3.21   The landlord condition has no relevance to this issue, but rather it is section 81 of the Housing Act 1985 that requires attention. This sets out the tenant condition simply as:

'… the tenant is an individual and occupies the dwelling-house as his *only or principal home*; or, where the tenancy is a joint tenancy, that each of the joint tenants is an individual and at least one of them occupies the dwelling-house as his only or principal home.' (emphasis added)

Assured tenancies

3.22   As with secure tenancies, section 1(1) of the Housing Act 1988 provides that an assured tenancy only remains as such if and for so long as:

'(b) the tenant or, as the case may be, at least one of the joint tenants occupies the dwelling-house as his only or principal home.'

Only or principal home

3.23   It follows from these statutory provisions that security of tenure cannot be retained for either secure or assured tenants if they do not remain in occupation as their only or principal home.

---

17 *Lam Kee Ying v Lam Shes Tong* [1975] AC 247 at [256C] *per* Sir Harry Gibbs.
18 Housing Act 1985, s 79(1).

3.24   That concept and the repercussions of its loss is dealt with, as previously noted, in appropriate detail in Chapter 4 and 3.3 above.

3.25   Paragraphs 3.31–3.42 look at with when sub-letting or parting with possession is only in respect of *part* of the premises. Where it concerns the whole premises, statutory provisions make the issue more straightforward.

Sub-letting or parting with possession of whole

3.26   Section 93 of the Housing Act 1985[19] confirms the permanent loss of security of tenure for secure tenants in such circumstances:

> '(2) If the tenant under a secure tenancy parts with the possession of the dwelling-house[20] or sublets the whole of it (or sublets first part of it and then the remainder), the tenancy ceases to be a secure tenancy and cannot subsequently become a secure tenancy.'

3.27   If an introductory tenant sub-lets the whole then they similarly lose that status if there has been sub-letting or parting with possession of the whole. Section 125 of the Housing Act 1996 provides:

> '(5) A tenancy ceases to be an introductory tenancy if, before the end of the trial period—
>
> (a) *the circumstances are such that the tenancy would not otherwise be a secure tenancy,*
>
> (b) a person or body other than a local housing authority or housing action trust becomes the landlord under the tenancy,
>
> (c) the election in force when the tenancy was entered into or adopted is revoked, or
>
> (d) the tenancy ceases to be an introductory tenancy by virtue of section 133(3) (succession)' (emphasis added).

3.28   As with 3.26 above, section 15A of the Housing Act 1988 has provided, with effect from 5 November 2013,[21] for assured tenants to also permanently lose security of tenure in such circumstances:

> '(1) Subsection (2) applies if, in breach of an express or implied term of the tenancy, a tenant of a dwelling-house let under an assured tenancy to which this section applies—

---

19 This section is not applicable to a secure tenancy from a co-operative housing association by reason of s 109.

20 Defined at s 112 as 'a house or a part of a house'.

21 Prior to this time a tenant was able to argue that even if they had sub-let or parted with possession of the whole of their premises then as long as they had a genuine intention to return there was no loss of security of tenure: *Ujima Housing Association v Ansah* (1997) 30 HLR 831 and *Waltham Forest Community Based Housing Association v Fanning* [2001] L&TR 41.

(a) parts with possession of the dwelling-house, or

(b) sub-lets the whole of the dwelling-house (or sub-lets first part of it and then the remainder).

(2) The tenancy ceases to be an assured tenancy and cannot subsequently become an assured tenancy.'

3.29   Section 15A of the 1988 Act does not apply to shared ownership leases.[22]

3.30   It follows that for periodic secure and assured tenancies, and introductory tenancies, a notice to quit should be served to bring the remaining common law tenancy to an end:[23]

● prior to taking possession action; and

● prior to following the necessary protocol (see 3.5).

Notice to Quit

To: Edward Hazard, 2 Stamford Bridge, London, SW18 1DD

From: Ferguson Housing Association, Andrew Herrera Way, Pocket, Manchester, M20 1LV

We give you NOTICE TO QUIT and deliver up possession of 2 Stamford Bridge, London, SW18 1DD on 27 November 20XX or the day on which a complete period of your tenancy expires next after the end of four weeks from the date of service of this notice

Dated: 16 October 20XX

Signed:................................

Position:

Important Information for tenants[24]

1   If the tenant or licensee does not leave the dwelling, the landlord or licensor must get an order for possession from the court before the tenant or licensee can lawfully be evicted. The landlord or licensor cannot apply for such an order before the notice to quit or notice to determine has run out.

2   A tenant or licensee who does not know if he has any right to remain in possession after a notice to quit or a notice to determine runs out can obtain advice from a solicitor. Help with all or part of the cost of legal advice and assistance may be available under the Legal Aid Scheme. He should also be able to obtain information from a Citizens' Advice Bureau, a Housing Aid Centre or a rent officer.

---

22   As defined in Housing Act 1988, s 15(5).
23   Housing Act 1996, s 125(6).
24   Notices to Quit etc. (Prescribed Information) Regulations 1988/2201, Sch 1.

WHAT IF THE SUB-LETTING/PARTING WITH POSSESSION ONLY RELATES TO *PART* OF THE PREMISES?

3.31   We know from 3.3 above that:

(a) A secure or periodic assured tenant[25] is entitled to sub-let or part with possession of part of the premises as long as:[26]
   - they have the (written[27] consent) of the landlord; and
   - *they themselves, or at least one of joint tenants or their spouses/civil partners, continue to live at the premises as their only or principal home.*

(b) Consent of the landlord in a secure tenancy case should not be unreasonably withheld and will be treated as given if it is so.[28]

(c) A secure tenant is also entitled to have lodgers (as opposed to sub-tenants) in the premises, and does not need the consent of the landlord to do so[29] (see 3.35).

(d) Despite the more restrictive nature of periodic assured tenancies, an assured tenant will be able to take in lodgers in so far as in those cases no possession in fact passes[30] (see 3.36).

3.32   If, therefore, a tenant lets out a room, say, in their three-bedroom property and moves out themselves to live elsewhere then, as indicated above at 3.3 and 3.31:

(a) they may well have lost security of tenure *not* because of the sub-letting/ parting with possession – because they have not done this in respect of the *whole* of the premises – but due to the fact that they no longer live at the premises as their only or principal home (see Chapter 4);

(b) this activity is almost certainly also a breach of tenancy both in respect of the letting the room, if without consent of the landlord and the failure of the tenant to live at the premises as their only or principal home (and probably also a failure to advise their landlord of absence from the home for longer than the specified period, usually 21 or 28 days, if that is such an express term).

3.33   It necessarily follows that if the sub-letting or parting with possession of part of the demised premises represents a breach of tenancy – whether of an express or implied term – and the tenant continues to live there, then the proper notice to serve prior to any possession proceedings is a notice seeking possession and *not* a notice to quit (which would not be available anyway for a fixed term or

---

25 A periodic assured tenancy can have a condition prohibiting or allowing any such sub-letting or parting with possession unless it is a statutory periodic tenancy or one arising under Local Government and Housing Act 1989, Sch 10 (see Housing Act 1988, s 15(3)).

26 Housing Act 1985, s 93(1)(a) (secure tenancies)/Housing Act 1988, s 15(1) (assured tenancies).

27 Housing Act 1988, s 15(1) dealing with assured tenancies, does not specify that the consent must be in writing.

28 Housing Act 1985, s 94(2) – there is no such restriction in periodic assured tenancy cases.

29 Ibid, s 93(1)(b).

30 *Edwards v Barrington* [1901] 85 LT 650 HL; *Segal Securities Ltd v Thoseby* [1963] 1 QB 887.

flexible tenancy, as is clear from 3.51–3.57 which also cautions about use of the section 146 notice for the reasons raised at 2.27–2.33).

3.34   To put it another way, the tenancy would continue in its secure/assured/ introductory tenancy form despite the breach of tenancy *unless* the tenant(s) have also themselves moved out such that they can be properly said to no longer live there as their only or principal home (in which case the Housing Acts are of no application in determining the tenancy, and a notice to quit is required in periodic tenancy cases, forfeiture otherwise).

3.35   Sub-letting or parting with possession of *part* of the relevant premises is not without some statutory restriction. For secure tenants, section 93 of the Housing Act 1985 provides:

'(1) It is a term of every secure tenancy that the tenant—

(a)   may allow any persons to reside as lodgers in the dwelling-house, but

(b)   will not, without the written consent of the landlord, sublet or part with possession of part of the dwelling-house.'

3.36   As for assured *periodic* tenants section 15 provides:

'(1) Subject to subsection (3) below, it shall be an implied term of every assured tenancy which is a periodic tenancy that, except with the consent of the landlord, the tenant shall not—

(a)   assign the tenancy (in whole or in part); or

(b)   sub-let or part with possession of the whole or any part of the dwelling-house let on the tenancy.

…

(3) In the case of a periodic tenancy which is not a statutory periodic tenancy or an assured periodic tenancy arising under Schedule 10 to the Local Government and Housing Act 1989 subsection (1) above does not apply if—

(a)   there is a provision (whether contained in the tenancy or not) under which the tenant is prohibited (whether absolutely or conditionally) from assigning or sub-letting or parting with possession or is permitted (whether absolutely or conditionally) to assign, sub-let or part with possession; or

(b)   a premium is required to be paid on the grant or renewal of the tenancy.'

3.37   It follows that the primary issues in a periodic tenancy scenario, where only part of the premises is subject to investigation and inquiry, are:

(1) Does the tenant(s) still live at the premises as their only or principal home?

(2) If not, security of tenure has been lost whilst that remains the case (as with any only or principal home case) and a notice to quit is required to end the remaining common law tenancy (see 3.30).

(3) If the tenant remains living at the premises, have they the permission of the landlord for any sub-letting or parting with possession *of part*?

(4) If not, this will be a breach of tenancy and a notice seeking possession could be served in reliance on:
   – Grounds 1 (secure tenancies) 'Rent lawfully due from the tenant has not been paid or an obligation of the tenancy has been broken or not performed'; or
   – 12 (assured tenancies) 'Any obligation of the tenancy (other than one related to the payment of rent) has been broken or not performed'

   to Schedule 2 to the Housing Acts of 1985 and 1988 respectively.

(5) Is it sensible to serve both a notice to quit and, in the alternative, a notice seeking possession (breach of tenancy) and rely on and plead both in any subsequent possession claim?

(6) This could be especially helpful and appropriate where the evidence for the landlord of misuse of the whole premises is not necessarily compelling, or the tenant may have resumed occupation of the premises, in an only or principal home case, prior to the expiry of the notice to quit, thereby coming back under the auspices and protection of the relevant Housing Act, and requiring a notice seeking possession as the first step in any possession claim.

3.38   The concern of landlords with sub-letting or parting with possession of part of the demised premises without consent is primarily the potential to cause problems elsewhere (eg anti-social behaviour of the new occupiers, housing benefit fraud, etc). In any event, as seen above:

- this may be a breach of tenancy warranting the service of a notice seeking possession (and possession proceedings);

- the tenant may not be living at the premises (another breach of tenancy and if security of tenure has been lost – see 'only or principal home' section above at 3.23 – may justify the service of a notice to quit);

- this maybe a criminal offence pursuant to sections 1 or 2 of the Prevention of Social Housing Fraud Act 2013 (see Chapter 7); and

- the arrangement may attract and warrant an unlawful profit order application, whether that be as part of a possession claim, criminal proceedings (see Chapter 7) or by means of separate Part 7 claim (see Chapter 5).

3.39   The most striking recent example of sub-letting of part was seen earlier this year in the case of *Poplar HARCA v Begum and anor*.[31] In *Begum* the tenants had moved away from the demised premises – a two-bedroom flat – and had

---

31   [2017] EWHC 2040 (QB).

let it out to a family, save for one of the bedrooms which they kept locked. The Recorder found at trial that the tenants had:

> '... deliberately kept the locked second bedroom at the flat containing toys and a cot as camouflage to deceive the appellant into believing, in the event of an inspection, that they and their children were still living at the flat'.

3.40   Because of the treatment of the second bedroom, the claim for possession based on the notice to quit was not accepted because there had been no parting with possession *of the whole*.

3.41   Mr Justice Turner overturned the suspended possession order made by the Recorder on discretionary grounds, and instead substituted it with a 21-day outright possession order. He remarked:

> '39. Putting it bluntly, I am entirely satisfied that the Recorder was taken in by the respondents. I make the following observations:
>
> (i)   The respondents' case was so clouded by a miasma of lies that there was no evidence to support the Recorder's conclusion that they, with their children, had decided to move in with the first respondent's mother for wholly altruistic reasons. Indeed, on their case, they had never moved in at all.
>
> (ii) If the real reason for moving in were to look after the first respondent's brother, they could have done this without, at the same time, renting out their flat for profit to Ms Rehana and Mr Ahmed.
>
> (iii) It was but a short walk from the flat to the first respondent's home, a fact which further undermines the conclusion that it was necessary for the whole family to decamp completely to allow the first defendant access to attend to her brother when needed.
>
> 40. The fact that the Recorder exercised his discretion on a demonstrably flawed basis means that this Court must exercise that discretion afresh. In doing so, notwithstanding the passage of time since the hearing before the Recorder, I am entirely satisfied that it would be wrong to exercise my discretion to suspend the possession order in this case. In particular, the sheer scale and persistence of the respondent's initial fraudulent deceit aggravated by further and subsequent drug-related offending wholly justifies the condign consequences of an outright order. I would stress that it is not compassionate to allow profiteering fraudsters indefinitely to continue to occupy premises and thereby exclude from such accommodation more needy and deserving families. In particular, in this case, there was a complete dearth of material which could amount to cogent evidence that the respondents would mend their ways in future. Accordingly, possession will be granted to take effect in 21 days from the date of this judgment.'

3.42   Whilst not precisely on all fours with the public policy approach towards Grounds 5 and 17 as described in Chapter 2, and there were other (drug) issues present, this authority does stress the high hurdle an errant tenant may have to overcome to avoid an outright possession order, especially if caught breaching their tenancy by moving out and sub-letting or parting with possession of part of the demise.

POSSESSION CLAIMS (PERIODIC TENANCIES)

3.43   The possession claim will be issued in the county court[32] and will follow the usual:

- N5 Claim form

- N119 Particulars of claim

- Annex to particulars of claim format.[33]

3.44   There is no reason why claims cannot be pleaded in the alternative as suggested in 3.37(5), and it is the practice of some landlords not to use the N119 particulars of claim, but to simply draft their own.[34] Whichever approach they adopt – N119 plus annex or separate particulars of claim – this must be served with the N5 Claim Form.[35]

3.45   Paragraph 2.1 to Practice Direction 55A states:[36]

'**2.1** In a possession claim the particulars of claim must:

(1) identify the land to which the claim relates;

---

32 PD55A.1.1 – although para 1.3 goes on to say – '**1.3** Circumstances which may, in an appropriate case, justify starting a claim in the High Court are if – (1) there are complicated disputes of fact; (2) there are points of law of general importance; or (3) the claim is against trespassers and there is a substantial risk of public disturbance or of serious harm to persons or property which properly require immediate determination.'

33 PD 55A.1.5 states: '**1.5** The claimant must use the appropriate claim form and particulars of claim form set out in Table 1 to Practice Direction 4 ... ' – this includes the N5 and N119.

34 Though see fn 33 above.

35 CPR 55.4.

36 Also note that CPR 16.4 provides: '**16.4** (1) Particulars of claim must include – (a) a concise statement of the facts on which the claimant relies; (b) if the claimant is seeking interest, a statement to that effect and the details set out in paragraph (2); (c) if the claimant is seeking aggravated damages or exemplary damages, a statement to that effect and his grounds for claiming them; (d) if the claimant is seeking provisional damages, a statement to that effect and his grounds for claiming them; and (e) such other matters as may be set out in a practice direction. (2) If the claimant is seeking interest he must – (a) state whether he is doing so – (i) under the terms of a contract; (ii) under an enactment and if so which; or (iii) on some other basis and if so what that basis is; and (b) if the claim is for a specified amount of money, state – (i) the percentage rate at which interest is claimed; (ii) the date from which it is claimed; (iii) the date to which it is calculated, which must not be later than the date on which the claim form is issued; (iv) the total amount of interest claimed to the date of calculation; and (v) the daily rate at which interest accrues after that date. (Part 22 requires particulars of claim to be verified by a statement of truth.)'

(2) state whether the claim relates to residential property;

(3) state the ground on which possession is claimed;

(4) give full details about any mortgage or tenancy agreement; and

(5) give details of every person who, to the best of the claimant's knowledge, is in possession of the property.

Residential property let on a tenancy

2.2 Paragraphs 2.3 to 2.4B apply if the claim relates to residential property let on a tenancy.

2.3 If the claim includes a claim for non-payment of rent the particulars of claim must set out:

(1) the amount due at the start of the proceedings;

(2) in schedule form, the dates and amounts of all payments due and payments made under the tenancy agreement for a period of two years immediately preceding the date of issue, or if the first date of default occurred less than two years before the date of issue from the first date of default and a running total of the arrears;

(3) the daily rate of any rent and interest;

(4) any previous steps taken to recover the arrears of rent with full details of any court proceedings; and

(5) any relevant information about the defendant's circumstances, in particular:

   (a) whether the defendant is in receipt of social security benefits; and

   (b) whether any payments are made on his behalf directly to the claimant under the Social Security Contributions and Benefits Act 1992.

2.3A If the claimant wishes to rely on a history of arrears which is longer than two years, he should state this in his particulars and exhibit a full (or longer) schedule to a witness statement.

2.4 If the claimant knows of any person (including a mortgagee) entitled to claim relief against forfeiture as underlessee under section 146(4) of the Law of Property Act 1925 (or in accordance with section 38 of the Senior Courts Act 1981, or section 138(9C) of the County Courts Act 1984):

(1) the particulars of claim must state the name and address of that person; and

(2) the claimant must file a copy of the particulars of claim for service on him.

2.4A If the claim for possession relates to the conduct of the tenant, the particulars of claim must state details of the conduct alleged.

2.4B If the possession claim relies on a statutory ground or grounds for possession, the particulars of claim must specify the ground or grounds relied on.'

3.46   As for the pleading of any claim, an example is set out below:

Example Particulars of Claim/Annex to Particulars of Claim (if N119 used as well)

Introduction

1. The claimant is a registered provider of social housing and the freehold owner of 7 Best Avenue, Charlton, BC9 7GG ('the premises'), a three-bedroom house. On 1 May 2009 they entered into an assured non-shorthold tenancy agreement ('the Agreement') with the defendant in respect of the (residential) premises, to commence on 4 May 2009. A copy of the said agreement and current conditions is attached at Exhibit A.

2. The defendant was born on 20 June 1962 and at the commencement of his tenancy stated, as contained in the Agreement, that he would reside there with his partner and two children, then aged four and two years.

3. The weekly rent at the premises was £83.15 at the tenancy's commencement and would now be £92.10 per week if the tenancy had persisted. Use and occupation charges in respect of the same are currently £13.16 per day.

4. As at the date this statement of case is being prepared, 2 October 2017, the rent/use and occupation account is in arrears in the sum of £3,412.55. A Schedule of account detailing the said arrears is attached at Exhibit B.

Grounds for possession

5. Possession of the premises is being sought on the primary basis that:
    (a) The defendant sub-let the whole of the premises to Ms Tyra Moss.
    (b) This arrangement commenced on or around 7 November 2016 to on or around 16 September 2017.

6. The defendant thereby permanently lost security of tenure pursuant to section 15A(1) and (2) of the Housing Act 1988 (and in any event security of tenure was lost pursuant to section 1(1)(b) of the Housing Act 1988).

7. A notice to quit served on the premises in accordance with clause 6.1 of the agreement on 18 July 2017 brought the remaining common law tenancy to an end at its expiry. A copy of the said notice is attached at Exhibit C.

---

8. In the alternative, the claimant relies on Ground 12 of Schedule 2 to the Housing Act 1988:

   'Any obligation of the tenancy (other than one related to the payment of rent) has been broken or not performed.'

9. A notice seeking possession was served on the premises – a copy of the said notice is attached at Exhibit D – in accordance with clause 6.1 of the Agreement on 18 July 2017 and the breaches of tenancy alleged are clause 3.1 and clause 3.3 of the Agreement:

   '3.1 The tenant shall live at the premises as their only or principal home.

   3.3 The tenant shall not sub-let or part with possession of the premises at any time save that so long as they comply with clause 3.1:

   (a) They may have a lodger if the premises is a two-bedroom property or above, or

   (b) They may sub-let or part with possession of part of the premises only with the express and prior written agreement of the landlord.'

10. In so far as paragraphs 5 to 7 above are not made out, the claimant maintains:
    (a) The tenant has at times during the tenancy not lived at the premises as his only or principal home. This is a breach of clause 3.1 of the agreement.
    (b) Further, or in the alternative, he has at times sub-let part of the premises, in particular to Ms Tyra Moss, without obtaining the prior consent of the claimant. This is in breach of clause 3.3(b) of the agreement.

11. For the avoidance of doubt, paragraphs 5 to 7 above represent the claimant's primary position, with paragraphs 8 to 10 being their case in the alternative.

Relevant matters

12. The defendant was interviewed under caution by Charlton District Council on 9 May 2017. He admitted that he and his family had been living in alternative accommodation since early November 2016. He denied that he had sub-let the Premises to Ms Tyra Moss, but admitted that she lived there. He said she was a family friend who did not pay rent and that he had moved out temporarily because of his partner's employment.

13. The claimant believes the defendant returned to live at the premises with his family on or around 16 September 2017 and required Ms Moss to leave forthwith (which she did).

14. In so far as the claimant is required to rely on Ground 12, it is averred that it would be reasonable to make a possession order, and that such an order should be outright, because:
    (a) Social housing is a scarce resource.
    (b) Even if only part of the premises was sub-let, then this may be an offence pursuant to section 2 of the Prevention of Social Housing Fraud Act 2013.
    (c) There are currently 1,232 households on the claimant's waiting list for three-bedroom properties.
    (d) The defendant has not been open or forthcoming with the claimant or the local authority investigating this matter.

15. There is no underlessee or mortgagee entitled to claim relief from forfeiture.

Unlawful profit order

16. The claimant also seeks an unlawful profit order pursuant to section 5 of the Prevention of Social Housing Fraud Act 2013. In particular, the claimant satisfies the requirements for such an order provided for at section 5(4) of the said Act:
    (a) the claimant is a private registered provider of social housing;
    (b) the tenancy between the parties is not a shared ownership lease;
    (c) in breach of an express or implied term of the tenancy, the defendant has sub-let or parted with possession of the whole or part of the premises;
    (d) the defendant ceased to occupy the premises as their only or principal home; and
    (e) the defendant received money as a result of the conduct described in paragraph (c).

17. Attached at Exhibit E is a schedule detailing the unlawful profit order sought by the claimant. It confirms:
    (a) The relevant sub-letting period is from 7 November 2016 to 16 September 2017.
    (b) During that period the defendant received £7,000 from Ms Moss.
    (c) During the same period, the claimant received £2,300 from the defendant, purporting to be rent.

18. The appropriate sum therefore sought by the claimant is £4,700.00.

19. The claimant also seeks interest on such sum pursuant to section 69 of the County Courts Act 1984 for such period and at such a rate as the court shall deem fit.

AND the claimant claims:

1. Possession of the premises.

2. A judgment for arrears of rent and/or use and occupation.

3. An unlawful profit order.

4. An order that the defendant pay use and occupation charges until possession of the premises is given up.

5. Interest pursuant to section 69 of the County Courts Act 1984.

6. Costs.

Statement of truth

3.47   If the mandatory claim succeeds (eg sub-letting of the whole is found) then the court's powers are limited in the order it can make. Section 89 of the Housing Act 1980 allows a 14-day maximum for any order unless exceptional hardship can be shown by the defendant, in which case that period can be extended for up to six weeks:

'89.— Restriction on discretion of court in making orders for possession of land.

(1) Where a court makes an order for the possession of any land in a case not falling within the exceptions mentioned in subsection (2) below, the giving up of possession shall not be postponed (whether by the order or any variation, suspension or stay of execution) to a date later than fourteen days after the making of the order, unless it appears to the court that exceptional hardship would be caused by requiring possession to be given up by that date; and shall not in any event be postponed to a date later than six weeks after the making of the order.

(2) The restrictions in subsection (1) above do not apply if—

(a) the order is made in an action by a mortgagee for possession; or

(b) the order is made in an action for forfeiture of a lease; or

(c) the court had power to make the order only if it considered it reasonable to make it; or

(d) the order relates to a dwelling-house which is the subject of a restricted contract (within the meaning of section 19 of the 1977 Act); or

(e) the order is made in proceedings brought as mentioned in section 88(1) above.'

3.48   An order for possession in such a case would normally read along the following lines:

Example Possession Order (based on a notice to quit)

1. The defendant do give the claimant possession of [the premises] on or before [date] *or* forthwith. This is a mandatory ground.

2. There be judgment for the claimant against the defendant in the sum of £x in respect of rent/use and occupation arrears, and the defendant do pay the claimant use and occupation charges at the daily rate of £x from [date of order] until possession is given up.

3. There be an unlawful profit order against the defendant in the sum of £x, including interest.

4. The defendant do pay the claimant's costs summarily assessed at £x (assuming a fast-track/one-day trial – otherwise they are likely to go off for detailed assessment, if not agreed). If the defendant is legally aided then the following will be added:

    '… to be subject to a determination of the defendant's ability to pay such costs pursuant to section 26 of the Legal Aid, Sentencing and Punishment of Offenders Act 2012, such determination to be adjourned generally with permission to restore.

5. There be a detailed assessment of the defendant's legal aid costs.

3.49   One argument that is sometimes used in possession claims by a landlord in cases where the tenant retains security of tenure, and as such questions of reasonableness arise, is that misuse of social housing stock is an especially serious matter. It may even represent an offence, such as under the Prevention of Social Housing Fraud Act 2013.[37]

3.50   Here, the more 'hard-line' approach, such as can be seen from the Grounds 5 and 17 cases described at Chapter 2 and at 3.38–3.42, is *prima facie* appropriate.

FIXED-TERM/FLEXIBLE TENANCIES

3.51   If one is considering a fixed-term or flexible tenancy then if security of tenure has been lost, the remedy for the landlord is usually by way of forfeiture proceedings. Some of the issues concerning these forms of tenancy are set out in Chapter 2 at 2.23–2.34, in particular the approach in discretionary ground cases (which will apply in breach of tenancy cases such as where the sub-letting or parting with possession is of part only of the premises).

3.52   Whilst possession action is by way of forfeiture and service of a section 146 notice, and not notice to quit, the usual requirements for a landlord to obtain a determination from the First-tier tribunal (Property Chamber) as to the breach of agreement, pursuant to section 168(4) of the Commonhold and Leasehold Reform Act 2002, before they can issue the required section 146 notice is not required (save in some shared ownership cases – see 3.53) as this provision only applies to long leases.

---

37 Sections 1 or 2 – see Chapter 7.

3.53   Sections 76 and 77 of the same Act define long leases as those exceeding 21 years, and expressly excludes from the definition right-to-buy leases, and shared ownership leases where the tenant's share has stair-cased to 100%.[38]

3.54   What is clear, from *Scala House & District Property Company Ltd v Forbes and others*,[39] is that a breach of covenant not to assign underlet or part with possession is *not* a breach capable of remedy within the meaning of section 146(1) of the Law of Property Act 1925. Lord Justice Russell said in this regard:[40]

> 'After this review of the cases I come to the conclusion that breach by an unlawful subletting is not capable of remedy at all. In my judgment the introduction of such breaches into the relevant section for the first time by section 146 of the Act of 1925 operates only to confer a statutory ability to relieve the lessee from forfeiture on that ground. The subterm has been effectively created subject only to risks of forfeiture: it is a complete breach once and for all: it is not in any sense a continuing breach. If the law were otherwise, a lessee, when a subtenancy is current at the time of the section 146 notice, would have a chance of remedying the situation without having to apply for relief. But if the unlawful subletting had been determined before the notice, the lessee could only seek relief from forfeiture. The only escape from that wholly unsatisfactory difference would be to hold that in the second example by some analogy the lessor was disabled from issuing a writ for possession. But I can find nothing in the section to justify that limitation on the common law right of re-entry, bearing especially in mind that a lessor might discover a whole series of past expired unlawful sublettings which might well justify a refusal to grant relief in forfeiture proceedings.
>
> I stress again that where there has been an unlawful subletting which has determined (and which has not been waived) there has been a breach which at common law entitles the lessor to re-enter: nothing can be done to remedy that breach: the expiry of the subterm has not annulled or remedied the breach: in such case the lessor plainly need not, in his section 146 notice, call upon the lessee to remedy the breach which is not capable of remedy, and is free to issue his writ for possession, the possibility of relief remaining. Can it possibly be that, while that is the situation in such case, it is otherwise if the lessee has failed to get rid of the subterm until after a notice served? Is the lessee then in a stronger position and the lessor in a weaker position? In my judgment not so. These problems and questions arise only if such a breach is capable of remedy, which in my judgment it is not. I consider that *Capital & Counties Property Co. Ltd. v. Mills* [1966] E.G.D. 96, if correctly reported, was wrongly decided. I should add that I find some support for my opinion in the comments of Fraser J. in *Abrahams v. Mac Fisheries Ltd.* [1925] 2 K.B. 18, 35, who expressed

---

38   Section 76(2).
39   [1973] 3 WLR 14.
40   Ibid at [588–589].

the view that the exceptions in section 14(6) of the Act of 1881 (as to, *inter alia*, subletting) were made to cover cases where the breach cannot be remedied specifically.'

3.55   The usual forfeiture issues such as waiver may be relevant in preventing a landlord from relying on any sub-letting/parting with possession breach (not least of course where the complained of activity has ceased), though the irredeemable nature of the breach means that this is less likely to happen 'by accident'.

3.56   If relief from forfeiture is granted this may be conditional, and is in any event difficult to achieve (though in consent cases, that is partial sub-letting/ parting with possession, the question of whether the landlord would have granted permission if asked, or could not reasonably have withheld consent, may well be relevant).[41]

3.57   For the sake of accuracy it should also be noted that in *Scala House* relief from forfeiture was given. Part of the rationale for this was:[42]

'Third: as I have indicated, the defendants did unscramble the situation in June by an agreement which involved surrender of the subtenancy and a discontinuance of any parting with possession. The agreement envisages the possibility of a future assignment of the lease by the first defendant to the second and third defendants, and erroneously provided that if that should happen the second and third defendants, in addition to continuing to pay the £25 to £35 weekly to the first defendant, should also bear the rent under the lease which hitherto has, of course, been borne by the first defendant. This was admittedly an error in drafting: it was intended that the first defendant in effect should continue to bear the lease rent by equivalent reduction of the weekly payments. This error, which remains in the documents, I record.'

EVIDENCE

3.58   It is frequently the case that evidence in support of any sub-letting or parting with possession case is perceived as being limited and inconclusive. Where a sole tenant of a one-bedroom flat has been found to be sub-letting and evidence is available of the tenancy agreement they entered into with the sub-tenant, which contains an address for the tenant other than the demised premises, makes for an easy case, this is not the norm.

3.59   More usually there are suggestions and indications of such activity – neighbour reports of other persons living at the premises, contractors and repair operatives finding persons other than the tenant answering the door when they visit the premises, etc. Chapter 6 gives further details as to measures that may

---

41 *West Layton Ltd v Ford (Executrix of the Estate of Louis Joseph, deceased) and another* [1979] 3 WLR 14.
42 *Scala House* at [590] *per* Russell LJ.

be taken by a landlord to improve their chances of success in any legal action they take.

3.60 To give one well-known example, in *Hussey v London Borough of Camden*,[43] the local authority argued that their tenant had sub-let his flat to the second defendant whilst he lived elsewhere. Indeed, the trial judge found:

(a) that the tenant *had* occupied other premises as his only or principal home in the latter part of 1986 and 1987.

(b) The only person shown on the electoral register for the relevant premises in 1987 was the second defendant.

(c) From 1989 to 1990 the tenant occupied yet another flat as his principal residence.

(d) The tenant had thereby lost security of tenure, and therefore the judge made a possession order.

3.61 There was, however, no evidence of any tenancy agreement between the first and second defendants or that rent was paid, and also no evidence that the first defendant did not occupy the flat as his only or principal home on the expiry of the notice to quit, which had not been served by the plaintiffs until January 1991.

3.62 In allowing the tenant's appeal, Lord Justice Leggatt was compelled to remark:[44]

'It is obvious that from time to time others were in sole occupation of it, but it does not follow that they enjoyed exclusive possession. Mr Hussey's right to enter and use the premises if and when he chose was not negatived. There might have been proof that he gave up his key, or of the manner in which rent was paid either to him by another or by another in his stead. There was no such evidence.

In my judgment the vital ingredient necessary to prove that Mr Hussey had ceased to be a secure tenant, that he had for some period or periods parted with possession of 10 Brockham House, was simply not proved either by direct evidence or by way of inference from the proven facts. Even though, for some periods, he did cease to occupy 10 Brockham House as his principal home, he was not shown to have parted with possession of it. Since there was no evidence that Mr Hussey was not occupying the flat as his only or principal home upon expiry of the notice to quit, despite his absence in Greece, the tenant condition was satisfied and the possession order ought not to have been made.'

3.63 In short, the judge had asked himself the wrong questions; this defect could not on the findings as presented be corrected by way of 'inference evidence'.

43 (1995) 27 HLR 5.
44 Ibid at [11].

3.64   Some ten years later Lord Justice Mummery addressed the issue of a lack of direct evidence again in *Lambeth LBC v Vandra*:[45]

> '8. In my judgment, the fact that there is another possible explanation for the state of affairs found by the housing officer does not mean that there was no evidence or insufficient evidence for the inferences made by the district judge as to subletting of the whole. The absence of direct evidence is not fatal. Judges are entitled, when finding facts, to make inferences as a matter of probability from the primary facts which are established.'

3.65   In *Vandra* the so-called primary facts were:

(a) The tenant was not in occupation of the premises on either of the authority's two visits.

(b) Conversely, five other people were seen at the premises at these two visits.

(c) There was no evidence or signs of occupation by Miss Vandra and her four children.

(d) There were Yale locks on all rooms (and an additional padlock on one).

(e) There were no signs of any room being used as a living room.

(f) Four of the occupants said they paid rent to Kim (the name of Miss Vandra's caretaker).

3.66   The Court of Appeal found that the authority was entitled to claim that an explanation was called for from Miss Vandra as to why she was not at the premises, and why others were paying to be there. The district judge, in turn, was entitled to reject her explanations. The authority's appeal was allowed and the district judge's possession order restored.

3.67   These two authorities illustrate that the court must direct itself to the right questions. For example:

(a) Has the tenant sub-let or parted with possession of the whole? If so and a valid notice to quit has been properly served, then a possession order should be made. It is irrelevant in such circumstances if the 'tenant' has returned to live at the premises.

(b) If not, have they sub-let or parted with possession of *part* of the demised premises?

(c) If so, was this in breach of tenancy (ie without consent)? Would it be reasonable – in reliance on a notice seeking possession[46] – to make a possession order (and should that order be suspended on terms or made outright)?

---

45 [2005] EWCA Civ 1801, [2006] HLR 19.
46 Although the court has the power to dispense with the requirement for such a notice if they consider it just and equitable to do so – Housing Act 1985, s 83(1)(b) (secure tenancies)/ Housing Act 1988, s 8(1)(b) (assured tenancies).

(d) If there was sub-letting or parting with possession of part *and* the tenant(s) were not themselves living at the premises as their only or principal home at the time of the expiry date in any valid notice to quit properly served then a possession order should be made.

(e) Lack of direct evidence (eg tenancy agreement between the tenant and sub-tenant) is not necessarily fatal to any possession claim.

(f) The stronger the evidence, the more likely it is that the *'tenant'* is going to be required by the court to explain away the seemingly compelling evidence.

3.68 Chapter 6 deals with the question of investigation and evidence in more focused detail, while Chapter 7 covers criminal sanctions including those flowing from sub-letting or parting with possession activities.

CONCLUSION

3.69 If sub-letting or parting with possession is properly evidenced then there are obvious remedies available to the landlord, both in terms of repossession of the demised premises and, at times, recovery of compensation and other monies (as addressed in Chapters 5 and 7).

3.70 When it is obvious that someone other than the tenant(s) have been living at the premises then there are often questions as to the nature of this third-party's occupation – family friend 'loose' arrangement, 'caretaker' scenario in the enforced absence of the tenant abroad, in prison, etc, temporary 'let', unpaid scenario or, of course, a true sub-let.

3.71 Evidence is, of course, key as to the true nature of the occupation, but it may in any event be such as to if not shift the burden of proof to the tenant, at least require an explanation as to the apparent improper use of the premises.

3.72 Possession claims pleaded in the alternative (eg by way of notice to quit and notice seeking possession in an assured tenancy case) are not uncommon as the true facts remain unclear pre-trial. As if to demonstrate the inherent problems of accuracy and consistency in many cases (not least between tenant and sub-tenant), Mr Justice Turner remarked somewhat witheringly in a non-housing case, *McClelland v Elvin* [2017] EWHC 2795 (QB):

> '31 ... The murky absence of documentary formality formed a background against which both the claimant and defendant appeared for much of the time to have assumed the roles of determined competitors in an implausibility contest.'

3.73 Finally, as with many of the civil scenarios dealt with in this book, criminal sanctions may also apply alongside the civil remedy sought. See Chapter 7 for further details.

CHAPTER 4

Only or Principal Home/Succession

- Not using premises as main home
- Succession to tenancy

Key points

- To retain security of tenure a tenant – or at least one of joint tenants – must live at the demised premises as their only or principal home.

- However, occupation by a spouse or civil partner is to be treated as occupation by the tenant for these purposes.

- A tenant can go in and out of security of tenure, as long as they do not sub-let or part with possession of the whole of the premises; if the premises in a periodic tenancy case are not their only or principal home upon the expiration date specified in a properly served and valid notice to quit, then security is lost permanently.

- If the tenant does return to live at the premises prior to the expiry of any notice to quit then they will have acted in breach of their tenancy by living away and possession action can be taken on discretionary grounds for breach of tenancy in reliance on a notice seeking possession (periodic tenancy or assured fixed term) or forfeiture and notice seeking possession (flexible tenancy) – see 2.20–2.32.

- The ending of a tenancy for premises not used by the tenant(s) as their only or principal home will either by way of forfeiture (fixed-term/ flexible tenancies) – see 2.20–2.32 and 3.51 – or in reliance on a notice to quit (periodic tenancies).

- A social landlord can extend the statutory rights of succession beyond the basic provision for spouses and civil partners (and those living together as such) – see 4.20–4.28 below.

- See Chapter 3, paragraph 3.3 for a 'round-up' of security of tenure issues.

INTRODUCTION

4.1   The previous chapters have dealt with the most obvious social housing fraud topics: obtaining the property by misrepresentation and sub-letting or parting with possession of the whole or part of the premises. Here we address the issues of:

(a) the tenant not living in the allocated property as their only or principal home; and

(b) 'fraudulent' succession to a social tenancy.

4.2   Whilst the only or principal home topic does not necessarily indicate fraud in the strict sense, it is certainly 'misuse' of a property (not simply as an undoubted breach of tenancy but also by way of preventing its use by some other person or family in housing need) and relevant as a concept in any event (eg when dealing with unlawful profit orders).[1]

4.3   As was made clear in Chapter 3, sub-letting the whole of premises – or parting with possession of the same – is an obvious example of the tenant not living there as their only or principal home. This chapter goes on to address situations which are, perhaps, not so straightforward and sets out the important principles in issue, including by way of decided court authorities. Any possession claim alleged no succession or a loss of security of tenure by an existing tenant will, in broad terms and as discussed in Chapters 2 and 3, be by way of reliance on a properly served notice to quit for periodic tenancies (see an example at 3.30, and note 4.32) or use of the forfeiture procedure in fixed-term tenancy cases.

ONLY OR PRINCIPAL HOME

Overview

4.4   It is invariably an express, but in any event an implied,[2] term of secure and assured tenancies that the tenant(s) must live in their premises as their only or principal home. Chapter 3 explains, in particular at 3.3 and 3.23–3.25. To recap:

(a) The requirement for the tenant to live at the demised premises as their only or principal home is ambulatory[3] such that whilst security of tenure may be lost during periods of absence it is capable of being regained as long as:

- the tenant has not sub-let or parted with possession of the *whole* of the premises (in which case security of tenure is, as shown in Chapter 3, permanently lost); and

- the tenant returns to live at the said premises prior to the expiry of any valid notice to quit properly served.[4]

(b) If it is a joint tenancy, as long as one of the joint tenants lives at the premises then it is irrelevant and of no effect if the others do not.

---

1   See Chapter 5.
2   Housing Act 1985, s 81 (secure tenancies)/Housing Act 1988, s1(1)(b) (assured tenancies).
3   *Crawley Borough Council v Sawyer* (1987) 20 HLR 98, CA.
4   See *Hussey v Camden LBC* (1995) 27 HLR 5 at [7–8] *per* Leggatt LJ.

(c) If the tenant's spouse or civil partner lives at the premises then that is treated as occupation by the tenant. Section 30(4) of the Family Law Act 1996[5] provides (with A as the tenant and B as the spouse/civil partner):

'(4) B's occupation by virtue of this section—

...

(b) if B occupies the dwelling-house as B's only or principal home, is to be treated, for the purposes of the Housing Act 1985, Part I of the Housing Act 1988, Chapter 1 of Part 5 of the Housing Act 1996 and the Prevention of Social Housing Fraud Act 2013, as occupation by A as A's only or principal home.'

4.5 In relation to the last point, it followed that in *Derwent Housing Association v Taylor*,[6] where the tenant wife left the demised premises whilst her non-tenant husband remained, she was still required to serve a notice to quit to bring the tenancy to an end:

'11 It follows, in my judgement, that as a matter of interpretation of the Family Law Act, 1996, B has no home rights once A has validly terminated the tenancy. I do not consider that this conclusion is called in question by the Human Rights Act 1988 . B has, of course, the right under art.8 of the European Convention on Human Rights and Fundamental Freedoms to respect for his home. In *Sims v Dacorum Borough Council* [2015] UK SC 63; [2015] A.C. 133 the Supreme Court decided that the common law rule which enabled one of two joint tenants to terminate a periodic tenancy by notice to quit without the consent of the other was not incompatible with art. 8 or with art. 1 of the First Protocol. The ability of the sole tenant to terminate the tenancy without the consent of her spouse is, in my judgment, an even stronger case. However, as the Supreme Court held in *Simms*, B would, at least in principle, be entitled to raise the proportionality of his eviction, thus giving effect to art. 8. That has not thus far been raised in this case, and whether such an argument would succeed is, of course, a different matter. For these reasons, I would dismiss the appeal.'

4.6 In that case the husband had unsuccessfully argued that once his wife had left the marital home he had, in effect, become the tenant such that her notice to quit was of no effect. This was given short shrift by the Court of Appeal who reminded the parties that the Family Law Act 1996 was merely regulating the rights of spouses *as between themselves*.[7]

---

5 Amended by the Civil Partnership Act 2004, Sch 9.
6 [2016] EWCA Civ 508, [2016] HLR 25.
7 *Sanctuary Housing Association v Campbell* [1999] 1 WLR 1279 concerning the 1996 Act's predecessor, the Matrimonial Homes Act 1983.

4.7   As an aside, it is open to a landlord and tenant to agree to waive the requirements of section 5 of the Protection from Eviction Act 1977 (four weeks' notice to quit):[8]

> '22 It is open to the landlord and the tenant, for whose sole benefit section 5 of the 1977 Act was enacted, to waive its requirements. Mr Alomo contended that, as a matter of public policy or public interest, the court should be slow to infer an intention or agreement to waive a requirement such as that imposed by section 5 of the 1977 Act, particularly in the absence of any evidence that the parties had specifically addressed their minds to that requirement.'

If there are joint tenants though, *all* must agree.[9]

Defining the term

4.8   Turning to the substantive issue of how 'only or principal home' is properly defined, it should first be noted that it is a *question of fact* for the court to decide,[10] though a simple 'day count' comparison for times spent at the premises and time spent away is unlikely to be sufficient or determinative on its own.[11]

4.9   Indeed, the day count issue was most obviously disregarded in *Hammersmith & Fulham LBC v Clarke*[12] where Lord Justice Keene remarked, in rejecting the authority's appeal against a trial judge's finding that the tenant had an objective and enduring intention to return to her home despite being a permanent resident in a nursing home:

> '28 Was there then no evidence on which he could have come to the conclusion which he did? Certainly there was evidence pointing towards an intention to remain in the nursing home. Mrs Clarke had a permanent placement there. She did sign the note of 14 January and she did spend the vast majority of her time between then and the trial at the nursing home. On the other hand, her grandson and his wife continued occupying the premises as they had previously done with her. They would undoubtedly have allowed her back, as indeed they did from time to time, so there was no impediment to her return. It does seem probable, as Mr Wragg conceded at one point, that her furniture remained there. Certainly there was no evidence that it had been moved elsewhere. She was, after all, back living there at the date of the trial, so it seems that her furniture was probably there. That is not only relevant to occupation generally but it may also assist on the issue of intention.'

---

8   *Hackney LBC v Snowden* (2001) 33 HLR 49, para 22 *per* Peter Gibson LJ.
9   *Hounslow LBC v Pilling* (1993) 25 HLR 305.
10 *Ujima Housing Association v Ansah* (1998) 30 HLR 31 and *Peabody Donation Fund Governors v Grant* (1982) 6 HLR 41 (the latter being a succession case).
11 *Dove v Havering LBC* [2017] EWCA Civ 156, [2017] HLR 19, para 34 *per* Lewison LJ.
12 (2001) 33 HLR 77.

4.10   The *length of the tenant's absence* from the premises of which possession is sought, or other circumstances relevant to that absence, may however raise the presumption that the premises have ceased to be the tenant's principal home.[13]

4.11   Where the tenant's absence is *sufficiently prolonged* to raise the inference that they have ceased to occupy the dwelling, the burden the falls on the tenant to demonstrate that their only or principal residence continues.[14]

4.12   In *Islington LBC v Boyle*,[15] Lord Justice Etherton (now Master of the Rolls) helpfully summarised the relevant principles at paragraphs 55 and 65 of his judgment:

(a) The length or other circumstances of the tenant's absence may raise the inference that the premises ceased to be their principal home, and the burden of proving the contrary then falls on the tenant.

(b) To rebut that presumption, it is not sufficient for the tenant to simply prove that at the material time it was their *subjective* intention to return and belief that the dwelling remained their principal home. The *objective* facts must bear out the reality of that belief and intention both in the sense that:

- the intention and belief are or were genuinely held;

- the intention and belief themselves reflect reality (though a date or time period of return is not necessarily required); and

- there must be some 'formal, outward and visible sign of the intention to return'.

The reason for the absence, the length and other circumstances of the absence and (where relevant) the anticipated future duration of the absence, as well as statements and conduct of the tenant, will all be relevant to that objective assessment.

(c) The court's focus is on the enduring intention of the tenant, which, depending on the circumstances, may not be displaced by fleeting changes of mind.

(d) 'Second home' cases must be looked at with particular care.

(e) The issue is *one of fact* to be determined in the light of the evidence as a whole, and in respect of which the trial judge's findings of primary fact can only be overturned on appeal if they were perverse (the Appeal Court may, in an appropriate case, substitute its own inferences drawn from those primary facts).

---

13 *Brown v Brash* [1948] 2 KB 247 CA and *Islington LBC v Boyle* [2011] EWCA Civ 1450, [2012] HLR 18.
14 *Brown v Brash* [1948] 2 KB 247 CA at [254].
15 [2011] EWCA Civ 1450, [2012] HLR 18.

4.13 It follows that, for example, a visit to see family abroad for six months may be perfectly in order, especially where that family live some way off and/or face-to-face contact is otherwise rare. Similarly, a placement abroad for work purposes may be equally as explicable and will not fall foul of the only or principal home condition.

4.14 Looking at an 'extreme' example of the approach – and one which may not be decided the same today, though the principles it established remain good law – in the Rent Act[16] authority of *Tickner v Hearn*[17] the Court of Appeal upheld the decision of the trial judge that the tenant was still protected *despite* the fact that she had been in a mental hospital for six years, was 73 years of age and was unlikely ever to return to her home. It was found that she always considered the premises as her home and hoped to return, a hope for which there was *some* chance.

4.15 A note of caution was though given by Lord Justice Ormerod:[18]

'For my part, however, I am of the opinion that to establish an intention to return by itself is not necessarily sufficient to obtain the protection of the Acts. The ultimate fact to be established is the fact of occupation, for it is only those in occupation whom the Act protects. If a tenant is out of occupation for some time he must at least prove an intention to return; but if the circumstances of the case are such that by reason of mental or physical illness or for some other reason the intention, even if clearly and bona fide held, seems most unlikely to be achieved within a reasonable time, it must surely be open to the judge in a proper case to find as a fact that the tenant is not in occupation. It seems to me that some of the reported cases have gone very far in the protection of the tenant.'

4.16 In the more modern authority of *Crawley BC v Sawyer*,[19] the tenant went to live with his girlfriend in 1985 and in the following year both his electricity and gas at his local authority flat were disconnected. The local authority became aware of the situation the following year; when they spoke to the tenant he admitted that he was living with his girlfriend and that they intended to purchase her home.

4.17 A notice to quit was served soon after and, although the tenant broke up with his girlfriend shortly afterwards, he did not return to the premises until *after* the expiry date in the notice to quit.

---

16 In contrast to the position under the Rent Acts, a secure or assured tenant must not only show that the premises remain his home, but that they are their only or principal home: *Ujima Housing Association v Ansah* (1998) 30 HLR 31. The Court of Appeal in *Crawley BC v Sawyer* (1988) 20 HLR 98 held that there was no material difference between occupation as a 'home' under the Housing Act 1985 (and by extension the Housing Act 1988) and a 'residence' required to sustain a statutory tenancy under the Rent Acts (see Rent Act 1977, s 2).
17 [1960] 1 WLR 1406.
18 Ibid at [1416].
19 (1988) 20 HLR 98.

4.18   The Court of Appeal dismissed the local authority's appeal from their failed possession claim and found that, following on from the Rent Act approach, the temporary absence of a tenant who intended to return to live in the premises did not deprive them of statutory protection. Lord Justice Parker explained at [102]:

> 'The position as at the time the notice to quit was served was that the girlfriend had already told him that he had to get out. He did not, in fact, move back into Cobnor Close until after the expiry of the notice to quit, but in my view it was well open to the learned judge to have come to the conclusion that, both when the notice to quit was served and when it expired and indeed throughout the whole period, Cobnor Close remained his principal home. That the matter was a matter for the learned judge to conclude on the facts appears clearly from the decision of this court in *Peabody Donation Fund Governors v. Grant* (1982) 6 H.L.R. 41. The learned judge reached his conclusion here on evidence on which he was, in my view, entitled to reach that conclusion. I am unable to accept that in reaching it he misdirected himself in any way as to the law.'

4.19   The lessons to be learned from a plethora of cases under the Rent Acts, and the Housing Acts of 1985 and 1988 are therefore:

- Evidence, as so often, is key. If it is said that an individual is not living at the demised premises as their only or principal home, it is important, where possible, to gather evidence as to where the landlord says that individual *is* living. Credit reference reports and correspondence may, though, only take matters so far. Contemporaneous neighbour evidence may have a role to play too, as will evidence from internal inspections of the premises. See Chapter 6 for further details as to evidence and information gathering.

- Whilst there is no absolute necessity to have details of where the tenant is in fact living, it may therefore strengthen the case if evidence of such accommodation and its enduring value to the tenant is available.

- Proper service of a valid notice to quit in a periodic tenancy case (including introductory tenancies) is key, but in many instances a landlord will also serve a notice seeking possession at the same time (expressed to be without prejudice to the notice to quit) and rely on both in the alternative in any subsequent possession proceedings. Mr Sawyer (see 4.16), for example, would have been in breach of his tenancy had the trial judge determined that there were periods when he had not lived at the demised premises as his only or principal home but that at the expiry of the notice to quit he did so reside.

- In such circumstances the primary case is reliance on the notice to quit, but if the finding is that the tenant has 'returned home' prior to the expiry of such a notice then their behaviour and conduct may still represent a breach of tenancy (see 4.4 above), allowing discretionary possession proceedings.[20]

- The remedy is, therefore, by way of Part 55 possession proceedings relying on:
  - a notice to quit based on the argument that security of tenure has been lost by reason of the tenant not living at the premises as their only or principal home;
  - in the alternative and if the tenant 'moves back in' prior to the expiry of the notice to quit, a notice seeking possession citing the breach of tenancy grounds of Ground 1 (secure tenancy) or Ground 12 (assured tenancy) of Schedule 2 to the Housing Acts of 1985 and 1988 respectively.
  - in flexible and fixed-term tenancy cases action is by forfeiture if it is said the only or principal home situation continues, service of a s 146 notice and notice seeking possession if the tenant has returned (flexible tenancy) or just a notice seeking possession (assured fixed-term tenancy). See 2.20–2.32.

- As a question of fact, an appeal is only likely to succeed if there has been some misapplication of the law and principles pertaining to this area or the trial judge's findings of primary facts are perverse and without proper or rational or any basis.

SUCCESSION

Right of succession – secure tenancies (overview)

4.20 The right of succession to a secure tenancy is now governed by sections 86A (England) and 87 (Wales) of the Housing Act 1985 and the former provides in the case of post-1 April 2012[21] tenancies:

(a) If the deceased tenant was a sole tenant then their spouse or civil partner (or person living with the tenant as a spouse or civil partner) would succeed so long as:

- they were living at the premises as their only or principal home;[22]

- the tenant was not themselves a successor.[23]

---

20 Housing Act 1985, Ground 1 (secure tenancies)/ Housing Act 1988, Ground 12 (assured tenancies), to be found in Schedule 2 in both Acts.
21 Localism Act 2011, s 160(6). As noted at 4.24, the Housing and Planning Act 2016, s 120 Sch 8, will, when brought into force, amend the Housing Act 1985 further so as to bring the succession provisions for pre-1 April 2012 secure tenancies into line with those for tenancies granted since that date. It will only do so where the tenant dies after the amendment has come into force.
22 Housing Act 1985, s 86A(1)(5).
23 Ibid, s 88(1)(b) – remembering that, as always, a change from joint to sole tenancy upon death of a tenant counts as a succession (see s 86A(3)).

(b) Second successions are though possible under the new statutory scheme if the express term of the deceased tenant's agreement provides as much.[24]

(c) If there was no spouse, civil partner, etc. to succeed to the tenancy in the circumstances described above, then an extended succession right provided for in the tenancy agreement (eg carer, family member) is enforceable as a statutory succession.[25]

4.21 Statutory succession does not apply to joint tenancies – where one of joint tenants dies the remaining joint tenant(s) succeed to the tenancy under the doctrine of survivorship.[26]

4.22 For Wales – and at the time of writing pre-1 April 2012 tenancies in England[27] – the 'old' section 87 remains:

> 'A person is qualified to succeed the tenant under a secure tenancy of a dwelling house in Wales if he occupies the dwelling-house as his only or principal home at the time of the tenant's death and either—
>
> (a) he is the tenant's spouse or civil partner; or
>
> (b) he is another member of the tenant's family[28] and has resided with the tenant throughout the period of 12 months[29] ending with the tenant's death,

unless, in either case, the tenant was himself a successor, as defined in section 88.'

4.23 In *Turley v (1) Wandsworth LBC (2) Secretary of State for Communities and Local Government*,[30] the Court of Appeal held that a tenancy condition which required for succession purposes the long-term partner of a secure tenant to have resided with them throughout the 12-month period immediately prior to the secure tenant's death (ie the position in 4.22) was not discriminatory or

---

24 Ibid, s 86A(4).

25 Ibid, s 86A(2).

26 *Cunningham-Reid v Public Trustee* [1944] KB 602 – though it is not treated as a transmission of tenancy (*Tennant v Hutton* (unreported) 9 July 1996; Court of Appeal (Civil Division) Transcript No 904 of 1996 as reported in *Solihull MBC v Hickin* [2012] UKSC 39, [2012] 1 WLR 2295, para 8 *per* Lord Sumption JSC).

27 See n 21. Localism Act 2011, s 160(6) – this includes s 86 periodic tenancies arising after termination of pre-1 April 2012 secure fixed-term tenancies.

28 Housing Act 1985, s 113 – '(1) A person is a member of another's family within the meaning of this Part if – (a) he is the spouse or civil partner of that person, or he and that person live together as husband and wife or as if they were civil partners, or (b) he is that person's parent, grandparent, child, grandchild, brother, sister, uncle, aunt, nephew or niece. (2) For the purpose of subsection (1)(b) – (a) a relationship by marriage or civil partnership shall be treated as a relationship by blood, (b) a relationship of the half-blood shall be treated as a relationship of the whole blood, (c) the stepchild of a person shall be treated as his child, and (d) an illegitimate child shall be treated as the legitimate child of his mother and reputed father.'

29 See *Turley v (1) Wandsworth LBC (2) Secretary of State for Communities and Local Gov* [2017] EWCA Civ 189 at para 4.23.

30 [2017] EWCA Civ 189, [2017] HLR 21.

incompatible with her rights under Articles 8 and 14 of the European Convention of Human Rights but rather justified as the provision was not 'manifestly without reasonable foundation'. Lord Justice Underhill concluded:

> '42 I would dismiss this appeal. I am sorry for the appellant because the comparatively brief interruption in her relationship with Mr Doyle after a long period of living together has had the consequence of depriving her of the right to succeed to the tenancy of the house which has been her home for many years. But bright-line rules will sometimes have hard effects, and they are not for that reason unlawful. The Council cannot be blamed for insisting on the rules, in circumstances where there is an acute shortage of social housing, particularly no doubt of flats of the size occupied by the appellant. In that connection I should record that at an early stage, before the commencement of these proceedings, it offered her a three-bedroom flat in exchange for her current home; but she did not accept the offer.'

4.24   When section 120 and Schedule 8 of the Housing and Planning Act 2016 are brought into force, the more potentially restrictive succession rights for secure tenancies brought in for post-1 April 2012 secure tenancies and set out at 4.20 will apply to *all* secure tenancies.

Right of succession – assured tenancies (overview)

4.25   The assured periodic tenancy regime, to be found at section 17 of the Housing Act 1988, was always more restrictive when it came to succession compared with that applicable for secure tenancies, until the recent changes brought in by the Localism Act 2011.

4.26   Private registered providers of social housing, such as housing associations, frequently had and still have tenancy provisions seeking to extend or add to the statutory rule but as a matter of statutory succession, that was previously only possible to spouses, civil partners or those living together as husband and wife or as civil partners *and* occupying the premises as their only or principal home.[31]

4.27   Amendments brought in by the Localism Act 2011 changed that position for some tenancies provided for by private registered providers from 1 April 2012[32] and further alterations were made with effect from 13 March 2014 so that we now have the following position:

(a) Statutory succession still does not apply to joint tenancies – where one of joint tenants dies the remaining joint tenant(s) succeeds to the tenancy under the doctrine of survivorship (see 4.21).

---

31 Housing Act 1988, s 17.
32 Localism Act 2011, s 161 – periodic tenancies arising after the end of a fixed-term tenancy (granted prior to 1 April 2012) by virtue of Housing Act 1988, s 5 are also exempt from the Localism Act amendments.

(b) If the deceased tenant – whether periodic[33] or fixed-term (of not less than two years)[34] – was a sole tenant, then their spouse or civil partner (or person living with the tenant as a spouse or civil partner) would succeed as long as:

- they were living at the premises as their only or principal home;[35] and

- the tenant was not themselves a successor.[36]

(c) If the assured tenancy is a periodic arrangement (ie not fixed-term) and there was no spouse, civil partner, etc to succeed to the tenancy in the circumstances described above, then as long as the deceased tenant was not himself a successor an extended succession right provided for in the tenancy agreement (eg to a carer, or family member living at the premises) is enforceable as a statutory succession.[37]

(d) Save for section 17(1B) – see sub-paragraph (b) above – the statutory succession provisions apply to periodic tenancies and for fixed-term tenancies succession is only by any provision in a will or the intestacy rules.[38]

4.28   Pre-1 April 2012, periodic assured tenancies simply follow the approach set out at 4.26 above.[39] Tenancy terms (in agreements from 11 November 1999) seeking to extend rights of succession, though not statutory or enforceable as such, can be enforced by the would-be successor pursuant to section 1 of the Contracts (Rights of Third Parties) Act 1999:

'(1) Subject to the provisions of this Act, a person who is not a party to a contract (a 'third party') may in his own right enforce a term of the contract if—

(a) the contract expressly provides that he may, or

(b) subject to subsection (2), the term purports to confer a benefit on him.

(2) Subsection (1)(b) does not apply if on a proper construction of the contract it appears that the parties did not intend the term to be enforceable by the third party.

(3) The third party must be expressly identified in the contract by name, as a member of a class or as answering a particular description but need not be in existence when the contract is entered into.'

---

33 Housing Act 1988, s 17(1A).
34 Ibid, s 17(1B)(1C).
35 Ibid, s 17(1A)(4).
36 Ibid, s 17(1D) – remembering that, as always, a change from joint to sole tenancy upon death of a tenant counts as a succession (see s 17(2)(b)).
37 Ibid, s 17(1A)(1D)(1E) – prior to these changes would-be 'successors' relied on Contracts (Rights of Third Parties) Act 1999, s 1 for post-11 November 1999 tenancies – see 4.28.
38 The successor in these circumstances will be treated as a successor, but enjoy an assured tenancy with the consequential right to a statutory periodic tenancy at the end of the fixed term: see s 17(2)(a).
39 Localism Act 2011, s 161(7).

Fraudulent 'succession'

4.29   The question of succession is raised here in the context of a purported or claimed succession to a tenancy later found to have been without factual or legal merit.[40] This is an issue frequently resolved by means of the landlord taking possession action against the would-be successor (on the basis that they have *not* in fact succeeded to the deceased tenant's tenancy).

4.30   For example, this may arise in a pre-1 April 2012 secure tenancy where it is later discovered that the 'family' member was not, in fact, related to the deceased tenant or even if they were, then the would-be successor only moved in with the tenant three months before the latter's death rather than the required and stated 12 months.

4.31   The temptation to claim succession when there is, in fact, no such entitlement is obvious for three primary reasons:

(a) the would-be successor will usually have been living in the subject premises as their home and a failed succession could lead to homelessness;

(b) social housing attracts lower rents than those seen in the private rented sector, with frequently better records of management and repair; and

(c) depending upon the nature of the tenancy, the would-successor may enjoy a right to buy if their request to succeed is accepted.

4.32   The obvious remedy for a landlord faced with such a situation is to seek possession of the premises on the basis that the would-be successor is not, in fact, a tenant by reason of succession; once the deceased tenant's remaining common-law tenancy is brought to an end by way of service and expiry of a notice to quit,[41] they are actually a trespasser.

4.33   The proper analysis can be best described as follows:

Overview

A. Succession to a tenancy is by operation of law and as such, even if not confirmed for some months after the death of a tenant (or even after contested possession proceedings), the statutory successor becomes the tenant from the point of death of the deceased tenant by operation of law.

---

40 In *Thurrock BC v West* [2012] EWCA Civ 1435, [2013] HLR 5, the Court of Appeal rejected a grandchild's Art 8 defence to a possession claim in a case where he had no right to succeed to the tenancy as it was a second succession. In *R (on the application of Gangera) v Hounslow LBC* [2003] EWHC 794 (Admin), [2003] HLR 68 Mr Justice Moses, the applicant, failed in his Art 14 challenge to the succession provisions of the Housing Act 1985.

41 Served on the executors or administrators of the deceased's estate or, if no will or letters of administration were taken out, on the Public Trustee: Law of Property (Miscellaneous Provisions) Act 1994, s 18; Public Trustee (Notices Affecting Land) (Title on Death) Regulations 1995 (as amended); *Wirral BC v Smith* (1982) 4 HLR 81.

Grounds 5/17

B. If there was, in fact, no right to succession and it was 'allowed' by the landlord because of a false representation made by or on behalf of the would-be successor then Grounds 5 or 17 *may* apply (but see Chapter 2 and D below).

This depends, however, on the 'successor' having in fact and in law a tenancy. If they do not (because, for example, they were not sufficiently related to the deceased tenant, or residing with them for any required period), then the Housing Acts of 1985 and 1988 do not apply, and the Grounds of Possession in Schedule 2 in either Act similarly are of no application.

Possession action in such circumstances can be taken as indicated at 4.31 above.

If they do have a tenancy, such as by means of the landlord granting them a fresh tenancy (see, for example, D(a) below) it is not by reason of statutory succession of course but rather by agreement with the landlord. In such a case a Ground 5/17 case may be arguable if they came to the tenancy by reason of a false statement or omission to 'update' the landlord of the true state of affairs.

Rescission

C. There is also question of the landlord seeking the remedy of rescission on the basis of fraudulent misrepresentation if a tenancy has been created but there is no security of tenure (if there is then Grounds 5 and 17 must be applied instead[42] – also see D below). If there is no security of tenure it will presumably be because the 'successor' has sub-let or parted with possession of the whole, or no longer lives at the premises as their only or principal home – in such a case the 'easier' option maybe to issue a notice to quit and end the tenancy in this manner.

It follows that rescission is not going to be a usual remedy in cases of disputed succession.

Trespasser action

D. Even before that however unless:

(a) the landlord and would-be successor signed a fresh tenancy agreement (sometimes done to ensure the current tenancy conditions, especially in a stock transfer scenario, apply to the new tenant); or

(b) it was possible to argue that a new tenancy had been created by reason of the parties' actions; or

---

42 *Islington LBC v Uckac* [2006] EWCA Civ 340, [2006] 1 WLR 1303.

(c) there was no *statutory* succession but the landlord had granted a fresh tenancy in reliance on the tenancy terms of the deceased tenant (eg pre-1 April 2012 secure tenancy),

there would have been no grant or assumption of tenancy whatsoever and the landlord would be entitled to seek possession on the basis of trespasser possession proceedings (once they had determined the original tenancy agreement by means of a notice to quit served at the premises in accordance with the deceased tenant's tenancy conditions, and on the Public Trustee, or executor/personal representative).

This will be the usual action taken by the landlord.

Appeal

E. If a possession trial has already been held and the court has found that the defendant *has* succeeded to the tenancy then, by way of a late appeal, it can only be re-opened by way of a re-trial where:[43]

(a) new evidence has come to light which was not reasonably available to the landlord at trial;

(b) this suggests that the defendant may have given and/or presented false evidence;

(c) the new evidence is credible and would have an important influence on the case; *and*

(d) there were no other factors in the interests of justice which dictated that the matter should be re-opened.

Set aside

F. The even better route (than E) in cases where the evidence of fraud is strong would be by means of an application to set aside any order in reliance on CPR 3.1(7):

'*(7) A power of the court under these Rules to make an order includes a power to vary or revoke the order.*'

G. In *Lloyds Investment (Scandinavia) Ltd v Ager-Hanssen*,[44] Mr Justice Patten said at para 7:

'It seems to me that the only power available to me on this application is that contained in CPR r 3.1(7), which enables the court to vary or revoke an order. This is not confined to purely procedural orders and there is no real guidance in the White Book as to the possible limits of the jurisdiction. Although this is not intended to be an exhaustive

---

43 *London Borough of Barnet v Smart* [2005] EWCA Civ 434, paras 27–31 *per* LJ Rix, applying the traditional *Ladd v Marshall* test.
44 [2003] EWHC 1740 (Ch).

definition of the circumstances in which the power under CPR r 3.1(7) is exercisable, **it seems to me that, for the High Court to revisit one of its earlier orders, the applicant must either show some material change of circumstances or that the judge who made the earlier order was misled in some way, whether innocently or otherwise, as to the correct factual position before him**. The latter type of case would include, for example, a case of material non-disclosure on an application for an injunction. If all that is sought is a reconsideration of the order on the basis of the same material, then that can only be done, in my judgment, in the context of an appeal. Similarly it is not, I think, open to a party to the earlier application to seek in effect to reargue that application by relying on submissions and evidence which were available to him at the time of the earlier hearing, but which, for whatever reason, he or his legal representatives chose not to deploy' (emphasis added).

H.   This authority was referred to in *Tibbles v SIG Plc (t/a Asphaltic Roofing Supplies)*[45] in which Lord Justice Rix drew the following conclusions from the jurisprudence relevant to CPR 3.1(7) para 39 (with emphasis added in italic):

'(i)   Despite occasional references to a possible distinction between jurisdiction and discretion in the operation of CPR r 3.1(7) , there is in all probability no line to be drawn between the two. The rule is apparently broad and unfettered, but considerations of finality, the undesirability of allowing litigants to have two bites at the cherry, and the need to avoid undermining the concept of appeal, all push towards a principled curtailment of an otherwise apparently open discretion. Whether that curtailment goes even further in the case of a final order does not arise in this appeal.

(ii)   The cases all warn against an attempt at an exhaustive definition of the circumstances in which a principled exercise of the discretion may arise. Subject to that, however, the jurisprudence has laid down firm guidance as to the primary circumstances in which the discretion may, as a matter of principle, be appropriately exercised, namely *normally only (a) where there has been a material change of circumstances since the order was made, or (b) where the facts on which the original decision was made were (innocently or otherwise) misstated.*

(iii)   It would be dangerous to treat the statement of these primary circumstances, originating with Patten J and approved in this court, as though it were a statute. That is not how jurisprudence operates, especially where there is a warning against the attempt at exhaustive definition.

---

45   [2012] EWCA Civ 518, [2012] 1 WLR 2591.

(iv) Thus there is room for debate in any particular case as to whether and to what extent, in the context of principle (b) in (ii) above, misstatement may include omission as well as positive misstatement, or concern argument as distinct from facts. In my judgment, this debate is likely ultimately to be a matter for the exercise of discretion in the circumstances of each case.

(v) Similarly, questions may arise as to whether the misstatement (or omission) is conscious or unconscious; and whether the facts (or arguments) were known or unknown, knowable or unknowable. These, as it seems to me, are also factors going to discretion: but where the facts or arguments are known or ought to have been known as at the time of the original order, it is unlikely that the order can be revisited, and that must be still more strongly the case where the decision not to mention them is conscious or deliberate.

....

(vii) The cases considered above suggest that the successful invocation of the rule is rare. Exceptional is a dangerous and sometimes misleading word: however, such is the interest of justice in the finality of a court's orders that it ought normally to take something out of the ordinary to lead to variation or revocation of an order, especially in the absence of a change of circumstances in an interlocutory situation.'

I. The High Court judgment of *Satoshi Kojima v HSBC Bank Plc*[46] confirms the likely applicability of using 3.1(7) rather than appeal in respect of final orders, such as an order following trial, albeit in exceptional cases.

J. More recently, on 20 June 2017, in *Prompt Motor Limited v HSBC Bank PLC*[47] HHJ Paul Matthews reviewed the authorities and concluded:

> '31. I accept that even a final judgment obtained by fraud can be set aside. But, as at present advised, I doubt whether anything less will do. Nor do I consider that a final judgment can be set aside merely because fresh evidence comes to light or, worse, evidence that was available at the time that the final judgment was given but which was not deployed is now put forward for the first time. A party has the obligation to fight a case, and the whole case, on one occasion, and cannot deal with it in stages as and when convenient; cf Henderson v Henderson (1843) 3 Hare 100.'

---

46 [2011] EWHC 611 (Ch), para 34 *per* Mr Justice Briggs – the judgment was affirmed on appeal.
47 [2017] EWHC 1487 (Ch).

CONCLUSION

4.34 'Only or principal home' cases cover a multitude of scenarios but share one quality – they represent a use of the premises not anticipated by or allowed for in the tenancy agreement (by reason of express or implied terms).

4.35 Action in respect of the same may result in anything from a warning as to future use of the premises, through to the obtaining of a possession order (whether that be suspended on terms or outright, discretionary or mandatory) and even leading potentially to criminal prosecution (see Chapter 7).

4.36 'False' succession claims also involve a misuse of property and are most commonly 'tested' where the landlord does not itself accept succession, by means of possession proceedings, with the court ultimately determining whether the defendant is entitled to succeed to the tenancy in issue.

4.37 These issues of fact are rarely clear and straightforward, and whilst the litigation process is not inherently uncontroversial, the evidential strength of any case is often difficult to accurately gauge.

CHAPTER 5

Civil Financial Remedies

- Unlawful profit orders
- Damages for misrepresentation
- The tort of deceit and unjust enrichment
- [Rescission]

Key points

- Unlawful profit orders (UPOs) allow for the recovery by the social landlord of the profits achieved by a tenant sub-letting or parting with possession of some or all of their premises.

- UPOs do not apply to shared ownership arrangements.

- Civil financial remedies for social housing fraud above and beyond a UPO are limited and rarely used.

- Rescission as a remedy is available for cases of fraudulent misrepresentation (unless the false representation possession grounds are available[1]) and is usually considered in cases of right to buy/acquire or shared ownership fraud. Damages may not be awarded in lieu of rescission in such a case.

- Damages may be claimed in deceit in addition to or instead of possession claims on the false representation ground or those seeking rescission.

INTRODUCTION

5.1   Social housing fraud has an obvious cost to landlords, as is clear from Chapter 1 and whilst the emphasis upon its discovery is often the return of the premises in issue, there is also the question of financial compensation which can and should be addressed.

5.2   When criminal proceedings are brought in relation to social housing fraud the magistrates' and Crown Courts enjoy powers to make compensation orders in favour of the social landlord: these are dealt with in more detail at

---

1   Housing Act 1985, Sch 2, Ground 5 (secure tenancies); Housing Act 1988, Sch 2, Ground 17 (assured tenancies) – see Chapter 2.

Chapter 7.[2] This chapter addresses instead the options available to landlords in seeking to recover monies in civil proceedings in the county court or (more rarely) the High Court, and the remedy of rescission in so far as it is related to the question of damages for misrepresentation. The financial options may be exercised in addition to or as an alternative to proceedings for possession of the premises, in particular in the following scenarios:

- Sub-letting/parting with possession of let premises.

- Fraudulent misrepresentation and the tort of deceit.

UNLAWFUL PROFIT ORDERS (UPOs)

5.3 The clearest route for a social landlord to financial recompense for fraudulent misuse of their properties is to be found within the provisions set down in the Prevention of Social Housing Fraud Act 2013 (PSHF).[3] This legislation applies to England and Wales and is focused on the twin issues of sub-letting and the parting with possession of demised premises. Chapter 3 provides detailed analysis on the meaning of these terms and the procedure for seeking possession of premises in these circumstances. In this section we are concerned with the procedure for recovery of monies received by tenants, either at the same time as, or separate to, any possession proceedings.

5.4 The PSHF gives two clear benefits to social landlords in terms of their civil rights and remedies in dealing with such a misuse of their stock:

(a) It introduces a new procedure for recovering the profit element of the tenant's activities which is very clear, simple and straightforward (PSHF, s 5).

(b) It extends to assured tenancies the approach which has long applied to secure tenancies: where the *whole* of the demised premises are sub-let or the tenant(s) part with possession of the same, security of tenure is not only lost but it cannot be restored save by the grant of a fresh tenancy (Housing Act 1988, s 15A as inserted by PSHF, s 6).[4]

5.5 Earlier legislation, such as the Theft Act 1968, the Proceeds of Crime Act 2002 and the Fraud Act 2006, does still apply to social housing fraud scenarios. However, in the context of recovering 'compensation' for the types of housing

---

2   24 Housing, *'Illegal right to buy claim ends in conviction'* 6 August 2015: a former local authority tenant was convicted for attempting to defraud £66,500 in an illegal right-to-buy claim and also ordered to pay £7,376 for the costs incurred by the Royal Borough of Greenwich placing homeless persons in emergency accommodation when the property should have been available to them.

3   In force from 15 October 2013 (England) and 5 November 2013 (Wales).

4   The ambulatory nature of security of tenure *previously* extended to such arrangements for assured tenancies and as long as the tenant(s) – or at least one of them – was treated as living at the demised premises prior to the expiry of the notice to quit as their only or principal home then the said notice was of no effect.

fraud to which it applies, the UPO approach found in the PSHF is expressly designed to be:

(a) simpler,

(b) readily available in conjunction with existing criminal/civil proceedings, and

(c) easier to obtain.

Conditions

5.6   Where a secure or assured tenant has sub-let their premises or allowed others to stay there in their absence, then they will often have done so, at least in part, with a view to making a profit on such an enterprise.[5] Social housing rents, even at affordable rent levels, are lower than those seen in the private rented sector. The profit possibilities are all the greater if continuing (fraudulent) housing benefit awards are factored in.

5.7   The PSHF provides that UPOs can be obtained in both criminal[6] and civil[7] proceedings under the Act, the former being dealt with at Chapter 7. For civil recovery, section 5 of PSHF, requires that four basic conditions must all be satisfied for recovery in civil proceedings:[8]

(a) the sub-letting/parting with possession has taken place in breach of an express or implied condition of the tenancy (knowledge that such actions constitute a breach on the part of the tenant or dishonesty is not required);

(b) the sub-letting/parting with possession can be of the whole or, in a secure tenancy case, if the landlord's written consent has not been given, part of the premises;

(c) the tenant has ceased to occupy the premises as their only or principal home; *and*

(d) the tenant has received money as a result of the sub-letting/parting with possession.

5.8   In addition, for assured tenancy cases:

(a) the landlord must be a private registered provider of social housing (England)[9] or registered social landlord (Wales[10]),[11] invariably a housing association; *and*

(b) the tenancy must not be a shared ownership lease.[12]

---

5   An assured tenant refers to both an assured and an assured shorthold tenant.
6   PSHF, s 4.
7   Ibid, s 5.
8   Ibid, ss 5(3) and 5(4).
9   Housing and Regeneration Act 2008, s 80.
10   Housing Act 1996, s 1; Housing and Regeneration Act 2008, s 61.
11   PSHF, s 5(4)(a).
12   Ibid, s 5(4)(b).

5.9   The first two conditions at 5.7 are addressed in detail in Chapter 3 and, in reality, are unlikely to provide a difficult obstacle to obtaining a UPO – once the sub-letting or parting with possession is shown and the position of the tenant(s) sufficiently demonstrated to satisfy the condition at 5.7(c) then to some extent the question of a UPO is one of mathematics.

5.10   That is not, though, to ignore the fact that if these conditions are satisfied the court *'may'* make a UPO but is not bound to do so.[13] There are no reported cases as yet to demonstrate when a court may decide *not* to make a UPO, despite the conditions for one being satisfied, but factors such as:

(a) length of time since the offending period occurred;

(b) some fault on the part of the landlord in not detecting the fraud earlier;

(c) a particular joint tenant not being the main instigator of the arrangement; or

(d) the tenant's circumstances having dramatically changed for the worse since their activities came to light

may be four examples where, on the facts of a particular case, a court declines to make a UPO.

The application

5.11   Applications for UPOs in the civil courts must be made by a landlord,[14] either by way of a Part 7 claim:

Separate Part 7 claim for UPO

GREENHOFF HOUSING ASSOCIATION

Claimant

-and-

MR BARRY KANE

Defendant

PARTICULARS OF CLAIM

Introduction

1. The Claimant is a private registered provider of social housing and the freehold owner of 19B Di Maria Way, Angelford, AD1 5DD ('the Premises').

---

13 Ibid, s 5(1).
14 Ibid, s 5(1).

2. The defendant is an individual aged 53 years of age who on 5 May 2010 entered into an assured non-shorthold weekly periodic tenancy agreement ('the Agreement') with the Claimant in respect of the Premises.

The Agreement

3. The Agreement provided at clauses 3.4 and 3.5:

   '3.4 You must at all times live at the Premises as your only or principal home.

   3.5 You are not entitled to sub-let or part with possession of any part of the Premises without our prior written consent.'

Breach

4. On 12 March 2017 an officer of the Claimant visited the Premises for the purposes of a tenancy audit and spoke to a Mr John Evans there. Mr Evans showed the officer the tenancy agreement he had entered into on 13 June 2016 with the Defendant in respect of a bedroom therein and use of the bathroom, kitchen, lounge and hallway.

5. The said tenancy agreement is exhibited to these particulars at 'Annex A' and shows that Mr Evans was to pay to the Defendant £120.00 per week under the terms of his tenancy. He showed the officer a rent book demonstrating that he had, in fact, paid the Defendant such sums every week from 13 June 2016.

6. Mr Evans also advised that the Defendant did not live at the Premises – and no one else did aside from himself – but stayed with his partner nearby and only visited to collect the rent each week. He further advised that the second bedroom was locked and not in use.

7. The Claimant has at no stage been asked for, or given, permission to the Defendant to sub-let part of the Premises and he is accordingly in breach of both clauses 3.4 and 3.5 of the Agreement.

Basis of claim

8. It is known that the Defendant told Mr Evans to leave the Premises shortly after the visit on 12 March 2017 and that he is now back living at the Premises.

9. The Premises were sub-let to Mr Evans from 13 June 2016 until on or around 12 March 2017 ('the sub-letting period') and during this time the Defendant was not living there as his only or principal home.

10. The conditions for an unlawful profit order provided for at section 5(4) of the Prevention of Social Housing Fraud Act 2013 are satisfied:

    (a) The Claimant is a private registered provider of social housing.

> (b) The tenancy of the Premises is not a shared ownership lease.
>
> (c) The Defendant sub-let part of the Premises.
>
> (d) During the period of the sub-letting the Defendant ceased to occupy the Premises as his only or principal home.
>
> (e) The Defendant received money from the sub-letting.
>
> 11. The Premises are a two-bedroom flat on the third floor of a four-storey block and the current weekly rent applicable to the Premises is £85.00 per week.
>
> *Sums claimed*
>
> 12. The Defendant received 40 weeks' payment of £120.00 from Mr Evans as rent for the latter's sub-letting of the Premises. This totals £4,800.00.
>
> 13. The Defendant paid £3,000.00 to the Claimant in respect of his gross rent for the Premises during the sub-letting period.
>
> 14. The Claimant therefore claims £1,800.00 in addition to interest pursuant to section 69 of the County Courts Act 1984 at such rate as the court shall determine.
>
> AND the Claimant claims:
>
> 1. An Unlawful Profit Order against the Defendant in the sum of £1,800.
>
> 2. Interest pursuant to section 69.
>
> 3. Costs.
>
> **Statement of truth**

or (more normally) as part of ongoing possession proceedings, whether in the original pleading or in a statement of case varied to include the UPO claim by way of an N244 Application Notice.

> **Example Particulars of Claim (part)**
>
> *(Possession claim and UPO)*
>
> …
>
> **Unlawful profit order (UPO)**
>
> 8. Paragraph 5 is repeated herein.
>
> 9. The conditions for a UPO provided for at section 5(4) of the Prevention of Social Housing Fraud Act 2013 are met:
>   (a) The Premises were let to the Defendant under an assured tenancy and the Claimant is a private registered provider of social housing.
>   (b) In breach of clause 3(2)(b) of the said tenancy agreement, the Defendant sub-let the whole of the Premises for the period 1 January 2016 to 26 February 2017 ('the sub-letting period') to Ms Louise Macari.

> (c) During this period he was not living at the Premises as his only or principal home and rather was residing at the Second Premises.
>
> (d) The Defendant received £12,545.00 from Ms Macari during the sub-letting period.
>
> 10. The Claimant seeks and is entitled to a UPO for the maximum amount in the sum of £5,500 having only received £7,045 from the defendant during the sub-letting period in respect of what was purported to be rent.
>
> 11. The Claimant further seeks interest pursuant to section 69 of the County Courts Act 1984 at such a rate and for such a period as the court thinks fit.
>
> AND the Claimant claims:
>
> 1. Possession of the Premises forthwith (mandatory ground).
>
> 2. A money judgment in respect of any outstanding arrears of rent and use and occupation charges as at the date of the final hearing.
>
> 3. Use and Occupation charges at the daily rate of £13.71 from the date of the final hearing until possession is given up.
>
> 4. An unlawful profit order in the sum of £5,500 with interest pursuant to section 69 of the County Courts Act 1984.
>
> 5. Costs.
>
> **Statement of truth**

5.12 Although section 5(8) of PSHF provides that an application can be made to the High Court *or* county court, the usual application will be to the county court. Claims and/or applications to the High Court should be limited to cases involving unusually large sums of money or complex points of law of public importance.[15]

5.13 It is clear from section 5(2) of PSHF that the claim/application can only be made against the tenant. The conditions at sections 5(3) and 5(4) expressly refer to 'a tenant under the tenancy' having 'received money as a result of the [sub-letting/parting with possession]'.

5.14 For example, if the tenant has left the premises and allowed a friend to have use of them, and that friend 'sub-lets' it and keeps all the proceeds, then a UPO is not available because the tenant has not received money as a result of this conduct. However, if the friend in fact passed all or some of the money to the tenant, then even though it may be argued that it is not the tenant who has sub-let all or part of the premises, the tenant is likely to be caught by the provisions as he or she will likely be found to have 'parted with possession'.

---

15 Ibid, s 5(9). It also states that: 'Section 110(3) of the Housing Act 1985 (by which the claimant in proceedings relating to a secure tenancy may not recover the claimant's costs if the proceedings are taken in the High Court) does not apply to proceedings under this section.'

The amount sought

5.15   Section 5 of PSHF provides:

'(5) The amount payable under an unlawful profit order must be such amount as the court considers appropriate, having regard to any evidence and to any representations that are made by or on behalf of the landlord or the tenant, but subject to subsections (6) and (7).

(6) The maximum amount payable under an unlawful profit order is calculated as follows–

Step 1

Determine the total amount the tenant received as a result of the conduct described in subsection (3)(a) or (4)(c) (or the best estimate of that amount).

Step 2

Deduct from the amount determined under step 1 the total amount, if any, paid by the tenant as rent to the landlord (including service charges) over the period during which the conduct described in subsection (3) (a) or (4)(c) took place.'

5.16   It follows that:

(a)   the court has a wide discretion about whether to make an award at all and, if it does, its quantum; and

(b)   the award is subject to a maximum figure, namely the 'true profit' element (ie the amount received as a result of the sub-letting or parting with possession, less that paid by the tenant to her/his landlord *during the relevant period*).

5.17   A tenant who sub-lets for less than the rent they pay during the offending period cannot therefore have a UPO made against them. Similarly, no UPO is available where the tenant has parted with possession without asking for any monies from those allowed to reside in the premises in their stead.[16]

5.18   Conversely, if a tenant does not pay rent to their landlord during the sub-letting period or does not pay the full rent required, a payment to make-up for or exceed such a shortfall *after* any sub-letting period does not count towards step 2 of the section 5(6) calculation because it is not paid 'over a period during which the conduct … took place'. A judge would, though, have the discretion to factor it in when determining the 'appropriate' UPO, in addition to making an order for payment of arrears in the usual way.

---

16   PSHF, s 5(2) – there is, by definition, no profit element in such a case.

Example calculation

A is a (sole) secure tenant of a three-bedroom property. Her landlord is a local housing authority (LHA).

The LHA find out in January 2017 that A has been sub-letting the property since June 2012 at a weekly rent of £230.00 (plus utility charges which remained in A's name) and since then has been living in another house which she co-owns with her partner. A notice to quit is served and A arranges for the sub-tenants to leave, clears all arrears that had arisen on her rent account and hands in the keys to the property, which is now vacant.

A refuses to deal further with the LHA who thereupon decide against criminal prosecution under PSHF, but rather seek a UPO in a Part 7 claim brought in the county court. They assert that during the period of the sub-letting, A paid £25,000 to them towards the property's rent.

The amount sought is:

246 weeks of sub-letting × £230.00 = £56,580.00

Plus utility payments received by A from sub-tenants = £2,460.

Less £25,000 received by LHA from A *during the sub-letting period.*

Total Claim = £34,040 (plus interest)

5.19   If a criminal UPO has been made under s 4 of PSHF, then a civil court may only make an additional UPO if:

(a) the second UPO does not exceed in amount the aggregate of:

- the sum by which the tenant's profit found under section 5 of PSHF exceeds that ordered by the magistrates' court or Crown Court, and

- the amount that has not been recovered under the criminal UPO.[17]

(b) Permission is granted by the county court or High Court when enforcement is sought to recover the sum not recovered under the criminal UPO.[18]

5.20   A UPO made by the civil courts is treated as a judgment debt. Therefore if the amount of the Order is £5,000 or more, an applicant may also seek statutory interest.[19]

5.21   The recent High Court authority of *Poplar HARCA v Begum and anor*,[20] referred to in Chapter 3,[21] dealt effectively with the question of how (fraudulent) housing benefit payments during the sub-letting period should be treated.

---

17 Ibid, s 5(7).
18 Ibid, s 5(8).
19 County Courts Act 1984, s 74; County Courts (Interest on Judgment Debts) Order SI 1991/1184.
20 [2017] EWHC 2040 (QB).
21 See 3.39–3.41.

5.22 Mr Justice Turner also confirmed in *Begum* that a UPO was appropriate and that housing benefit received during the sub-letting period should be treated as monies received:

> '42. In this case, it is evident that each and every condition under section 1(4) has been fulfilled. The issue arises, however, as to the calculation of the maximum amount payable. The appellant points to the fact that a net sum of £1,550 was received by the respondents from Ms Rehana and Mr Ahmed and this is the sum which should be ordered to be paid. The Recorder, however, concluded that the rent which the respondents were collecting was less than the rent they were paying the applicants and thus assumed that the maximum payment was zero. In so doing, he left out of account the fact that the rent for the flat was covered entirely by Housing Benefit and so the monies received by the respondents from Ms Rehana and Mr Ahmed was pure profit.
>
> 43. I am satisfied that the total amount referred to under step 1 does not exclude the element of Housing Benefit. It is argued on behalf of the respondents that, on a strict interpretation of the statute, the Housing Benefit was not, in itself, received as a result of their breach of the tenancy agreement and so should be disregarded. I do not agree. The inclusion of the word "total" indicates that the gross receipts secured and consequent upon the dishonest relinquishment of possession should be considered under step 1. To hold otherwise would be to render all but nugatory the clear purpose of the section. A very considerable proportion of tenants in socially rented homes are in receipt of Housing Benefit and those who have their rents paid for them are those in the best position to be able to benefit from unlawful profiteering of this type. To disregard Housing Benefit under Step 1 but include it to the ill-gotten advantage of the fraudster under Step 2 would be to thwart the obvious intention of Parliament to provide a mechanism with which to strip him of his spoils.'

FRAUDULENT MISREPRESENTATION

Overview

5.23 Obtaining a UPO under PSHF is, as can be seen above, a comparatively straightforward and regulated process. The situation becomes more complicated, however, where the fraud alleged does not fall within PSHF and involves, for example, the right to buy, right to acquire or a shared ownership transaction, or the misrepresentation factors dealt with in Chapter 2.

5.24 Chapter 2 necessarily deals with a number of issues concerning misrepresentation, including questions as to the duty to disclose changes of circumstance and reliance, and this is further alluded to at 5.37 below. What is common ground, however, is that the proper focus here is on the fact that one of the parties to a contract, whether it be:

- a tenancy agreement;

- shared ownership lease; or

- right to buy/right to acquire sale,

has entered into the arrangement on the basis of a misrepresentation.

5.25   We are concerned in this book with matters of fraud, but whether the misrepresentation was fraudulent, negligent or innocent the other party may, in principle, seek the remedy of rescission – the 'normal' remedy for misrepresentation[22] – which will have the effect of setting aside the transaction and putting the parties back into the position they were in prior to the agreement or contract. This is addressed below from 5.33, as well as being explained in Chapter 2.

5.26   The other remedy for misrepresentation we are concerned with in this chapter is *damages*, whether under section 2 of the Misrepresentation Act 1967 for innocent or negligent misrepresentation:

> '(1) Where a person has entered into a contract after a misrepresentation has been made to him by another party thereto and as a result thereof he has suffered loss, then, if the person making the misrepresentation would be liable to damages in respect thereof had the misrepresentation been made fraudulently, that person shall be so liable notwithstanding that the misrepresentation was not made fraudulently, unless he proves that he had reasonable ground to believe and did believe up to the time the contract was made the facts represented were true.

> (2) Where a person has entered into a contract after a misrepresentation has been made to him otherwise than fraudulently, and he would be entitled, by reason of the misrepresentation, to rescind the contract, then, if it is claimed, in any proceedings arising out of the contract, that the contract ought to be or has been rescinded, the court or arbitrator may declare the contract subsisting and award damages in lieu of rescission, if of opinion that it would be equitable to do so, having regard to the nature of the misrepresentation and the loss that would be caused by it if the contract were upheld, as well as to the loss that rescission would cause to the other party.'

or by way of the tort of deceit if fraudulent. In the latter instance, that may be in addition to or instead of any claim seeking the remedy of rescission or possession (as described in Chapter 2).

---

22 *British and Commonwealth Holdings v Quadrex* [1995] CLC 1169 at 1199–1200.

Right to buy/acquire

5.27   Part 5 of the Housing Act 1985 gives secure tenants of more than three years' tenure (including those with the preserved right to buy[23]) in England[24] the right to buy a freehold or long leasehold interest in their homes, depending on the nature of the property and the landlord's interest in it. The great attraction of this right is the significant[25] statutory discounts available to such tenants.[26]

5.28   An application to exercise the right to buy commences when the tenant serves a notice claiming the right,[27] followed by a landlord admitting or denying that right[28] and identifying the proposed price.[29]

5.29   The most obvious fraud is where a tenant seeks to exercise their apparent right to buy and yet no longer satisfies the required conditions at the time of sale (if they ever did). To give an obvious example, if the tenancy ceases to be secure at any time before completion of the right to buy (eg by reason of death of the tenant, sub-letting or the tenant ceasing to use the premises as their only or principal home) the tenant loses their entitlement to exercise it.[30]

5.30   Lord Justice Mann said in *Muir Group Housing Association Ltd v Thornley*[31] where the tenants moved out and sub-let the subject premises after their right-to-buy application had been admitted by the landlord:

> 'I accordingly conclude that a tenant who has ceased to be a secure tenant has no right which he can enforce under section 138(3).[32] The conclusion

---

23 Housing Act 1985, s 171A. In particular, tenants of local housing authorities whose home is part of their landlord's stock transferred to a private registered provider such as a housing association become assured tenants: see Housing (Preservation of Right to Buy) Regulations (SI 1993/2241).

24 Housing Act 1985, s 119(A1) – in Wales it is five years (s 119(1)) though the Abolition of the Right to Buy and Associated Rights (Wales) Bill going through the Welsh Assembly will end the right to buy, the preserved right to buy and the right to acquire in Wales.

25 The maximum discount was set in 2014 as £102,700 (now £104,900) in respect of dwelling-houses situated within the areas of London authorities and as £77,000 (now £78,600) in respect of dwelling-houses not situated within the areas of London authorities. These amounts have increased each year (from 6 April 2015) by the percentage change in the consumer prices index published by the Statistics Board from the September before the previous year to the September of the previous year: Housing (Right to Buy) (Limit on Discount) (England) Order 2014 (SI 1994/1378). By reason of Housing Act 1985, s 129, the amount of the discount, or more precisely, the maximum percentage discount, will vary depending upon whether the property is a house or flat.

26 Housing Act 1985 (HA85), ss 129–131, and Sch 4.

27 Ibid, s 122(1).

28 Ibid, s 124(1).

29 Ibid, s 125.

30 *Bradford City Metropolitan Council v McMahon* [1994] 1 WLR 52, (1993) 25 HLR 534 CA (death); *Sutton LBC v Swann* (1986) 18 HLR 140 CA (no longer only or principal home); *Muir Group Housing Association Ltd v Thornley* (1993) 25 HLR 89 CA (sub-letting).

31 (1993) 25 HLR 89 CA at [97].

32 This provision allows a secure tenant, who has established the right to buy and all matters relating to the grant have been agreed or determined, to enforce the said grant of the freehold (house) or leasehold (flat) interest.

accords with my belief that most people would find it surprising if Parliament had enacted right to buy provisions which enabled a person to acquire a house at a discount when he no longer occupied it as his only, or principal, home.'

5.31   The difficulty arising from right-to-buy cases where the fraud is *not* identified prior to the sale – where the remedies are much more obvious by way of stopping the right-to-buy process and taking any necessary action in the normal way as a result of the newly discovered sub-letting, etc. – is that identified in *Haringey LBC v Hines* at 5.42 below. If there is no contract, then save for the ingenious argument not dealt with by the Court of Appeal there that it would have to be viewed as a disposal outside of the Part 5 scheme and thus the 'no contract' approach would not 'bite', it could rather encourage the greater reliance on criminal sanctions and activity.

5.32   Some tenants of housing associations[33] enjoy the right to acquire their properties after three years as a public sector tenant,[34] though the discounts are significantly below that for the right to buy.[35] Despite that, the same principles described above apply as for the right to buy.

Rescission

5.33   Rescission is not, of course, a financial remedy strictly speaking, but it is closely connected with the issues surrounding fraudulent misrepresentation and the tort of deceit. In broad terms and, as noted at 5.25 above, any misrepresentation which induces a party to enter a contract gives that party the right to seek the remedy of rescission of that contract. That is, a right to treat the arrangement as void, whereby the defendant in such circumstances no longer has the tenancy or right to buy arrangement, etc.

5.34   Rescission for fraudulent misrepresentation is an absolute right[36] and first requires the party affected to show that they were induced to enter into a contract as a result of a false statement made dishonestly so that they have the right to avoid and rescind that contract. In the context of tenancy fraud, therefore, it is necessary to show that there has been an incorrect statement of fact which is intended to, and did, induce the landlord to enter into a contract such as a tenancy agreement or lease.[37]

---

33 Registered with the Homes and Communities Agency. As of the summer of 2017, the government is running pilot schemes allowing for an extension of the right-to-buy process to housing associations on a voluntary basis, with a view to this becoming more widespread across the sector: funding arrangements to be provided for by means of Housing and Planning Act 2016, ss 64–68.

34 See Housing Act 1996, ss 16, 16A and 17; Housing and Regeneration Act 2008 (England) ss 180–185 and the Housing (Right to Acquire) Regulations 1997 (SI 1997/619).

35 Between £9,000 and £16,000: Housing (Right to Acquire) (Discount) Order 2002 (SI 2002/1091).

36 *Cavaliero v Puget* (1865) 4 F & F 537.

37 *Chitty on Contracts*, 30th edn, paras 6-001 *et seq.*

5.35   Housing practitioners will be well used to this concept when dealing with the Grounds 5 and 17 possession claims discussed in Chapter 2. This includes the rule that, where Grounds 5 and 17 are made out, rescission is *not* available as an alternative option for ending the tenancy.[38]

5.36   It follows from the above that this remedy is likely to be used in social housing fraud cases to recover premises obtained by fraudulent misrepresentation where the particular focus is on:

(a) right to buy, right to acquire and shared ownership fraudulent arrangements; and

(b) grants of tenancy where security of tenure is not retained, such that Grounds 5 and 17 are not available (see Chapter 2 at 2.8–2.19).

5.37   Any possession claim seeking the remedy of rescission[39] would need in particular to address the following matters:

(a) If the false representation is made in an application form or similar document which warns the writer of the need to be accurate and advise of changing circumstances,[40] or if the false statement was inaccurate from the start, then such a claim starts off in a straightforward manner.

(b) Otherwise, there *may* be issues where the false statement is outside such processes and it is argued that there is no common law duty to disclose material facts.[41] This is discussed further in Chapter 2; *Haringey LBC v Hines* referred to at 5.43–5.46 below is illustrative of the difficulties that can arise if the right analysis is not followed and the right questions are not asked. At the very least it confirms the common sense in local housing authorities and others making it absolutely clear on the face of any application form of the ongoing duty of disclosure to ensure that the applicant is expressly aware that any relevant change of circumstances must be disclosed.

(c) The pleaded claim needs to set out the alleged fraudulent misrepresentations clearly[42] and fully.[43]

(d) In cases based on fraud:[44]

---

38 *Islington London Borough Council v Uckac and another* [2006] EWCA Civ 340, [2006] 1 WLR 1303. See 2.12–2.13.
39 Rescission is, in fact, simply communicated by the innocent party to the other, though a declaration would ordinarily be sought and (of course) if property is not voluntarily returned, possession action will be required (where one might expect the fact of rescission to be disputed).
40 Or there is a statutory requirement to disclose such as is found in Housing Act 1996, ss 171 and 214 (reallocation and homelessness duties and powers).
41 *Ward v Hobbs* (1878) 4 App Cas 13, but see *Hurley v Dyke* [1979] RTR 265.
42 *Wallingford v Mutual Society* (1879–1880) LR 5 App Cas 685; *Abbey Forwarding Ltd (In Liquidation) v Hone* [2010] EWHC 2029 (Ch) – see CPR PD16, para 8.2(1).
43 *Lowe v Machell* [2012] 1 All ER (Comm) 153 at 74 *per* Lewison LJ; *NGM Sustainable Developments Ltd v Phillip Wallis, Lizzano Ltd, Cascina Ltd, Kevin Reardon, Hydro Properties Ltd, Hydro Property Holdings Ltd* [2015] EWHC 2089 (Ch) at 55 *per* Peter Smith J.
44 *Re: H (Sexual abuse, standard of proof)* [1996] AC 563 at 586 *per* Lord Nicholls.

'The more serious the allegation the less likely it is the event occurred and hence the stronger should be the evidence before the court concludes that the allegation is established on the balance of probability. Fraud is less likely than negligence …'

(e) The tort of deceit, which is covered below at 5.40–5.49, and damages for innocent or negligent misrepresentation (see 5.26) may be available in addition to the rescission claim.

(f) As an equitable remedy rescission may not always be available. For example:

- Has too long elapsed such that rescission would be inequitable?[45]

- Is it simply not possible to restore the parties to their pre-contract position?

- Has the innocent party affirmed the contract?

- Have third-party rights, such as a mortgagee, intervened?

- Would the remedy of rescission lead to an unjust enrichment?[46]

5.38 If the fact of rescission is, though, clear and sustainable then:

(a) In a right to buy/right to acquire scenario, it leaves the parties in their previous position of landlord and tenant. If, then, the reason for the rescission is, say, that the tenant had sub-let the whole of the premises at any time prior to the grant of the freehold/leasehold interest then a notice to quit can be served and possession proceedings taken.[47]

(b) If the problem was that the tenant 'simply' was not living at the premises as their only or principal home, but had not sub-let or parted with possession of the whole, then again a notice to quit could be served but it may be advisable to also serve a notice seeking possession (breach of tenancy) because the loss of security of tenure here – as previously explained – is ambulatory and the tenant may move back in prior to the expiry of any notice to quit.

(c) In a shared ownership case, once rescission is achieved the occupants would have no tenancy at all, having moved into the premises at the outset under a (now voided) shared ownership arrangement. Possession, thereafter, should then be straightforward, assuming the basis for rescission is clear, as the defendant would have no rights of occupation.

Damages

5.39 As referred to at 5.26, damages are available to a successful claimant landlord, though this is not achieved under the Misrepresentation Act 1967 in

45 *Fisher v Brooker* [2009] UKHL 41, [2009] 1 WLR 1764 at 64 *per* Lord Neuberger.
46 *Halpern v Halpern* [2007] 1 CLC 527, [2008] QB 195 at 61–75 *per* Carnwath LJ.
47 Given that rescission is 'declared' by the innocent party prior to any possession claim, then such a claim will likely seek a declaration of the rescission as well as a possession order in reliance on the notice to quit.

a case of fraudulent misrepresentation. Rather, any such claim – if not seeking a remedy under the 1967 Act for innocent or negligent misrepresentation in the alternative – would be in deceit.

DECEIT

5.40   The tort of deceit is a separate cause of action[48] which *may* provide grounds for damages in and of itself,[49] though it is fair to report that it is not a common basis of action at all in the social housing context. The Supreme Court recently summarised the tort as follows:

> '18 Subject to one point, the ingredients of a claim for deceit based upon an alleged fraudulent misrepresentation are not in dispute. It must be shown that the defendant made a materially false representation which was intended to, and did, induce the representee to act to its detriment. To my mind it is not necessary, as a matter of law, to prove that the representee believed that the representation was true. In my opinion there is no clear authority to the contrary. However, that is not to say that the representee's state of mind may not be relevant to the issue of inducement. Indeed, it may be very relevant. For example, if the representee does not believe that the representation is true, he may have serious difficulty in establishing that he was induced to enter into the contract or that he has suffered loss as a result ...'[50]

5.41   To establish deceit, therefore, a claimant must show that:

(a) the defendant dishonestly made the false representation with the intention that the claimant would act on it;

(b) the claimant was induced,[51] at least in part by reason of the misrepresentation,[52] to so act. This is a question of fact,[53] and the burden is on the defendant if they claim that the claimant knew the truth;[54] *and*

(c) the claimant suffered loss as a consequence.[55]

---

48 And separate, for example, to a claim in fraudulent misrepresentation (though the elements of the respective causes of action are similar), the latter, as explained at 5.26, being restricted in remedy to rescission.
49 *Derry v Peek* (1889) LR 14 App Cas 337 HL.
50 *Zurich Insurance Co plc v Hayward* [2016] UKSC 48, [2017] AC 142 *per* Lord Clarke JSC.
51 Lord Mustill said in *Pan Atlantic Insurance Co Ltd v Pine Top Insurance Co Ltd (No 2)* [1995] 1 AC 501 at 542:
    'In the general law it is beyond doubt that even a fraudulent misrepresentation must be shown to have induced the contract before the promisor has a right to avoid, although the task of proof may be made easier by a presumption of inducement.'
52 *Zurich Insurance Co plc v Hayward* [2016] UKSC 48, [2017] AC 142, at 26, 33 *per* Lord Clarke JSC.
53 Ibid at 25 *per* Lord Clarke JSC.
54 Ibid at 43 – Mere suspicion on the part of the claimant is not sufficient.
55 *Smith v Chadwick* (1883–84) LR 9 App Cas 187 HL – this is another question of fact.

5.42   As with the analysis of Grounds 5 and 17 in Chapter 2, the more material the statement, the stronger the presumption that it induced the claimant to enter into it.[56] That is clear from *Hines* referred to at 5.37 and below; further, Lord Justice Hobhouse said in *Downs v Chappell*:[57]

> 'The judge was wrong to ask how they [the representees] would have acted if they had been told the truth. They were never told the truth. They were told lies in order to induce them to enter into the contract. The lies were material and successful ... The judge should have concluded that the plaintiffs had proved their case on causation ...'

5.43   Putting all the above in a social housing context, and appreciating the potential pitfalls of such a claim, in *Haringey LBC v Hines*,[58] the defendant sought to exercise her right to buy and in the statutory notice she stated (wrongly) that the relevant premises were her only or principal home. She was granted a long lease, but six years later the local authority discovered that she had, in fact, lived elsewhere at the time of purchase.

5.44   In July 2008, the authority brought a claim in the county court against the defendant contending that, by accepting the offer to buy the flat, she had falsely represented:

(a) that she was still occupying it as her only or principal home; and

(b) that she was entitled to exercise the right to buy.

It was alleged that these representations were fraudulent because she knew that they were untrue. The authority claimed, amongst other remedies, damages for misrepresentation.

5.45   The trial judge held that the authority did not have a claim in misrepresentation because an acquisition under the right to buy was not a contract,[59] but that they had succeeded in establishing a claim in deceit. He awarded the authority damages of £38,000 plus interest.

5.46   The Court of Appeal allowed the tenant's appeal and held that the judge's finding that the defendant knew that her flat had ceased to be her only or principal home before the 16 May 2002 acceptance of the section 125 offer notice did not, of itself, establish the claim in deceit. Rather the authority had to also demonstrate that, as at that date, the defendant:

(a) knew, as a matter of law, that the flat had to remain her only or principal home throughout the right to buy process;

(b) knew that the flat was no longer her only or principal home; and

---

56 *Ross River Ltd v Cambridge City Football Club Ltd* [2008] 1 All ER 1004 at 241 *per* Briggs J.

57 [1997] 1 WLR 426 at 433.

58 [2010] EWCA Civ 1111, [2011] HLR 6.

59 Thereby following *Rushton v Worcester City Council* [2001] EWCA Civ 367, [2002] HLR 9.

(c) dishonestly intended her acceptance of the authority's proposed terms of acquisition to mislead the authority so that she could acquire the flat even though she was no longer entitled to do so.

5.47 If those hurdles can be overcome, however, the correct measure of damages in deceit is an award which serves to put the claimant into the position they would have been in if the representation had not been made to them.[60]

5.48 As the misrepresentation will have been made fraudulently, all losses flowing from it can be recovered, even if they are not reasonably foreseeable.[61] For example, if a claim in deceit is brought alongside a Ground 5 possession claim brought by a local housing authority, as described at Chapter 2, this may potentially include the cost of temporary accommodation for a third-party household who would have been granted the tenancy were it not for the defendant's fraud which led to the premises being allocated elsewhere.

5.49 Finally, it is worth noting that whereas in a claim under section 2(1) of the Misrepresentation Act 1967 it is for the defendant to show that they had reasonable grounds for believing the offending statement to be true, in the tort of deceit that burden (ie knowledge/recklessness as to the falsity) falls on the claimant.

CONCLUSION

5.50 In a case covered by the PSHF, a UPO will be commonplace and, usually, advisable in any sub-letting case. Otherwise, as Chapter 7 makes clear, there may be criminal compensation orders, but rarely consideration of much else.

5.51 The tort of deceit presents a useful 'bargaining chip' where fraud is discovered, as well as, in appropriate cases, a potentially fruitful cause of action.

---

60 *Doyle v Olby (Ironmongers) Ltd* [1969] 2 QB 158.
61 *Royscott Trust v Rogerson* [1991] 2 QB 297, CA.

CHAPTER 6

Investigation and Evidence

- Data Protection Act 1998
- Data sharing
- PSHF Regulations
- Court powers

Key points

- The Data Protection Act 1998 (DPA) does not provide an absolute bar on the obtaining of private information as it does allow for the disclosure of private data in defined circumstances – for example, cases of one-off requests in connection with legal proceedings or for the prevention or detection of a crime may allow information to be provided to a social landlord by a third party, such as the police, housing benefit department or a credit reference agency.

- Local authorities have particular powers to request information from banks, utility providers, etc, as provided for in the Prevention of Social Housing Fraud Act 2013 (PSHF) and attendant regulations.

- Local Authorities frequently interview, under caution, those tenants suspected of benefit fraud and for offences under the PSHF.

- The Civil Procedure Rules 1998 allow a social landlord to obtain further details of a defendant's case and its evidential basis before trial, such as by way of an application for specific disclosure or a request for further information.

INTRODUCTION

6.1 The successful detection and prosecution of social housing fraud invariably depends on good and reliable information. You often hear the phrase 'something smells' particularly when it comes to potential sub-letting and only or principal home cases, and the social landlord concerned frequently has a sound basis for investigation. But do they have enough evidence to proceed to court?

6.2 Some information is easily come by, such as reports from neighbours or the social landlord's own records. For example, the landlord may have received complaints of anti-social behaviour in one of their properties, yet the alleged perpetrators do not match the expected occupants.

6.3   Similarly, the social landlord's gas contractor may have visited premises to carry out an annual inspection and been met by an individual, other than the tenant, who states that they are living there with their family and not the tenant.

6.4   Obtaining sufficient evidence to justify further action such as a claim for possession of premises or an unlawful profit order can be more difficult and requires ingenuity, persistence and a sound understanding of the tools at the social landlord's (and their 'partners') disposal.

6.5   This chapter considers those tools and their legislative underpinning, both in the context of pre- and post-court issue activity. If used effectively, they may ensure the relevant disclosure and obtaining of data such as:

- housing benefit/council tax support records;

- electoral roll information;

- credit applications and use;

- utility bills;

- police information; and

- bank statements.

6.6   They may also ensure that the defendant in any claim is required to provide more information and explanation than a bare denial, however eloquently put.

DATA PROTECTION ACT 1998

Introduction

6.7   The Preamble to the Data Protection Act 1998 (DPA) explains that it is:

> 'An Act to make new provision for the regulation of the processing of information relating to individuals, including the obtaining, holding, use or disclosure[1] of such information.'

6.8   HHJ Behrens further explained its purpose in *Dawson-Damer v Taylor Wessing LLP*:[2]

> '33 The 1998 Act was enacted, in part, to give effect to Parliament and Council Directive 95/46/EC of 24 October 1995 on the protection of individuals with regard to the processing of personal data and on the free movement of such data ... The primary objective of the 1995 Directive is to protect individuals' fundamental rights, notably the right to privacy

---

1   Including to the individual themselves of course – see DPA, s 7.
2   [2015] EWHC 2366 (Ch), [2016] 1 WLR 28 – reversed on appeal [2017] EWCA Civ 74 – but the explanation here holds good.

and accuracy of their personal data held by others ('data controllers') in computerised form or similarly organised manual filing systems...'

6.9   In essence, the DPA provides controls on what a 'data controller' – that is, a person or organisation who (either alone or jointly or in common with other persons) determines both the purposes for and the manner in which any personal data is, or is to be, 'processed'[3] – can do with personal data.

6.10   In terms of social housing fraud, this could impact upon what information the social landlord can obtain from third parties about an allegedly errant tenant or others (such as their partner or supposed sub-tenants) and, to a lesser degree, what data a social landlord can hold on their tenants.

6.11   The Information Commissioner's Office (ICO) is the regulator responsible for making sure that organisations comply with the DPA. It also has a remit for promoting good practice in information handling. For example, the ICO have provided invaluable guidance on data protection and data sharing[4] which is discussed below.

6.12   Finally, it should be noted that the European Union General Data Protection Regulation 2016/679 (GDPR) comes into force on 25 May 2018. This will impact on social landlords in terms of security of data, lawful processing and responsibility for breach of data protection in particular. The ICO has produced a helpful overview on the GDPR,[5] although the information as to the processing of data dealt with below should be largely unaffected in practice.

Data protection

6.13   The DPA is, as already noted, concerned with the protection of 'data' and 'personal data' which are both defined at section 1(1) of the DPA as information which:

Data

(a) is being processed by means of equipment operating automatically in response to instructions given for that purpose;

(b) is recorded with the intention that it should be processed by means of such equipment;

(c) is recorded as part of a relevant filing system or with the intention that is should form part of a relevant filing system;

---

3   DPA, s 1(1) – there is an exception to this definition of 'data controller' at s 1(4) – 'Where personal data are processed only for purposes for which they are required by or under any enactment to be processed, the person on whom the obligation to process the data is imposed by or under that enactment is for the purposes of this Act the data controller.'
4   See www.ico.org.uk/for-organisations/guide-to-data-protection/.
5   See www ico.org.uk/for-organisations/data-protection-reform/overview-of-the-gdpr/.

(d) is a health, education or accessible public record.[6] The latter includes,[7] as explained at Schedule 12, information held for the purposes of a local authority's (or a housing trust's) tenancies[8] or social services functions; or

(e) is recorded information held by a public authority.[9]

Personal data

Relates to an an individual who can be identified –

(a) from those data; or

(b) from those data and other information which is either in the possession of, or is likely to come into the possession of, the data controller

and includes any expression of opinion about the individual and any indication of the intentions of the data controller or any other person in respect of the individual.

6.14   Lord Justice Auld considered the breadth of the definition of 'personal data' in *Durant v Financial Services Authority*[10] and concluded:

(a) not all information retrieved from a computer search against an individual's name or unique identifier is personal data within the DPA;

(b) mere mention of the data subject in a document held by a data controller does not necessarily amount to her or his 'personal data';

(c) whether it does so in any particular instance depends on *'where it falls in a continuum of relevance or proximity to the data subject as distinct, say, from transactions or matters in which he may have been involved to a greater or lesser degree'*;

(d) it may be relevant to consider whether the information is biographical in a significant sense (ie, it goes beyond the recording of the putative data subject's involvement in a matter or an event that has no personal connotations, a life event in respect of which his privacy could not be said to be compromised);

(e) the information should have the putative data subject as its focus rather than some other person with whom they may have been involved or some transaction or event in which they may have figured or have had an interest; and

6   DPA, s 68, Schs 11 and 12.
7   For England and Wales.
8   By reason of DPA 1998, Sch 12, para 3, the record falls within this definition if it is held for any purpose of the relationship of landlord and tenant of a dwelling which subsists, has subsisted or may subsist between the authority and any individual who is, has been or, as the case may be, has applied to be, a tenant of the authority.
9   DPA, s 1(1) – 'public authority' is as defined by the Freedom of Information Act 2000, s 3 and Sch 1 (or for a Scottish public authority, as defined by the Freedom of Information (Scotland) Act 2002) – this would include bodies such as the police, local authorities and the Homes and Communities Agency but not a private registered provider of social housing, such as a housing association.
10   [2003] EWCA Civ 1746, [2004] FSR 28 at para 28.

(f) in essence, it should be information that affects her or his privacy, whether in their personal or family life, business or professional capacity.[11]

6.15   Whatever the precise definition of 'data' and 'personal data', it is good practice for a social landlord to make clear to tenants and others that certain data is collected and may be shared in certain circumstances. This is usually done in the form of what is commonly known as a 'fair processing notice' and examples can be seen on a number of social landlords' websites.[12]

6.16   What information can be retained, however, in what form and for how long will be informed by the data protection principles set out at Schedule 1 of the DPA and referred to at 6.22.

6.17   As for the obtaining of information from a third party, *save for freely given responses to enquiries* from people such as:

(a) neighbours of the premises under investigation or of where the tenant is thought to be living in cases of only or principal home or sub-letting/parting with possession concerns;

(b) family of the tenant;

(c) sub-tenants in a sub-letting case; and occasionally

(d) the person(s) under investigation themselves given voluntarily to the social landlord or those investigating on their behalf (whether under caution or not),

the difficulty can often be as a result of the legitimate data protection rights of the individual.

6.18   In the context of a social housing fraud investigation and the gathering of evidence, the DPA therefore provides a potential 'hurdle' to obtaining access to information about the individual in issue held by other bodies, but one which is not necessarily insurmountable.

6.19   As indicated at 6.5, in addressing this issue we are concerned with data held by organisations such as the police, utility companies and the banks, as well as more general and widespread information such as may be secured by credit reference agencies and other companies.

6.20   This is in addition to the personal information already held by the social landlords themselves in respect of their tenants, such as:

(a) names, date of birth, contact details, religion, ethnicity, etc;

---

11 In Case C-101/01 *Criminal Proceedings against Lindquist* (6 November 2003), the court held, at para 27, that 'personal data' covered the name of a person or identification of him by some other means (eg by giving his telephone number or information regarding his working conditions or hobbies).

12 See, eg, Birmingham City Council's Privacy Notice. Available at: www.birmingham.gov.uk/privacy. See also that used by Hyde Housing. Available at: www.hyde-housing.co.uk/privacy/.

(b) complaints and correspondence;

(c) support contact details and physical/mental health information;

(d) tenancy agreements, repair requests, family members' details living at premises; and

the question of what can be 'processed' therefore has to be next considered once the definition of 'data' and 'personal data' is satisfied.

Processing

6.21   Paragraph 6.13 references the importance of data being 'processed' to the question of its availability; section 1(1) of the DPA defines 'processing' as including the:

(a) organisation, adaptation or alteration of the information or data;

(b) retrieval, consultation or use of the same;

(c) *disclosure of the information or data by transmission, dissemination or otherwise making available*; or

(d) alignment, combination, blocking, erasure or destruction of the information or data.

6.22   In addressing the question of 'processing', regard must be had, in particular, to the eight data protection principles set out in Part 1 of Schedule 1 DPA in respect of personal data.[13] A social landlord will need to comply with these principles and they are set out in full in Appendix A. In summary, they are as follows:

(1) Personal data is to be processed fairly and lawfully, and only where certain conditions are met (see further below)[14] – First Principle.

(2) It shall only be obtained for one or more specified and lawful purpose – Second Principle.

(3) It shall be adequate, relevant and not excessive to the purpose in question – Third Principle.

(4) Personal data shall be accurate and where necessary kept up to date – Fourth Principle.

(5) It shall not be kept longer than necessary for the purpose in question – Fifth Principle.

(6) It shall be processed in accordance with the individual's rights under the DPA – Sixth Principle.

---

13 DPA, s 4(4).
14 Ibid, Schs 2 and 3.

(7) Appropriate technical and organisational measures shall be taken against unauthorised or unlawful processing of personal data and against accidental loss or destruction of, or damage to, the same – Seventh Principle.

(8) It shall not be transferred to a country outside the European Economic Area unless there are adequate data protection safeguards in that country – Eighth Principle.

6.23 Schedule 1 of the DPA also provides, in Part II, a guide to the interpretation of the Data Protection Principles. For example, there is no breach of the Fourth Principle where the data controller has taken steps to ensure the accuracy of the data; if the data subject disagrees, this fact is recorded in the data. As for the Second Principle, a fair processing notice such as is described at 6.15 is recommended.

6.24 Most crucially, Schedule 2 of the DPA sets out the conditions referred to in the First Principle, at least one of which must be met[15] so that information can be lawfully processed:

- *The data subject has given their consent to the processing*: paragraph 1.

- The processing is necessary for the performance of a contract to which the data subject is a party or for the taking of steps at the request of the data subject with a view to entering into a contract: paragraph 2.

- *The processing is necessary for compliance with any legal obligation to which the data controller is subject,* other than an obligation imposed by contract: paragraph 3.

- The processing is necessary to protect the vital interests of the data subject: paragraph 4.

- *The processing is necessary for the administration of justice,* the exercise of any functions of either House of Parliament, *the exercise of any functions conferred on any person by or under any enactment* (see the reference to the regulations made under the PSHF at 6.38), the exercise of any functions of the Crown, a Minister of the Crown or a government department or the exercise of any other functions of a public nature exercised in the public interest by any person: paragraph 5.

- *The processing is necessary for the purposes of legitimate interests pursued by the data controller* or by the third party or parties to whom the data are disclosed, except where the processing is unwarranted in any particular case by reason of prejudice to the rights and freedoms or legitimate interests of the data subject. The Secretary of State may, by order, specify particular circumstances in which this condition is, or is not, to be taken to be satisfied: paragraph 6.

- The processing is necessary for the purposes of making a disclosure in good faith under a power conferred by – (a) section 21CA of the Terrorism Act

---

15 DPA, s 4(4).

2000 (disclosures between certain entities within regulated sector in relation to suspicion of commission of terrorist financing offence or for purposes of identifying terrorist property), or (b) section 339ZB of the Proceeds of Crime Act 2002 (disclosures between certain entities within regulated sector in relation to suspicions of money laundering): paragraph 7.

6.25   There is an additional requirement when it comes to what is referred to as 'sensitive personal data'. This latter term is defined at section 2 of DPA as consisting of information as to:

(a) the racial or ethnic origin of the data subject;

(b) her or his political opinions;

(c) her or his religious beliefs or other beliefs of a similar nature;

(d) whether they are a member of a trade union (within the meaning of the Trade Union and Labour Relations (Consolidation) Act 1992);

(e) her or his physical or mental health or condition;

(f) her or his sexual life;

(g) the commission or alleged commission by them of any offence; or

(h) any proceedings for any offence committed or alleged to have been committed by them, the disposal of such proceedings or the sentence of any court in such proceedings.

6.26   In those cases, at least one of the ten conditions set down at Schedule 3 must be satisfied for the First Principle to be capable of being satisfied. These conditions include, as for general data, where consent is given by the individual and for the administration of justice, etc but also, Schedule 3, paragraph 6 of the DPA states:

'The processing—

(a) is necessary for the purpose of, or in connection with, any legal proceedings (including prospective legal proceedings),

(b) is necessary for the purpose of obtaining legal advice, or

(c) is otherwise necessary for the purposes of establishing, exercising or defending legal rights.'

6.27   For example, this could allow the police to disclose information to a social landlord where confirmation is sought for the purposes of an absolute ground for possession[16] (condition 1 – serious offence). Disclosure of convictions, records and summaries of police activity are after all common in anti-social behaviour and absolute ground cases.

---

16 Housing Act 1985, s 84A (secure tenancies)/Housing Act 1988, Sch 2, Ground 7A (assured tenancies).

6.28 Indeed, they may be of use in confirming an individual's address (eg the tenant may have given the police a different address to that of the demised premises).

6.29 Under these principles and conditions therefore, information cannot be obtained from a third party in a social fraud investigation:

- without the consent of the individual;

- unless the PSHF Regulations are being used (as described at Section D);

- otherwise save as is described above (such as is referred to at 6.27).

This requires consideration of the exemptions to some or all of the data protection principles to be found at Part IV of the DPA.

Exemptions

6.30 The two provisions which are frequently cited as allowing the obtaining of such information about an individual without their consent or even knowledge in cases of social housing fraud are:

Section 29	Crime and taxation
Section 35	Disclosures required by law or made in connection with legal proceedings etc.

Crime and Taxation (section 29)

6.31 Section 29(1) of the DPA provides that the usual data protection is relaxed and the First Data Protection Principle is not relevant (see 6.22), though the conditions set out in Schedules 2 and 3 DPA (see 6.24 and 6.26) apply in cases where personal data is being processed for:

(a) the prevention or detection of crime;

(b) the apprehension or prosecution of offenders; or

(c) the assessment or collection of any tax or duty or of any imposition of a similar nature.

6.32 Further, non-disclosure provisions are not applicable (see 6.37).

6.33 Given that sub-letting and parting with the possession of the whole or part of let premises may well constitute a crime[17] and activities surrounding acquiring a tenancy, right to buy, shared ownership and right to acquire involving

---

17 Prevention of Social Housing Fraud Act 2013, ss 1 and 2.

false representations may similarly be a criminal offence,[18] it is not surprising that information is more readily disclosable in such cases.

6.34   This section is therefore frequently used by local authority or accredited fraud investigators.

6.35   In terms of information disclosing details of a third party – such as will invariably be the case with credit reference information (eg where electoral roll information will normally refer to persons other than the tenant) section 7 of the DPA provides that this should be acceptable where:

(a) the other individual has consented to the disclosure of the information to the person making the request; or more likely in social housing fraud investigations; *or*

(b) it is reasonable in all the circumstances to comply with the request without the consent of the other individual.[19]

Disclosure required by law (section 35)

6.36   The second exemption at 6.30 is provided by section 35 of the DPA:

'(1) Personal data are exempt from the non-disclosure provisions where the disclosure is required by or under any enactment, by any rule of law or by the order of a court.[20]

(2) Personal data are exempt from the non-disclosure provisions where the disclosure is necessary—

(a) *for the purpose of, or in connection with, any legal proceedings (including prospective legal proceedings),* or

(b) for the purpose of obtaining legal advice,

or is otherwise necessary for the purposes of establishing, exercising or defending legal rights'[21] (emphasis added).

6.37   The 'non-disclosure provisions' referred to in section 35(1) of the DPA means the provisions below:[22]

---

18 See Chapter 7 and in particular the reference to the Fraud Act 2006 and offences under Parts 6 and 7 of the Housing Act 1996.

19 Section 7 further provides: '(6) In determining for the purposes of subsection (4)(b) whether it is reasonable in all the circumstances to comply with the request without the consent of the other individual concerned, regard shall be had, in particular, to– (a) any duty of confidentiality owed to the other individual, (b) any steps taken by the data controller with a view to seeking the consent of the other individual, (c) whether the other individual is capable of giving consent, and (d) any express refusal of consent by the other individual.'

20 *R (on the application of Davies) v Commissioners Office* [2008] EWHC 334 (Admin), [2008] 1 FLR 1651.

21 DPA, s 35.

22 Ibid, s 27(3)(4).

(a) the First Data Protection Principle, except to the extent to which it requires compliance with the conditions in Schedules 2 and 3 of the DPA;

(b) the Second, Third, Fourth and Fifth Data Protection Principles; and

(c) sections 10 (right to prevent processing likely to cause damage or distress) and 14(1) to (3) (rectification, blocking, erasure and destruction of inaccurate data) of the DPA,

to the extent that that they are inconsistent with the disclosure in question.

6.38   To give an obvious example of section 35(1) of the DPA, a local authority seeking information from a bank as to a tenant's statements pursuant to the Prevention of Social Housing Fraud (Power to Require Information) (England) Regulations 2014, described further below, can do so without the restriction of the DPA by reason of this provision (and see 6.24).

6.39   As for section 35(2) of the DPA, this provision is commonly utilised in data sharing arrangements on the basis that the disclosure is necessary for the purposes of legitimate interests being pursued by the data controller (Schedule 2, paragraph 6).

DATA SHARING

'Any data controller who is involved in the sharing of personal data should use this code to help them to understand how to adopt good practice. Much of the good practice advice will be applicable to public, private and third sector organisations. Some parts of the code are necessarily focused on sector-specific issues. However, the majority of the code will apply to all data sharing regardless of its scale and context.'[23]

6.40   Data sharing is not in itself inherently controversial or commercially unusual. For example, a social landlord will, as a matter of course, provide necessary disclosures of information about a tenant and their premises to maintenance and gas contractors.

6.41   It is also not uncommon for local authorities and housing associations (and others) to enter into data-sharing protocols,[24] and even for different departments in, say, a local authority to do the same. The purpose will be to explain *what*, *why* and *when* specified personal data can be shared, though it should be stressed that the DPA still applies and such protocols are not a 'way around' the statutory disclosure restrictions.

---

23 See *Data Sharing Code of Practice* (Information Commissioner's Office), (May 2011) p 7 – prepared under DPA, s 52.
24 See Chartered Institute of Housing *Tenancy Fraud and Data Sharing: A Guide for Housing Associations* (Feb 2012) for some examples.

6.42   These protocols will invariably be informed by the (statutory) Data Sharing Code of Practice prepared by the Information Commissioner's Office.[25] The Code states:

> 'This code explains how the Data Protection Act 1998 (DPA) applies to the sharing of personal data. It also provides good practice advice that will be relevant to all organisations that share personal data.'[26]

6.43   Section 15 of the Code provides a checklist for both systematic and one-off checks, the latter being set out four questions:

---

1.   Is the sharing justified?

Key points to consider:

o   Do you think you should share the information?

o   Have you assessed the potential benefits and risks to individuals and/or society of sharing or not sharing?

o   Do you have concerns that an individual is at risk of serious harm?

o   Do you need to consider an exemption in the DPA to share?

2.   Do you have the power to share?

Key points to consider:

o   The type of organisation you work for.

o   Any relevant functions or powers of your organisation.

o   The nature of the information you have been asked to share (eg was it given in confidence?).

o   Any legal obligation to share information (eg a statutory requirement or a court order).

3.   If you decide to share

Key points to consider:

o   What information do you need to share?

–   Only share what is necessary.

–   Distinguish fact from opinion.

o   How should the information be shared?

–   Information must be shared securely.

–   Ensure you are giving information to the right person.

---

25 Prepared and published under DPA, s 52 and available at: https://ico.org.uk/media/for-organisations/documents/1068/data_sharing_code_of_practice.pdf.
26 See *Data Sharing Code of Practice* (Information Commissioner's Office), (May 2011) p 6.

○ Consider whether it is appropriate/safe to inform the individual that you have shared their information.

4. Record your decision

Record your data sharing decision and your reasoning – whether or not you shared the information.

If you share information you should record:

○ What information was shared and for what purpose.

○ Who it was shared with.

○ When it was shared.

○ Your justification for sharing.

○ Whether the information was shared with or without consent.

6.44 Further, the DPA expressly provides that disclosure of sensitive data may be possible where:[27]

'(1) The processing–

(a) is either–

(i) the disclosure of sensitive personal data by a person as a member of an anti-fraud organisation or otherwise in accordance with any arrangements made by such an organisation; or

(ii) any other processing by that person or another person of sensitive personal data so disclosed; and

(b) is necessary for the purposes of preventing fraud or a particular kind of fraud.

(2) In this paragraph 'an anti-fraud organisation' means any unincorporated association, body corporate or other person which enables or facilitates any sharing of information to prevent fraud or a particular kind of fraud or which has any of these functions as its purpose or one of its purposes.'

PSHF REGULATIONS

6.45 The Prevention of Social Housing Fraud (Power to Require Information) (England) Regulations 2014[28] ('the Regulations') came into force on 6 April 2014. The Regulations make express provision for powers to be given to an 'authorised

---

27 DPA, Sch 3, para 7A added by the Serious Crime Act 2007, s 72.
28 SI 2014/899 – made under PSHF, ss 7, 8 and 9(2)(b) and (c). There are also the Prevention of Social Housing Fraud (Detection of Fraud)(Wales) Regulations 2014/826 – made under PSHF, ss 7 and 8 to similar effect and in force from 28 March 2014.

officer' (see 6.50) to require information from third parties for housing fraud investigation purposes.

6.46   Prior to this, social landlords used the limited and more general data-sharing powers and ability to request information under the DPA[29] referred to above, and at times the surveillance powers to be found under legislation such as the Regulation of Investigatory Powers Act 2000.

6.47   The Regulations, however, essentially create a distinct power under regulation 4 to require information from certain identified third parties, *but only for housing fraud investigation purposes*,[30] a definition which extends beyond simply the PSHF sub-letting/parting with possession offences.

6.48   Section 7(7) of the PSHF defines 'housing fraud investigation purposes' as purposes relating to the prevention, detection or securing of evidence for a conviction of:

(a) a PSHF offence;

(b) an offence under the Fraud Act 2006 relating to the unlawful sub-letting or parting with possession of the whole or part of a dwelling-house let by a local authority, a private registered provider of social housing or a registered social landlord;

(c) an offence under the Fraud Act 2006 relating to an application for an allocation of housing accommodation under Part 6 of the Housing Act 1996;

(d) an offence under the Fraud Act 2006 relating to an application for accommodation or for assistance in obtaining accommodation, under Part 7 of the Housing Act 1996 or under Part 2 of the Housing (Wales) Act 2014;

(e) an offence under the Fraud Act 2006 relating to–
   (i)   a claim to exercise the right to buy under Part 5 of the Housing Act 1985,
   (ii) a claim to exercise the right to acquire under section 16 of the Housing Act 1996,
   (iii) a claim to exercise the right to acquire under section 180 of the Housing and Regeneration Act 2008, or

(f) an associated offence in relation to an offence mentioned in any of paragraphs (a) to (e).

6.49   Chapter 7 deals with some of these offences in more detail.

6.50   The local authority can grant authorisation to an individual to exercise the regulation 4 investigation powers – which can relate to matters beyond the authority's geographical boundary – if:[31]

---

29 DPA, ss 29 and 35, and Sch 2, para 6 – see the Chartered Institute of Housing's *Tenancy Fraud & Data Sharing* (February 2012).
30 See reg 4(1).
31 See reg 3.

(a) the authorisation is in writing; and

(b) the individual is employed by that or another local authority or by a joint committee that carries out functions relating to housing fraud investigation purposes on behalf of that authority.

6.51 To then exercise these powers under the Regulations, regulation 4 merely requires the authorised officer to have reasonable grounds for suspecting that:

(a) the person they require information from is a bank, building society, other provider of credit, telecommunications provider or utilities company (or employee of any of these bodies); and

(b) they either have or may have, possession of or access to, any information about any matter that is relevant to housing fraud investigation purposes.

6.52 Common examples of information obtained by this means are:

(a) Bank statements demonstrating:

- regular payments going into the account (eg the allegation being that they are rent payments from a sub-letting);
- regular payments of mortgage and (other) rent;
- address(es) used for bank purposes; and
- activity on the account and geographical location of the same.

(b) Utility accounts demonstrating:

- whose name the account is in;
- method of payment; and
- utility usage (especially in only or principal home cases).

(c) Telephone accounts demonstrating:

- how many accounts there are;
- whose name it/they are in;
- contact with particular individuals; and
- method of payment.

6.53 The operation of this power is unsurprisingly not without caveats and 'hurdles'. For example, regulation 4 states (with emphasis added in italics):

'(5) An authorised officer shall not, in exercise of those powers, require any information from any person by virtue of that person falling within paragraph (3) unless *it appears to that officer that there are reasonable grounds for believing that the person to whom it relates is—*

(a) a person who has committed, is committing or intends to commit an offence listed in section 7(7)[32] *of the Prevention of Social Housing Fraud Act 2013; or*

---

32 See 6.48.

(b) *a person who is **a member of the family** of a person falling within sub-paragraph (a).'*

6.54   It does not, therefore, assist in obtaining information from third parties, such as a 'reluctant' sub-tenant, who is unrelated to the tenant. Nor does it allow for a 'fishing expedition' as the relevant officer must have 'reasonable grounds' for believing that the individual in question has committed, is committing or intends to commit one of the offences set down at 6.48.

6.55   It is an offence under regulation 5 to not provide, intentionally delay, etc the information requested and conviction makes any defendant liable to a fine (ongoing breach thereafter is punishable by a fine not exceeding £40 per day).[33] The Regulations also provide in this respect a limitation on such action:

'7.— Legal proceedings

(1) Proceedings for an offence under regulation 5 may be brought within the period of 6 months beginning with the date on which evidence sufficient in the opinion of the prosecutor to warrant the proceedings came to the prosecutor's knowledge.

(2) But no such proceedings may be brought more than three years —

(a) after the commission of the offence, or

(b) in the case of a continuous contravention, after the last date on which the offence was committed.

(3) A certificate signed by the prosecutor and stating the date on which such evidence came to the prosecutor's knowledge is conclusive evidence of that fact; and a certificate to that effect and purporting to be signed is to be treated as being so signed unless the contrary is proved.'

COURT PROCESSES

6.56   Obtaining information via the routes described earlier in this chapter is largely, though by no means exclusively, confined to pre-court activities. Effective use of court procedures after the issue of proceedings may further help to 'fill in the gaps' and strengthen the evidence available to the social landlord to its optimum effect.

Pre-action

6.57   Most of the actions available through the civil courts relate to the post-issue period, though pre-action disclosure is available pursuant to Rule 31.16 of the Civil Procedure Rules 1998 (CPR).

33 The Regulations also deal with the liability of directors (reg 6) and legal proceedings under reg 5 (reg 7).

6.58 Any application for pre-action disclosure:

(a) can only be made against a would-be party;

(b) must identify the documents or class of documents to be disclosed (which would have been disclosable under standard disclosure if proceedings had been issued); and

(c) will only be considered if it is desirable to:

- dispose fairly of the anticipated proceedings;

- assist the dispute to be resolved without proceedings; or

- save costs.

6.59 This option is unlikely to be taken up in social housing fraud cases very often, not only because of the powers already available to a social landlord to obtain information (see above) but also because it is unlikely that such evidence will 'tip the balance' between issuing or not issuing proceedings (let alone disposing of them) in most instances.

Post-issue

6.60 A social landlord has four primary options available to them after proceedings have been issued in the County Court or High Court, all of which are generally under-used:

- Part 18 Request for Further Information;

- Specific disclosure;

- Disclosure against third party;

- Witness summonses.

6.61 Firstly, therefore, there is the *Part 18 Request for Further Information* procedure, whose purpose is to clarify a party's case. For example, it may be helpful where the defence is, in essence, a bare denial of subletting, but does not respond in substance or at all to the pleaded matters used to support the landlord's case, such as statements provided by the alleged sub-tenant, evidence of the defendant living elsewhere, credit reference information, etc.

6.62 The provision of a defence may therefore still leave unknown in such cases, to give three actual examples known to the author:

(1) What the defendant says about monthly (rent level) payments going into their account.

(2) How long they spend (and what they do) in another country, where their partner and any business are located.

105

(3) What the tenant lived on between 2012 and 2015 when they were not working and were not in receipt of social security benefits (the suspicion being it was from the income obtained from sub-letting her local authority flat).

6.63   It is important to note when considering use of the Part 18 process:[34]

(a) A preliminary written request should always be made first, providing a date when a response is expected and confirming that the request is made under Part 18. This should usually be served by e-mail if reasonably practicable.

(b) The request should be proportionate and with a genuine view of knowing the case the first party has to meet.

(c) Such a request should comply in full with the Practice Direction to Part 18.

Preliminary Request for Further Information or Clarification

1.1 Before making an application to the court for an order under Part 18, the party seeking clarification or information (the first party) should first serve on the party from whom it is sought (the second party) a written request for that clarification or information (a Request) stating a date by which the response to the Request should be served. The date must allow the second party a reasonable time to respond.

1.2 A Request should be concise and strictly confined to matters which are reasonably necessary and proportionate to enable the first party to prepare his own case or to understand the case he has to meet.

1.3 Requests must be made as far as possible in a single comprehensive document and not piecemeal.

1.4 A Request may be made by letter if the text of the Request is brief and the reply is likely to be brief; otherwise the Request should be made in a separate document.

1.5 If a Request is made in a letter, the letter should, in order to distinguish it from any other that might routinely be written in the course of a case,

   (1) state that it contains a Request made under Part 18, and

   (2) deal with no matters other than the Request.

1.6 (1) A Request (whether made by letter or in a separate document) must –

> (a) be headed with the name of the court and the title and number of the claim,
>
> (b) in its heading state that it is a Request made under Part 18, identify the first party and the second party and state the date on which it is made,

---

34 See the Practice Direction to CPR 18, paras 1 to 4 in particular, as set out after sub-paragraph (c).

(c) set out in a separate numbered paragraph each request for information or clarification,

(d) where a Request relates to a document, identify that document and (if relevant) the paragraph or words to which it relates,

(e) state the date by which the first party expects a response to the Request.

(2) (a) A Request which is not in the form of a letter may, if convenient, be prepared in such a way that the response may be given on the same document.

(b) To do this, the numbered paragraphs of the Request should appear on the left-hand half of each sheet so that the paragraphs of the response may then appear on the right.

(c) Where a Request is prepared in this form, an extra copy should be served for the use of the second party.

1.7 Subject to the provisions of rule 6.23(5) and (6) and paragraphs 4.1 to 4.3 of Practice Direction 6A, a request should be served by e-mail if reasonably practicable.

Responding to a Request

2.1 A response to a Request must be in writing, dated and signed by the second party or his legal representative.

2.2 (1) Where the Request is made in a letter, the second party may give his response in a letter or in a formal reply.

(2) Such a letter should identify itself as a response to the Request and deal with no other matters than the response.

2.3 (1) Unless the Request is in the format described in paragraph 1.6(2) and the second party uses the document supplied for the purpose, a response must:

(a) be headed with the name of the court and the title and number of the claim,

(b) in its heading identify itself as a response to that Request,

(c) repeat the text of each separate paragraph of the Request and set out under each paragraph the response to it,

(d) refer to and have attached to it a copy of any document not already in the possession of the first party which forms part of the response.

(2) A second or supplementary response to a Request must identify itself as such in its heading.

2.4 The second party must, when he serves his response on the first party, serve on every other party and file with the court a copy of the Request and of his response.

Statements of truth

3   Attention is drawn to Part 22 and to the definition of a statement of case in Part 2 of the rules; a response should be verified by a statement of truth.

General matters

4.1 (1) If the second party objects to complying with the Request or part of it or is unable to do so at all or within the time stated in the Request he must inform the first party promptly and in any event within that time.

(2) He may do so in a letter or in a separate document (a formal response), but in either case he must give reasons and, where relevant, give a date by which he expects to be able to comply.

4.2 (1) There is no need for a second party to apply to the court if he objects to a Request or is unable to comply with it at all or within the stated time. He need only comply with paragraph 4.1(1) above.

(2) Where a second party considers that a Request can only be complied with at disproportionate expense and objects to complying for that reason he should say so in his reply and explain briefly why he has taken that view.

(d) Any response should be verified by a statement of truth.

(e) If the second party objects to complying with the request (including on the basis that it would be disproportionately expensive) or any part of it, then they should inform the first party promptly.

(f) If no response at all is made, then the first party can seek an order requiring a response without a hearing and without serving the application on the second party.

(g) A court granting an order under Part 18 can make it subject to conditions, and with the application of a sanction, such as a striking out of the defence, for failure to comply.

(h) The court can make a Part 18 order of its own initiative or upon application by the requesting party (ie where the other party has failed to respond or failed to respond adequately).

(i) A request is necessarily made post-statement of case, but may be made prior to statements being served and more than once. A response may necessitate a further follow-up request for further information.

Request for Further Information

IN THE COUNTY COURT AT TRAFFORD   CLAIM NO: OT7456

BETWEEN:

PEARSON HEIGHTS HOUSING ASSOCIATION

Claimant

-and-

MR BRIAN GREENHOFF

Defendant

PART 18 REQUEST

The Claimant requires the Defendant to respond to the questions below by **4.00pm on Thursday 26 October 20XX**.

1. In paragraph 4 of the Defence dated 21 September 20XX it is said 'No admissions are made as to paragraph 5 of the Annex to the Particulars of Claim'.

    (a) Does the Defendant know Timothy Hill referred to at paragraph 5(b) of the Annex to the Particulars of Claim'?

    (b) Has the said Timothy Hill ever stayed overnight at Flat 3, Rosebush Avenue, Trafford, TF3 3DD ('the Premises') since the Defendant's tenancy commenced on 7 April 2014? If so when and was payment received?

    (c) Did the Defendant ever provide the said Timothy Hill with a tenancy agreement in respect of the Premises? If so:

    - When?

    - Can the Defendant please provide a copy to the Claimant's solicitors?

    - What were the terms of the tenancy?

    (d) Has the Defendant ever visited 12 Broom Heights, Manchester M13 1TT ('the Second Premises')?

    (e) Has the Defendant ever stayed overnight at the Second Premises? If so, when and how often?

    (f) Does the Defendant admit:

    - He was on the electoral register at the Second Premises from 2015? If so, why?

> - He used the Second Premises as his address for bank and correspondence purposes? If so, why?
>
> - He has use of the Second Premises? If so, under what arrangement?
>
> The response to this Part 18 Request for Further Information should be sent to: Gotcha Solicitors, Parting Way, Manchester M13 2KH. The Defendant is referred to paragraphs 2 and 3 of the Practice Direction to CPR 18, which is exhibited to this document.
>
> *27 September 20XX*

6.64   In many instances, allied to the Part 18 process, is the availability of powers under CPR Part 31 for a court to order *specific disclosure* of identified documents or classes of documents (31.12), or *disclosure against a person who is not a party* (31.17).

6.65   With respect to the former, the order will require the defendant to disclose the identified documents and carry out a search to the extent provided in the order. To give one example of the latter, it may be that the tenant does not, in fact, retain their bank statements or housing benefit decision letters but an order under 31.12 can require them to seek copies from the bank and local authority respectively and then disclose the results of their request.

6.66   As for third-party disclosure, the court must be satisfied that:

(a) the documents of which disclosure is sought are likely to support the case of the applicant or adversely affect the case of one of the other parties to the proceedings; and

(b) disclosure is necessary to dispose fairly of the claim or to save costs.

6.67   For example, the claimant social landlord may seek the bank accounts of the alleged sub-tenant, not available under the PSHF Regulations, or details in relation to where the tenant claims to have lived at the relevant time (such as household bills).

6.68   Finally, there is the question of witnesses and in particular the ability to *witness summons* an individual to attend court to give evidence or produce documents in court (CPR 34.2) by use of Form N20 or obtain the court's permission to call the other party's (identified) witness where they were not otherwise going to be called so that they may be cross examined (CPR 33.4).

6.69   A witness summons, which will be served by the Court unless the party advises otherwise,[35] does not require the permission of the Court unless it is issued less than seven days before trial or requires attendance of the witness on a day other than that fixed for the trial: CPR 34.3.

---

35 See CPR 34.6.

6.70   The party issuing the witness summons must pay in advance the witnesses reasonable travel expenses and (extremely modest[36]) compensation for loss of time.[37]

6.71   One has to be careful in the use of witness summonses because it can backfire and end up strengthening the case of the defendant. For example, if in a sub-letting case you want to hear evidence from neighbours of the relevant premises and decide to witness summons such people who have previously indicated they do not want to get involved, then they could end up not supporting the case that other persons (than the tenant(s)) were living at the premises.

6.72   An application under CPR 33.4 must be made not more than 14 days after the day on which a notice of intention to rely on the hearsay evidence was served on the applicant (though a party can seek permission to do so outside of this time).[38]

CONCLUSION

6.73   This chapter promotes the truism that 'a claim is only as good as the evidence in support of it'. Sometimes though, documentary evidence will be scarce and the case will turn upon the credibility of the witnesses and their performance, in particular, under cross examination.

6.74   At other times the evidence is so overwhelming one wonders why the defendant bothered to defend the proceedings. A successful conclusion for the social landlord should be then easily achievable.

6.75   More likely, however, is something in-between the two extremes; it is foolhardy not to ensure that the best evidence possible is put before the court. This is likely to require all or some of the following:

(a) proactive efforts to obtain information from relevant third parties;

(b) the application and invoking of data sharing arrangements;

(c) if the social landlord is not a local housing authority, the engagement with and use of the local authority to obtain information as part of any 'housing fraud

---

36 For example, the maximum rate at present for a period not exceeding four hours is £33.50 – see *Guide to Allowances under Part V of Costs in Criminal Cases (General) Regulations* (September 2016).

37 CPR 34.7 and CPR PD34A, para 3 – loss of time payments are allied to the criminal procedure and the Costs in Criminal Cases (General Regulations) 1986 (SI 1986/1335).

38 See CPR 3.1 –

"(2) Except where these Rules provide otherwise, the court may –
  (a) extend or shorten the time for compliance with any rule, practice direction or court order (even if an application for extension is made after the time for compliance has expired).

investigation' (including by the undertaking of 'under caution' interviews); and

(d) a proactive use of court procedures, and close regard to questions of disclosure and the availability of the Part 18 Request for Further Information.

CHAPTER 7

Criminal Sanctions

- Sub-letting offences
- Right to buy/right to acquire/shared ownership fraud
- Allocation and homelessness offences

Key points

- There are specific criminal offences relating to sub-letting and parting with possession, and the failure to provide accurate information for allocation and homelessness purposes to be found in the Prevention of Social Housing Fraud Act 2013 (PSHF) and Housing Act 1996 respectively.

- The Fraud Act 2006 creates a series of fraud offences and will be used, especially in a housing context, in false statement, right to buy, right to acquire and shared ownership cases.

- The making of an unlawful profit order should be considered by the court upon conviction for an offence under the PSHF.

- A local authority is able to prosecute an offence under PSHF even if the premises concerned are not let by them or are not even in their area.

- The Powers of Criminal Courts (Sentencing) Act 2000, s 130(1) allow a criminal court to make a compensation order to cover loss or damage resulting from the criminal offence of which the defendant has been convicted.

INTRODUCTION

7.1   Any book on social housing fraud is inevitably going to deal with the criminal aspect of such activity, as well as the more immediate and well-trodden civil remedies route of possession, damages and, perhaps, declaration.[1]

7.2   This chapter does not purport to be a definitive guide to all the criminal sanctions that may be available – for example, it does not deal with the related benefit fraud offences with the common law conspiracy to defraud or issues of false accounting under section 17 of the Theft Act 1968. However, it does seek to demonstrate the range of the most likely options available to the prosecuting authorities when faced with social housing fraud.

---

1   For rescission.

7.3   In particular, the PSHF has brought into sharp focus the inter-relationship between criminal sanctions and civil remedies, though alongside the more general Fraud Act 2006 there had been (and remain) earlier targeted criminal offences created, such as can be found at sections 171 and 214 of the Housing Act 1996 (both of which are dealt with below).

7.4   It is always worth remembering that in criminal proceedings the general rule is that the prosecution bears the legal burden of proving *all* elements of the offence[2] and that guilt must be established to the criminal standard of proof, beyond reasonable doubt.[3]

7.5   Those offences most obviously relevant to social housing fraud are identified and discussed below and if a conviction is achieved, this will provide conclusive proof of any of the matters that need to be proved for any civil action, particularly bearing in mind section 11 of the Civil Evidence Act 1968:

> '(1) In any civil proceedings the fact that a person has been convicted of an offence by or before any court in the United Kingdom or of a service offence (anywhere) shall (subject to subsection (3) below[4]) be admissible in evidence for the purpose of proving, where to do so is relevant to any issue in those proceedings, that he committed that offence, whether he was so convicted upon a plea of guilty or otherwise and whether or not he is a party to the civil proceedings; but no conviction other than a subsisting one shall be admissible in evidence by virtue of this section.'

ALLOCATION FRAUD

> (1) A person commits an offence if, in connection with the exercise by a local housing authority of their functions under this Part—
>
> > (a) he knowingly or recklessly makes a statement which is false in a material particular, or
> >
> > (b) he knowingly withholds information which the authority have reasonably required him to give in connection with the exercise of those functions.
>
> *Housing Act 1996, s 171*

---

2   This is in contrast to civil proceedings where, for example, the burden of proving the right to succession is on the would-be successor (*Governors of the Peabody Donation Fund v Grant* (1983) 6 HLR 41 at 44 *per* Donaldson LJ) and sufficient absence from a premises may lead to an explanation being required from the tenant in an only or principal home case: *Lambeth LBC v Vandra* [2005] EWCA Civ 1801, [2006] HLR 19 at 8–10 *per* Mummery LJ; *Islington LBC v Boyle* [2011] EWCA Civ 1450 at 65 *per* Etherton LJ.

3   *Woolmington v DPP* [1935] AC 462.

4   Section 11(3): 'Nothing in this section shall prejudice the operation of section 13 of this Act or any other enactment whereby a conviction or a finding of fact in any criminal proceedings is for the purposes of any other proceedings made conclusive evidence of any fact.'

7.6   Chapter 2 discusses the route to recovery of a social housing unit procured by a fraudulent misrepresentation. However, not only is such activity a ground for possession of the premises but it may also represent a specific criminal offence if the allocation is by way of a local housing authority's (LHA) allocation scheme.

7.7   The criminal offence, set out in section 171 above, requires the false statement(s) or withholding of information to be in relation to a LHA's operation of its allocation scheme. It should, therefore, be appreciated that:

(a) An LHA is required to comply with the provisions of Part 6 when allocating accommodation.[5]

(b) This includes nominations by a LHA to a private registered provider or registered social landlord (primarily housing associations).[6]

7.8   The section 171 offence can be committed in two different ways, broadly by giving or withholding information, and can best be explained by way of three questions:

● *First*, is the LHA exercising its functions under Part 6 of the Housing Act 1996? If yes,

● *Second*, has the defendant made a false statement? If so,
   –   Did the defendant knowingly or recklessly make the statement?
   –   Was the statement false in a material sense?

● *Third*, as an alternative to the second requirement, has the applicant knowingly withheld information which the LHA have reasonably required in the exercise of their allocation functions?

False statement

7.9   The most obvious starting point in considering the issue of false statement is to make the point that both the maker of the statement and the potential defendant need not be the applicant. Someone assisting the applicant to complete the form may therefore be caught by this provision.

7.10   The mere copying down of false information would not, however, be sufficient:

(a) absent any further evidence that the maker of the statement knew that it was false, or was reckless as to its accuracy, and

(b) absent evidence that they intended the LHA to believe in its accuracy,

no offence will have been committed.

---

5   Housing Act 1996, s 159(1).
6   Ibid, s 159(2)(c) – this would cover the nomination arrangements many LHAs have with housing associations in their area (see s 159(4)).

7.11   The *Allocation of Accommodation: Guidance for Local Housing Authorities in England* (June 2012)[7] helpfully confirms:[8]

> '5.11 The circumstances in which an offence is committed could include providing false information:
>
> - on an application form for social housing
>
> - in response to a request for further information in support of the application
>
> - during review proceedings.'

Withholding information

7.12   As with the making of a false statement, the offence of withholding relevant information can be committed by a person other than the applicant. The most obvious examples of who such other person may be are a partner, employer or landlord.

Sentence

7.13   The sentencing for a section 171 offence is dealt with at 7.17 below.

7.14   As a footnote to this discussion on allocation 'fraud' it is worth noting that the grant of a secure tenancy to someone to whom accommodation has been allocated inconsistently with the authority's allocation scheme does not of itself render the tenancy void or ineffective.[9]

HOMELESSNESS FRAUD

(1) It is an offence for a person, with intent to induce a local housing authority to believe in connection with the exercise of their functions under this Part that he or another person is entitled to accommodation or assistance in accordance with the provisions of this Part or is entitled to accommodation or assistance of a particular description–

---

7   Produced by the Department for Communities and Local Government under Housing Act 1996, s 169.
8   The above guidance states in relation to staff fraud or negligence:
     '5.13 Authorities may also wish to take action to minimise the risk of staff allocating incorrectly or even fraudulently, for example to applicants who do not have sufficient priority under the allocation scheme or do not meet the authority's qualification criteria. Appropriate steps might include vetting staff who take allocation decisions or providing for decisions to be validated by employing senior staff to undertake random checks.'
9   *Birmingham City Council v Qasim* [2009] EWCA Civ 1080, [2010] HLR 19 at 37 *per* Lord Neuberger and 46–48 *per* Lord Justice Sedley – see 2.15–2.17.

(a) knowingly or recklessly to make a statement which is false in a material particular, or

(b) knowingly to withhold information which the authority have reasonably required him to give in connection with the exercise of those functions.

(2) If before an applicant receives notification of the local housing authority's decision on his application there is any change of facts material to his case, he shall notify the authority as soon as possible.

The authority shall explain to every applicant, in ordinary language, the duty imposed on him by this subsection and the effect of subsection (3).

(3) A person who fails to comply with subsection (2) commits an offence unless he shows that he was not given the explanation required by that subsection or that he had some other reasonable excuse for non-compliance.

Housing Act 1996, s 214

7.15   The first two offences under section 214(1)(a) and (1)(b) mirror those seen above for allocation fraud. This is with the 'addition' of the need to demonstrate an intention to induce the LHA, in connection with the exercise of their homelessness (Part 7) functions, to believe that the homeless applicant is entitled to accommodation or assistance.

7.16   There is, though, an *additional* offence, under sub-paragraph (2) of failing to notify the LHA of material changes, which *is* restricted to the applicant. The reason is apparent when one considers the various elements of the offence:

(a) An applicant is under a positive duty to inform the LHA as soon as possible of any change of facts material to their application prior to the LHA's *original*[10] decision.

(b) What is a 'change of material fact' is a moot point and may provide a line of defence where the change is not of obvious relevance.

(c) Before such an offence can be committed, a LHA must explain to an applicant, in ordinary language, the nature of his duty to notify them of material changes and that any failure to do so is a criminal offence.[11] If the applicant can show that this advice was not given, it provides an absolute defence.

(d) Similarly, if the applicant can show that they had some other reasonable excuse for non-compliance then, again, this could constitute a complete defence to the charge.

---

10 Housing Act 1996, s 184 – it follows that the same obligation does not apply to any changes post-original decision and pre-s 202 review decision.

11 See *Homelessness Code of Guidance for Local Authorities*, para 6.11 (July 2006).

Sentence[12]

7.17 Offences under the allocation and homelessness provisions are prosecuted in the magistrates' court, and carry a maximum fine of level 5 on the standard scale.[13]

PREVENTION OF SOCIAL HOUSING FRAUD ACT 2013

7.18 The Prevention of Social Housing Fraud Act 2013 (PSHF) creates two criminal offences relating to the sub-letting or parting with possession of the whole of, or part of, demised premises let by a local authority or private registered provider of social housing[14] without the landlord's consent. There are broad similarities between the provisions concerning secure tenancies (s 1) and assured tenancies (s 2).

7.19 There is nothing to prevent a social landlord seeking *both* a criminal remedy by way of conviction[15] and a civil remedy through possession action or unlawful profit order application in the county court (see Chapters 3 and 5, and 7.5 above).

7.20 It follows that not only is a conviction admissible evidence in the civil courts of the sub-letting and parting with possession claimed by the landlord, but also, because of the higher standard of proof required in the criminal courts, a failure to secure a conviction is not necessarily fatal to a claim for possession of premises or an application for an unlawful profit order reliant on the same facts.

Major offence

7.21 A tenant will commit an offence if:[16]

(a) they sub-let or part with possession of the whole of the premises, or part thereof, without the landlord's written consent (for assured tenancies there is no reference to consent although this is likely to be a breach of tenancy);

(b) this is done dishonestly and in breach of an express or implied term of the tenancy; and

---

12 See Housing Act 1996, ss 171(2) and 214(4).
13 Criminal Justice Act 1982, s 37 – the Legal Aid, Sentencing and Punishment of Offenders Act 2012, s 85 has removed the £5,000 limit.
14 PSHF, s 2(3) or registered social landlord in Wales – a shared ownership lease is excluded from these provisions.
15 The prosecution, though, would be by a local authority even if the premises were owned or otherwise let by a housing association – PSHF, s 3(5).
16 PSHF, ss 1(2), 2(2).

(c) the tenant ceases to occupy the premises as their only or principal home. Of course, if the arrangement is a joint tenancy then no offence is committed if the joint tenant remains in occupation.

Lodgers

7.22   As has been made clear in Chapter 3, lodger and most licensee arrangements do not constitute either sub-letting or parting with possession.

Consent

7.23   Most tenancy agreements have express terms which prohibit sub-letting or parting with possession of the whole of the demised premises, only allowing the same of part with the landlord's written consent.

7.24   In any event, it is an implied term of every secure and assured tenancy agreement that the tenant will not sub-let or part with possession of part of the dwelling without the landlord's written consent,[17] which must not be unreasonably withheld (and will be treated as given if it is unreasonably withheld).[18]

Dishonesty

7.25   The test for 'dishonesty' is as recently confirmed by the Supreme Court in *Ivy v Genting Casinos (UK) Ltd t/a Crockfords*.[19] This is referred to in more detail at 7.51 below.

Only or principal home

7.26   This is considered in more detail at Chapter 4 but suffice to say here:

(a) it is a question of fact and degree;

(b) if the sub-letting or parting with possession is of the whole of the demised premises then this will be treated as being inconsistent with the premises still being the tenant's only or principal home;[20]

(c) physical occupation of the premises is not required to retain security of tenure, but the tenant will have to have an objective[21] intention to return to the premises (which must remain their only or principal home notwithstanding the tenant's non-occupation);[22]

---

17 Housing Act 1985, s 93(1)(b) (secure tenancies); HA 1988, s 15(1) (assured tenancies).
18 Housing Act 1985, s 94(2). For assured tenancies, the Housing Act 1988 expressly provides at s 15(2) that the usual statutory provision implying a condition that consent may not be unreasonably withheld; Landlord and Tenant Act 1927, s 19 does not apply.
19 [2017] UKSC 67.
20 *Ujima Housing Association v Ansah* (1998) 30 HLR 831, CA.
21 *Amoah v Barking and Dagenham LBC* (2001) 82 P & CR DG6, ChD.
22 *Crawley BC v Sawyer* (1988) 20 HLR 98, CA.

(d) a sufficiently lengthy or continuous absence from the premises could compel the inference that the tenant had ceased to occupy the property as his only or principal home, the onus then being on the tenant to rebut it.[23]

Less serious offence

7.27   For the less serious offence of 'knowingly' sub-letting, which does not require dishonesty, the prosecution must show that the tenant:[24]

(a) has sub-let or parted with possession of the whole or part of the premises without the landlord's written consent (for assured tenancies there is again no reference to consent);

(b) no longer lives at the premises as their only or principal home; and

(c) knows that this is contrary to the express or implied terms of their tenancy.

7.28   Knowledge that any sub-letting is a breach of tenancy can include where a defendant has 'deliberately shut their eyes' to the truth.[25]

Defences

7.29   There are two specified defences to the less serious crime.

7.30   First, where the tenant's actions are due to violence, or threats of violence, by a person either residing in, or in the locality[26] of, the premises.[27] The violence or threats of violence must either be towards:

● the tenant; or

● a member of the tenant's family[28] who was residing with the tenant immediately before they ceased to occupy the premises.

---

23 *London Borough of Islington v (1) Boyle (2) Collier* [2011] EWCA Civ 1450, [2012] HLR 19.

24 PSHF, s 1(1) for secure tenancies; s 2(1) for assured tenancies.

25 *Warner v Metropolitan Police Commr* [1969] 2 AC 256 at 279 *per* Lord Reid; *Atwal v Massey* (1972) 56 Cr App R 6, DC.

26 Not defined in the Act, but see anti-social behaviour injunction case of *Manchester City Council v Lawler* (1998) 31 HLR 119 – Butler Sloss LJ said at [124]: 'One purpose of the phrase "in the locality" was to avoid the often difficult, unrewarding and sometimes lengthy discussion of whether to identify one road rather than another which would meet the general need to keep the tiresome and obstreperous tenant under some control in the area where he/she was likely to be the most troublesome. That area may be the part or the whole of a housing estate. It may straddle parts of two housing estates or include local shops serving the housing estate but within its boundaries. In my view, if one asked a resident in Broadoak Drive if Haveley Circle and Haveley Road were in the locality, the answer would be yes, of course.'

27 Section 1(3).

28 Section 11(4) defines this by reference to HA 1985, s 113(5) – spouse or civil partner or person living together with another as if they were his spouse or civil partner; parent, grandparent, child, grandchild, brother, sister, uncle, aunt, nephew or niece. In this context: a relationship by marriage or civil partnership shall be treated as a relationship by blood; a relationship of half-blood shall be treated as a relationship of the whole blood; the stepchild of a person shall be treated as his child (including the stepchild of a civil partner) and an illegitimate child shall be treated as the legitimate child of his mother and reputed father. A foster child is not a 'child' for the purposes of s 113: *Sheffield City Council v Wall* [2010] EWCA Civ 922, [2011] 1 WLR 1342, [2010] HLR 47.

7.31   Though 'violence' is not formally defined in PSHF it is apparent from section 1(3) that it can concern domestic violence[29] as well as, for example, gang activity.[30]

7.32   The second defence is where a person who occupies the dwelling is a person entitled[31] to apply to the court for an order giving that person a right to occupy the dwelling, to have the tenancy transferred to him or a person in respect of whom an application may be made to have the tenancy transferred to him or to another person for his benefit.[32] This usually applies to the tenant's current or former spouse, civil partner, co-habitant or a child.

Proceedings

7.33   The major (dishonesty) offence can be tried summarily in the magistrates' court or on indictment in the Crown Court, whereas the lesser offence is summary only and heard in the magistrates' court. Precedents 7.1, 7.2 and 7.3 shown below, set out the documents and their required contents that will be needed to begin proceedings in the magistrates' court.

Precedent 7.1

PSHF INFORMATION
IN THE STILLOPEN MAGISTRATES' COURT (1910)
INFORMATION

Prosecutor: Stillopen Borough Council, 7 Trafford Place, Stillopen, ST1 2BM

Defendant: Mr Stuart Pearson, of 33 Devereux Close, Stillopen, ST17 1RR

1.   Between 29 July 20XX to 18 July 20XX *(Date of Information)*, Mr Stuart Pearson, being a tenant of 33 Devereux Close, Stillopen, ST17 1RR ('the Premises'), a dwelling-house owned by the Ferguson Heights Housing Association and let to him under an assured shorthold tenancy, did, knowing that it was in breach of the tenancy and in breach of an

---

29   See *Yemshaw v Hounslow London Borough Council (Secretary of State for Communities and Local Government and another Intervening)* [2011] UKSC 3, [2011] 1 WLR 433, [2011] HLR 16.
30   This type of behaviour was referred to by Jack Dromey MP during passage of the Bill, *Hansard*, HC, Deb, 23 October 2012, Vol 551, col 891.
31   Under Family Law Act 1996, ss 33–40, s 53, Sch 7 of the 1996 Act and Children Act 1989, Sch 1, para 1.
32   PSHF, s 1(4).

express or implied term of the tenancy, sub-let or part with possession of the whole of the Premises and ceased to occupy the Premises as his only or principal home **contrary to** section 2(1) and (6) of the Prevention of Social Housing Fraud Act 2013

2. Between 29 July 20XX to 18 July 20XX *(Date of Information)*, Mr Stuart Pearson being a tenant of 33 Devereux Close, Stuillopen, ST17 1RR ('the Premises'), a dwelling-house owned by the Ferguson Heights Housing Association and let to him under an assured shorthold tenancy, did dishonestly and in breach of an express or implied term of the tenancy, sub-let or part with possession of the whole of the Premises and ceased to occupy the Premises as his only or principal home **contrary to** section 2(2) and (7) of the Prevention of Social Housing Fraud Act 2013

DATED THE EIGHTEENTH DAY OF OCTOBER 20XX

....

Ms Fiona Giggs
Borough Solicitor
Stillopen Borough Council,
7 Trafford Place,
Stillopen,
ST1 2BM

Precedent 7.2

PSHF SUMMONS
IN THE STILLOPEN MAGISTRATES' COURT (1910)

To: Mr Stuart Pearson

Of: 33 Devereux Close, Stillopen, ST17 1RR
INFORMATION was on 18 February 20XX laid before me, the undersigned Justice of the Peace, by Fiona Giggs, Borough Solicitor for Stillopen Borough Council for and on behalf of the Council of such Borough of 7 TRAFFORD PLACE, STILLOPEN, ST1 2BM

1. Between 29 July 20XX to 18 July 20XX *(Date of Information)*, Mr Stuart Pearson being a tenant of 33 Devereux Close, Stillopen, ST17 1RR ('the Premises'), a dwelling-house owned by the Ferguson Heights Housing Association and let to him under an assured shorthold tenancy, did, knowing that it was in breach of the tenancy, and in breach of an express or implied term of the tenancy, sub-let or part with possession of the whole of the Premises and ceased to occupy the Premises as his only or principal home **contrary to** section 2(1) and (6) of the Prevention of Social Housing Fraud Act 2013

2. Between 29 July 2016 to 18 July 2017 *(Date of Information)*, Mr Stuart Pearson being a tenant of 33 Devereux Close, Stuillopen, ST17 1RR

('the Premises'), a dwelling-house owned by the Ferguson Heights Housing Association and let to him under an assured shorthold tenancy, did dishonestly and in breach of an express or implied term of the tenancy, sub-let or part with possession of the whole of the Premises and ceased to occupy the Premises as his only or principal home **contrary to** section 2(2) and (7) of the Prevention of Social Housing Fraud Act 2013

YOU ARE THEREFORE HEREBY SUMMONSED to appear on Friday, 3 November 20XX at the hour of 10am before the Stillopen Magistrates' Court sitting at The Civic Centre, Carrington Street, Stillopen, ST1 7DB to answer to the said Information.

DATED THE EIGHTEENTH DAY OF OCTOBER 20XX

Delegated Legal Adviser for the Area first above mentioned

Precedent 7.3

PSHF CERTIFICATE

CERTIFICATE

Prevention of Social Housing Fraud Act 2013

Stillopen Borough Council v Stuart Pearson

Evidence that was sufficient to warrant these proceedings in Stillopen Magistrates' Court came to the prosecutor's knowledge on 15 June 20XX

Fiona Giggs

Borough Solicitor

Stillopen Borough Council

18.10.20XX

7.34 It should be noted:

(a) A local authority can prosecute section 1, section 2 (and associated) offences even if the premises are not theirs (eg it is a housing association let) and if the property is not in their area.[33]

(b) For a summary offence, such as the lesser offence under sections 1(1) and 2(1) of the PSHF, a magistrates' court may ordinarily not try a person unless the information was 'laid' (served on) the court within six months of the time that the offence was committed.[34]

However, section 3(1) of PSHF provides that this six-month period does not start to run until 'the date on which evidence sufficient in the opinion of the prosecutor to warrant the proceedings came to the prosecutor's knowledge'.

---

33 Ibid, s 3(5)(6).
34 Magistrates' Courts Act 1980, s 127; Criminal Procedure Rules 2015, para 7.2(5).

This is subject to a long-stop of three years from the commission of the offence after which no prosecution of the lesser offence is possible.[35]

Example: A tenant has been sub-letting his one-bedroom flat since November 2013 to various sub-tenants under six-month lets. His landlord housing association only finds out about this in January 2017. He can be prosecuted for *all* this activity under section 2(1) even though the offences started more than six months ago and the latest arrangement has been running for nine months. The contravention is continuous as the time runs from the last day.

(c) Precedent 7.1 (see below) provides an example of such an Information. The Criminal Procedure Rules 2015 provide:

'7.3(1) An allegation of an offence in an information or charge must contain—

(a) a statement of the offence that—

(i) describes the offence in ordinary language, and

(ii) identifies any legislation that creates it; and

(b) such particulars of the conduct constituting the commission of the offence as to make clear what the prosecutor alleges against the defendant.

(2) More than one incident of the commission of the offence may be included in the allegation if those incidents taken together amount to a course of conduct having regard to the time, place or purpose of commission.'

(d) Precedent 7.3 (set out above) is an example certificate confirming when the prosecutor had knowledge, in their view, of sufficient evidence to warrant the prosecution of the lesser offence. This is provided for under section 3(3) of PSHFA and is conclusive proof of its contents.

(e) The more serious dishonesty offences at sections 1(2) and 2(2) are either-way offences – so can be tried in either the magistrates' court or the Crown Court. As such, they avoid the six-month limitation to prosecute provided for under section 127 of the Magistrates' Courts Act 1980.[36] Note that 'either way' offences must still begin with information 'laid' in a magistrates' court, from which they may then be committed to the Crown Court for trial on indictment.

Trial

7.35 For those used to civil proceedings, a PSHF trial in the criminal courts has some significant differences, not least in the areas of disclosure, the defendant's

---

35 PSHF, s 3(2).
36 *Kemp v Leibherr (Great Britain) Ltd* [1987] 1 WLR 607 at 615B *per* Glidewell LJ.

case, hearsay evidence and, of course, the standard of proof. It is important to have proper regard to the Criminal Procedure Rules 2015.

7.36 The standard of proof is straightforward. The prosecution must prove its case beyond reasonable doubt.

7.37 Yet while the prosecutor will inevitably have served its evidence as early as possible (and in any event before the first hearing),[37] including initial witness statements,[38] that is not necessarily the case with the defendant.

7.38 Indeed, for a trial in the magistrates' court, unlike in the Crown Court, a defendant does not even need to give a defence statement setting out their position, although they may do so.[39] What they must do, however, is give a defendant witness notice indicating if they will be calling other witnesses and, if so, who those witnesses will be.[40]

7.39 Much of the evidence in a sub-letting case could rely on hearsay evidence, which is dealt with at Part 20 of the Criminal Procedure Rules 2015 and Part 11 Chapter 2 of the Criminal Justice Act 2003.

7.40 Hearsay evidence may include for example:

(a) bank account details and statements obtained from the bank of either the defendant's or a third-party;

(b) utility accounts; and

(c) reports of visits to the subject premises by the social landlord or their contractors.

7.41 Hearsay evidence is not generally admissible in criminal proceedings, unless it is a statement[41] the admissibility of which is agreed by the parties[42] or it can fit through one of the gateways provided by the 2003 Act. These include:

(a) evidence admissible where the court is satisfied it is in the interests of justice to so admit (s 114(1)(d));

(b) unavailability of witness (health, out of UK due to fear of giving evidence, cannot be found or dead) (s 116);

---

37 Criminal Procedure Rules 2015, r 8.2.
38 Ibid, at Part 16.
39 Criminal Procedure and Investigations Act 1996, s 6; Criminal Procedure Rules 2015, r 15.4 – one advantage to a defendant of serving a defence statement may be that this then allows them, under r 15.5, to seek further prosecution disclosure.
40 Criminal Procedure and Investigations Act 1996, s 6C.
41 Under the Criminal Justice Act 2003, s 115 – (a) a 'statement' means any representation of fact or opinion, by any means, and includes a representation in pictorial form; and (b) a 'matter stated' is something stated by someone with the apparent purpose of— (i) causing another person to believe it, or (ii) causing another person, or a machine, to act or operate on the basis that the matter is as stated.
42 Ibid, at s 114(1)(c).

(c) evidence created in the course of a trade, business or profession where the maker of the statement had no personal knowledge of the matters dealt with (such as a statement from a bank worker exhibiting the defendant's bank statements)(s 117(1)(b)); and

(d) a rule of law preserved by section 118 of the Criminal Justice Act 2003 makes it admissible.

7.42   Reliance on hearsay must generally[43] be indicated by the service and lodging of a hearsay notice served not more than 28 days after a not guilty plea has been entered by the defendant (14 days in the Crown Court).[44]

7.43   Once the prosecution's evidence has been heard then – either of its own motion or upon application – the court may, after hearing any representations from the prosecution, acquit (or in the Crown Court direct the jury to acquit) on the ground that the prosecution evidence is insufficient for any reasonable court to properly convict.[45]

Sentence

7.44   A person convicted on summary conviction in the magistrates' court for the lesser offence can be liable for a fine not exceeding level 5 (unlimited for offences committed on or after 12 March 2015 or £5,000 if earlier).[46]

7.45   In respect of the major (dishonesty) offence, on summary conviction in the magistrates' court, the defendant will be liable to a maximum of six months' imprisonment and/or a fine not exceeding the statutory maximum (or both; if convicted on indictment in the Crown Court, they can be sentenced to a maximum of two years' imprisonment and/or a fine).[47]

7.46   Unlawful profit orders (UPOs), which are dealt with in Chapter 5 in respect of civil remedies, are available if the defendant is convicted under sections 1 or 2 of PSHF (or an associated offence[48]).[49] Section 4(3) of PSHF defines the UPO in this way:

43   Criminal Procedure Rules 2015, r 20.2(1) – Where admission is sought under the Criminal Justice Act 2003, ss 114(1)(d), 116, 117(1)(c) and 121 (multiple hearsay).
44   Ibid, at r 20.2(3).
45   Ibid, at rr 24.3(3)(d) (magistrates' court) or 25.9(2)(e) (Crown Court).
46   Section 1(5) (secure tenancies); s 2(6) (assured tenancies).
47   Section 1(6) (secure tenancies); s 2(7) (assured tenancies).
48   Defined at PSHF, s 11(10) as (a) an offence of aiding, abetting, counselling or procuring the commission of that offence, (b) an offence of attempting or conspiring to commit that offence, or (c) an offence under Part 2 of the Serious Crime Act 2007 (encouraging or assisting crime) in relation to that offence.
49   See PSHF, s 4.

'(3) An "unlawful profit order" is an order requiring the offender to pay the landlord[50] an amount representing the profit made by the offender as a result of the conduct constituting the offence.'

7.47 The court can either make such an order of its own motion, if it considers it appropriate to do so or accede to an application by the prosecution for a UPO.[51] If the court declines to make such an order they must give reasons during the sentencing.[52]

7.48 Section 4 further provides:

(a) There is a maximum UPO that can be ordered which mirrors that for civil UPOs (see Chapter 5). In essence, it is the 'profit element' of the activity after deducting what the tenant has paid in rent during the sub-letting period.

(b) If a civil UPO has already been made then the criminal UPO may only consist of the 'profit element' over and above the amount ordered in the civil court in addition to any unpaid portion of that order. Enforcement of that latter element by the landlord requires the leave of the court.[53]

(c) UPOs take priority over fines. If the defendant cannot afford both, then only a UPO will be made.[54]

(d) Interest is payable at the usual civil judgment rate if the UPO is not paid by the time ordered.[55]

FRAUD ACT 2006

'The Act provides for a general offence of fraud with three ways of committing it, which are by false representation, by failing to disclose information and by abuse of position.'

Paragraph 7 of the Explanatory Notes to the Fraud Act 2006

7.49 The Housing Act 1996 and PSHF deal with many of the primary areas of social housing fraud. However, a lacuna would certainly arise if they were the

---

50 Which s 4(13) explains 'means the landlord under the tenancy in respect of which the offence was committed'. Section 11(6) also states: 'References in this Act to the landlord under a secure or an assured tenancy include – (a) in a case where the tenancy has ended, a person who was the landlord under the tenancy, and (b) in a case where the tenancy has ceased to be a secure or an assured tenancy, the person who was the landlord under the tenancy when it was a secure or an assured tenancy.'
51 A section 4 UPO is enforced in the same way as for costs and compensation – see the Administration of Justice Act 1970, s 41 and Sch 9, para 12B and the Magistrates' Courts Act 1980, ss 75–85 (eg attachment of earnings, benefits reduction, means inquiry, distress warrant, imprisonment and the taking of civil proceedings).
52 PSHF, s 4(4).
53 Ibid, at s 4(7).
54 Ibid, at s 4(8)–(9).
55 Ibid, at s 4(10)–(11) – see Judgments Act 1838, s 17.

only pieces of legislation providing for criminal offences in this area, not least with respect to:

(a) right to buy fraud (and that relating to right to acquire and shared ownership), and

(b) fraud involving employees of the landlord.

7.50 The Fraud Act 2006, which received Royal Assent on 8 November 2006, outlines a general offence of fraud at section 1:

(a) by false representation (s 2);

(b) by failing to disclose information (s 3); and

(c) by abuse of position (s 4).

7.51 All these fraud offences require dishonesty to be shown. This is determined by answering the question – would the defendant's behaviour be regarded as dishonest by the ordinary standards of reasonable and honest people? Lord Hughes rejected, therefore, the long-standing two-stage *Ghosh* test:[56]

(1) Would the defendant's behaviour be regarded as dishonest by the ordinary standards of reasonable and honest people?

(2) Was the defendant aware that his conduct was dishonest and would be regarded as dishonest by reasonable and honest people?

in the *Ivy v Genting Casinos* case referred to at 7.25 above and rather preferred Lord Hoffman's analysis in *Barlow Clowes International v Eurotrust International Ltd*:[57]

> '10 The judge stated the law in terms largely derived from the advice of the Board given by Lord Nicholls of Birkenhead in *Royal Brunei Airlines Sdn Bhd v Tan* [1995] 2 AC 378. In summary, she said that liability for dishonest assistance requires a dishonest state of mind on the part of the person who assists in a breach of trust. Such a state of mind may consist in knowledge that the transaction is one in which he cannot honestly participate (for example, a misappropriation of other people's money) or it may consist in suspicion combined with a conscious decision not to make inquiries which might result in knowledge: *Manifest Shipping Co Ltd v Uni-Polaris Insurance Co Ltd* [2003] 1 AC 469. Although a dishonest state of mind is a subjective mental state, the standard by which the law determines whether it is dishonest is objective. If by ordinary standards a defendant's mental state would be characterised as dishonest, it is irrelevant that the defendant judges by different standards. The Court of Appeal held this to be a correct state of the law and their Lordships agree.'

---

56 *R v Ghosh* [1982] QB 1053.
57 [2005] UKPC 37, [2006] 1 WLR 1476 at 1479–1480.

False representation (section 2)

'(1) A person is in breach of this section if he–

    (a) dishonestly makes a false representation, and

    (b) intends, by making the representation–

        (i) to make a gain for himself or another, or

        (ii) to cause loss to another or to expose another to a risk of loss.'

Fraud Act 2006, s 2

7.52   The section 2 offence of fraud by false representation requires four elements:

(a) a false (ie untrue or misleading) representation must be made;[58]

(b) it must be made 'dishonestly';[59]

(c) the maker of the statement must know that it is false (or might be so);[60]

(d) it was made for the purpose of gain, or to cause loss to another (or expose them to it).[61]

7.53   An obvious example of a section 2 offence in a right-to-buy scenario is where the supposed tenant maintains in their application that they live at the relevant premises as their only or principal home, when that is not the case.

7.54   The representation can be either of fact or law[62] and can be express or implied.[63] Attempts to argue that the (obvious) fraud had nothing to do with the beneficiary may also be difficult for any defendant to pursue successfully.

7.55   In *Mohammed Idrees v Director of Public Prosecutions*,[64] the defendant had sought to argue that he had nothing to do with the fact that someone impersonating him had taken the theory driving test, which he had failed 15 times previously. Lord Justice Moses said:

'5 The issue on this appeal, as the magistrates posed in the question they asked, was whether there was sufficient evidence at the close of the prosecution case. In my judgment there plainly was. Indeed, any contrary view would have been perverse. The magistrates rightly focused upon the fact that the only person who could possibly have benefited from this attempt by the unknown person to impersonate Mr Idrees was Mr Idrees himself. No other sensible explanation has been advanced. Courageously

---

58 Fraud Act 2006, ss 2(1)(a), 2(2)(a).
59 Ibid, at s 2(1)(a).
60 Ibid, at s 2(2)(b).
61 Ibid, at s 1(b)(ii).
62 Ibid, at s 2(3).
63 Ibid, at s 2(4).
64 [2011] EWHC 624 (Admin).

Mr Smith today, landed with this brief, sought to submit that somebody might have taken pity on Mr Idrees' plight in failing to pass his test on 15 previous occasions and had arranged for the unknown man to impersonate him without Mr Idrees' knowledge. Anything is possible. The magistrates are required to confine their deliberations on the facts to that which is not fanciful. Such a possibility advanced by Mr Smith was wholly fanciful. If one adds to that benefit the circumstance that the test had been booked for Mr Idrees in English on this occasion, whereas previously he [had] taken it 15 times in Urdu, the evidence becomes overwhelming.'

7.56　To give one example of the particulars of an offence in a right-to-buy case:[65]

'[The appellants] on or about 31 January 2011, dishonestly and intending thereby to make a gain for themselves or another, made a representation to the London Borough of Lewisham in a "Notice Claiming the Right to Buy," in relation to the council property at 43 Frankham House, Crossfield Estate, London, SE8, which was and which they knew was or might be untrue or misleading, namely that the said property was their only or principal home, which was false because they were, in fact, the joint owners of a residential property at 102 Brookehowse Road, Bellingham, London, SE6 which was their principal home, in breach of section 2 of the Fraud Act 2006.'

Failure to disclose information (section 3)

'A person is in breach of this section if he–

(a) dishonestly fails to disclose to another person information which he is under a legal duty to disclose, and

(b) intends, by failing to disclose the information–

　(i) to make a gain for himself or another, or

　(ii) to cause loss to another or to expose another to a risk of loss.'

Fraud Act 2006, s 3

7.57　The section 3 offence of fraud by failing to disclose information can extend to obligations imposed by contract, such (arguably) as a housing association accommodation application.

7.58　This offence is generally straightforward. It is the concept of 'legal duty to disclose', which requires some explanation. The *Law Commission Report on Fraud*[66] explained it in this way:

65　*R v (1) Krissene Offormezie (2) Ngozika Eze* [2015] EWCA Crim 324 – the defendants both successfully appealing against conviction.
66　Number 276 of 2002 – referred to by Lord Justice Pitchford in *R v Forrest (Nathan)* [2014] EWCA Crim 308 at [10].

'7.28 ... Such a duty may derive from statute (such as the provisions governing company prospectuses) from the fact that the transaction in question is one of the utmost good faith (such as a contract of insurance), from the express or implied terms of a contract, from the custom of a particular trade or market, or from the existence of a fiduciary relationship between the parties (such as that of agent and principal).

7.29 For this purpose there is a legal duty to disclose information not only if the defendant's failure to disclose it gives the victim a cause of action for damages, but also if the law gives the victim a right to set aside any change in his or her legal position to which he or she may consent as a result of the non-disclosure. For example, a person in a fiduciary position has a duty to disclose material information when entering into a contract with his or her beneficiary, in the sense that a failure to make such disclosure will entitle the beneficiary to rescind the contract and to reclaim any property transferred under it.'

7.59 Establishing this legal duty in the housing context can be difficult. Whilst an obligation to provide information may be apparent in either a contract of employment or a tenancy agreement, it may be more tenuous to argue that legal obligations arise in an application for housing, in which case a different offence (such as fraud by false representation) may prove to be a more natural fit.

Abuse of position (section 4)

(1) A person is in breach of this section if he–
   (a) occupies a position in which he is expected to safeguard, or not to act against, the financial interests of another person,
   (b) dishonestly abuses that position, and
   (c) intends, by means of the abuse of that position–
       (i) to make a gain for himself or another, or
       (ii) to cause loss to another or to expose another to a risk of loss.

(2) A person may be regarded as having abused his position even though his conduct consisted of an omission rather than an act.

Fraud Act 2006, s 4

7.60 Section 4 makes it an offence to commit a fraud by dishonestly abusing one's position. It follows that this is the section usually applied where a staff member has, for example, been involved in right-to-buy, right-to-acquire, shared ownership or allocation fraud.

7.61 It applies in situations where the defendant has been put in a privileged position and, by virtue of this position, is expected positively to safeguard another's financial interests or at least not to act against those interests.

7.62 In the same report, referred to above at 7.58, the Law Commission explained the meaning of 'position':

'7.38 The necessary relationship will be present between trustee and beneficiary, director and company, professional person and client, agent and principal, employee and employer, or between partners. It may arise otherwise, for example within a family, or in the context of voluntary work, or in any context where the parties are not at arm's length. In nearly all cases where it arises, it will be recognised by the civil law as importing fiduciary duties, and any relationship that is so recognised will suffice. We see no reason, however, why the existence of such duties should be essential. This does not of course mean that it would be entirely a matter for the fact-finders whether the necessary relationship exists. The question whether the particular facts alleged can properly be described as giving rise to that relationship will be an issue capable of being ruled upon by the judge and, if the case goes to the jury, of being the subject of directions.'

7.63 In the context of allocation fraud, this may include cases where an employee of a LHA fraudulently allocates its properties outside the lawful allocation scheme, with the caveat provided by Lord Neuberger in *Birmingham City Council v Qasim*:[67]

'43 Equally, it should be emphasised, that this is a case where the selection of the applicants in breach of the terms of the allocation scheme was made by a person to whom, as Mr Arden accepts, the Council had properly delegated the tasks of granting residential tenancies on its behalf. Different considerations would presumably apply where a tenancy had been purportedly granted by a person with no such authority, even if he had been employed by the Council.'

Sentence

7.64 To give one example of sentence, in *R v Hamza & Ahmed*,[68] the defendants had pleaded guilty to eight counts of fraud pursuant to section 1 of the Fraud Act 2006. They made two right-to-buy applications, in 2011 and 2012, to Sandwell Metropolitan Borough Council concerning 245 Thimblemill Road in Smethwick. The first defendant was the tenant of this property. To be entitled to proceed with such an application:

(a) it had to be the first defendant's sole or principal residence (it was not and representations to the contrary were false); and

(b) the second defendant had to be related to her and to have lived at the property for the previous 12 months (both these representations were untrue).

---

67 Ibid. See also Lord Justice Sedley: '48 What then is the effect of a departure from the scheme? Clearly if an allocation bears what Lord Radcliffe in *Smith v East Elloe Rural DC* [1956] A.C. 736 called the brand of invalidity on its forehead (if, for example, it was issued by the doorkeeper) it is of no legal effect.'
68 [2014] EWCA Crim 2378.

7.65   Each defendant was sentenced to concurrent terms of 20 months' imprisonment on each of the counts applicable to them, making a total sentence in each case of 20 months' imprisonment.

COMPENSATION ORDERS
Section 6 of the Proceeds of Crime Act 2002 (POCA 2002) states:

'(1) The Crown Court must proceed under this section if the following two conditions are satisfied.

(2) The first condition is that a defendant falls within any of the following paragraphs—

(a) he is convicted of an offence or offences in proceedings before the Crown Court;

(b) he is committed to the Crown Court for sentence in respect of an offence or offences under sections 3, 3A, 3B, 3C , 4, 4A or 6 of the Sentencing Act;

(c) he is committed to the Crown Court in respect of an offence or offences under section 70 below (committal with a view to a confiscation order being considered).

(3) The second condition is that—

(a) the prosecutor asks the court to proceed under this section, or

(b) the court believes it is appropriate for it to do so.'

7.66   Chapter 5 deals with the unlawful profit orders that may be obtained by a landlord under the PSHF, along with other potential civil remedies allowing for some financial 'compensation' to be paid to the landlord as a result of social housing fraud.

7.67   Paragraphs 7.46 to 7.48 above also deal with UPOs in criminal proceedings in cases brought under the PSHF.

7.68   As well as providing for civil remedies for unlawful conduct under Part 5, POCA 2002 also allows the court to make a confiscation order in the following circumstances:[69]

(1) The matter is before the Crown Court (either after trial and conviction, or committal to the Crown Court for sentence).

(2) The prosecutor has asked for a confiscation order or the Court believes it appropriate to make such an order.

69 POCA 2002, s 6 – the legitimate aim of the penalty is to remove the financial proceeds of the crime from the criminal: *R v Waya (Terry)* [2012] UKSC 51, [2012] 3 WLR 1188.

(3) The Court decides, on the balance of probabilities,[70] that the defendant has a criminal lifestyle and has benefited from his criminal conduct or has simply so benefited from the particular criminal conduct before them.[71]

7.69 If those conditions are satisfied then the Court must decide, again on the balance of probabilities, the just recoverable amount – based on the benefit from the conduct concerned[72] – and make an order (unless civil recovery is being or is likely to be sought, when this duty becomes a power).

7.70 In practice, the Court will typically only invoke its confiscation powers if the prosecution invites it to do so. The prosecution must do this after conviction but before sentence and need not give any indication of its intention to take this step. POCA 2002 proceedings can only be dealt with in the Crown Court; the magistrates' court will commit summary proceedings to the Crown Court for this purpose upon the invitation of the prosecution under section 70. This is in contrast to UPOs, which can be made by the magistrates' court.[73]

7.71 POCA 2002 can be a time-consuming and costly process, involving disclosure by the defence and investigation by the prosecution, with exchange of reports and information with a view to agreeing two main figures: the 'benefit figure' (how much profit has been derived from criminality) and the 'available amount' (what assets are available for confiscation). A confiscation order is then made in the lower of these two amounts.

7.72 Under the Home Office Asset Recovery Incentivisation Scheme (ARIS), authorities that investigate and prosecute offences are entitled to recover approximately one-third of the total amount recovered by the court under a confiscation order. The UPO regime, however, provides for all monies recovered to be paid directly to the landlord.

7.73 The principal advantage of POCA 2002 proceedings over the UPO procedure is that there should be no deductions for expenditure incurred by offending. However, it is unlikely to be appropriate to pursue confiscation proceedings where a UPO would be available.

---

70 Ibid, at s 6(7).
71 Rental income from a criminally obtained house or flat constituted a 'benefit': see *R v Oyebola (Folarin)* [2013] EWCA Crim 1052, [2014] 1 Cr App R (S) 58.
72 Ibid, at s 7(1).
73 '130(1) A court by or before which a person is convicted of an offence, instead of or in addition to dealing with him in any other way, may, on application or otherwise, make an order (in this Act referred to as a "compensation order") requiring him—
  (a) to pay compensation for any personal injury, loss or damage resulting from that offence or any other offence which is taken into consideration by the court in determining sentence; or
  (b) to make payments for funeral expenses or bereavement in respect of a death resulting from any such offence, other than a death due to an accident arising out of the presence of a motor vehicle on a road;
but this is subject to the following provisions of this section and to s 131 below.'

Civil remedies

7.74   As noted at 7.68, POCA 2002 allows for the recovery in civil proceedings before the High Court of property obtained either through unlawful conduct[74] or the forfeiting of cash which is (or represents) property obtained through unlawful conduct (or which is intended to be so used) through the magistrates' court.[75]

7.75   To give one example of POCA 2002's use, in *Serious Organised Crime Agency v Olden*,[76] Mr Olden was said to have engaged in mortgage fraud and other deception. In February 2006, he was convicted of a number of offences, including three counts of obtaining property by deception. His conviction was set aside by the Court of Appeal (Criminal Division) on 9 March 2007 and thereafter the Assets Recovery Agency successfully applied to the High Court for a property freezing order and for an order for possession of a number of assets.

7.76   Mr Olden won his appeal in part, in relation to the possession order of the properties (although not in relation to recoveries of identified money sources). It was found that POCA 2002 did not provide power for a possession order but rather a recovery order vesting any property in the trustee (who could then seek a possession order in the usual way under CPR Part 55).

7.77   This book does not go into any further detail as to the POCA 2002 civil remedies because they are exercisable not by the social landlord but by the National Crime Agency, Director of Public Prosecutions or the Director of the Serious Fraud Office.[77]

CONCLUSION

7.78   Social landlords will be familiar by now with the criminal sanction possibilities of PSHF and no doubt will be aware, too, of its 'predecessor', the Fraud Act 2006, which of course remains very much in force.

7.79   They may also have had some success in recovery of monies pursuant to the Powers of Criminal Courts (Sentencing) Act 2000, s 130(1) to cover any losses resulting from the offence.

7.80   Save for 'sending out a message' and, upon any conviction, providing for incontrovertible evidence of wrongdoing, it may be argued that such matters are of limited interest to social landlords.

---

74   Ibid, at s 240(1)(a).
75   Ibid, at s 240(1)(b).
76   [2010] EWCA Civ 143, [2010] CP Rep 29.
77   The enforcement authority being so defined for England and Wales at POCA 2002, s 316(1).

7.81 They will naturally be more interested in recovering properties of theirs misused in a housing fraud sense, and the costs of so doing, as well as any orders available to recoup the perpetrators' illicit gains.

7.82 Yet the criminal options available are important not only to put the seriousness of social housing fraud in proper context, but also because civil remedies alone may not always encourage this context to be properly appreciated.

Excerpts from primary legislation

1. Protection from Eviction Act 1977
2. Housing Act 1985
3. Housing Act 1988
4. Data Protection Act 1998
5. Fraud Act 2006
6. Prevention of Social Housing Fraud Act 2013

I.   PROTECTION FROM EVICTION ACT 1977

2.—Restriction on re-entry without due process of law.

Where any premises are let as a dwelling on a lease which is subject to a right of re-entry or forfeiture it shall not be lawful to enforce that right otherwise than by proceedings in the court while any person is lawfully residing in the premises or part of them.

5.—Validity of notices to quit.

(1) Subject to subsection (1B) below no notice by a landlord or a tenant to quit any premises let (whether before or after the commencement of this Act) as a dwelling shall be valid unless—

   (a) it is in writing and contains such information as may be prescribed, and

   (b) it is given not less than 4 weeks before the date on which it is to take effect.

(1A) Subject to subsection (1B) below, no notice by a licensor or a licensee to determine a periodic licence to occupy premises as a dwelling (whether the licence was granted before or after the passing of this Act) shall be valid unless—

   (a) it is in writing and contains such information as may be prescribed, and

   (b) it is given not less than 4 weeks before the date on which it is to take effect.

(1B) Nothing in subsection (1) or subsection (1A) above applies to—

   (a) premises let on an excluded tenancy which is entered into on or after the date on which the Housing Act 1988 came into force unless it is entered into pursuant to a contract made before that date; or

   (b) premises occupied under an excluded licence.

(2) In this section *prescribed* means prescribed by regulations made by the Secretary of State by statutory instrument, and a statutory instrument containing any such regulations shall be subject to annulment in pursuance of a resolution of either House of Parliament.

(3) Regulations under this section may make different provision in relation to different descriptions of lettings and different circumstances.

2.   HOUSING ACT 1985

79.—Secure tenancies.

(1) A tenancy under which a dwelling-house is let as a separate dwelling is a secure tenancy at any time when the conditions described in sections 80 and 81 as the landlord condition and the tenant condition are satisfied.

(2) Subsection (1) has effect subject to—

    (a) the exceptions in Schedule 1 (tenancies which are not secure tenancies),

    (b) sections 89(3) and (4) and 90(3) and (4) (tenancies ceasing to be secure after death of tenant), and

    (c) sections 91(2) and 93(2) (tenancies ceasing to be secure in consequence of assignment or subletting).

(3) The provisions of this Part apply in relation to a licence to occupy a dwelling-house (whether or not granted for a consideration) as they apply in relation to a tenancy.

(4) Subsection (3) does not apply to a licence granted as a temporary expedient to a person who entered the dwelling-house or any other land as a trespasser (whether or not, before the grant of that licence, another licence to occupy that or another dwelling-house had been granted to him).

81.—The tenant condition.

The tenant condition is that the tenant is an individual and occupies the dwelling-house as his only or principal home; or, where the tenancy is a joint tenancy, that each of the joint tenants is an individual and at least one of them occupies the dwelling-house as his only or principal home.

82.—Security of tenure.

(1) A secure tenancy which is either—

    (a) a weekly or other periodic tenancy, or

    (b) a tenancy for a term certain but subject to termination by the landlord,

cannot be brought to an end by the landlord except as mentioned in subsection (1A).

(1A) The tenancy may be brought to an end by the landlord–

(a) obtaining–

   (i) an order of the court for the possession of the dwelling-house, and

   (ii) the execution of the order,

(b) obtaining an order under subsection (3), or

(c) obtaining a demotion order under section 82A.

(2) In the case mentioned in subsection (1A)(a), the tenancy ends when the order is executed.

(3) Where a secure tenancy is a tenancy for a term certain but with a provision for re-entry or forfeiture, the court shall not order possession of the dwelling-house in pursuance of that provision, but in a case where the court would have made such an order it shall instead make an order terminating the tenancy on a date specified in the order and section 86 (periodic tenancy arising on termination of fixed term) shall apply.

(4) Section 146 of the Law of Property Act 1925 (restriction on and relief against forfeiture), except subsection (4) (vesting in under-lessee), and any other enactment or rule of law relating to forfeiture, shall apply in relation to proceedings for an order under subsection (3) of this section as if they were proceedings to enforce a right of re-entry or forfeiture.

83.—Proceedings for possession or termination: general notice requirements.

(A1) This section applies in relation to proceedings for an order mentioned in section 82(1A) other than—

(a) proceedings for possession of a dwelling-house under section 84A (absolute ground for possession for anti-social behaviour), including proceedings where possession is also sought on one or more of the grounds set out in Schedule 2, or

(b) proceedings for possession of a dwelling-house under section 107D (recovery of possession on expiry of flexible tenancy).

(1) The court shall not entertain proceedings to which this section applies unless—

(a) the landlord has served a notice on the tenant complying with the provisions of this section, or

(b) the court considers it just and equitable to dispense with the requirement of such a notice.

(2) A notice under this section shall—

(a) be in a form prescribed by regulations made by the Secretary of State,

(b) specify the ground on which the court will be asked to make [the order] [5] , and

(c) give particulars of that ground.

139

(3) Where the tenancy is a periodic tenancy and the ground or one of the grounds specified in the notice is Ground 2 in Schedule 2 (nuisance or other anti-social behaviour), the notice—

    (a) shall also—

        (i) state that proceedings for the possession of the dwelling-house may be begun immediately, and

        (ii) specify the date sought by the landlord as the date on which the tenant is to give up possession of the dwelling-house, and

    (b) ceases to be in force twelve months after the date so specified.

(4) Where the tenancy is a periodic tenancy and Ground 2 in Schedule 2 is not specified in the notice, the notice—

    (a) shall also specify the date after which proceedings for the possession of the dwelling-house may be begun, and

    (b) ceases to be in force twelve months after the date so specified.

(4A) If the proceedings are for a demotion order under section 82A the notice–

    (a) must specify the date after which the proceedings may be begun;

    (b) ceases to be in force twelve months after the date so specified.

(5) The date specified in accordance with subsection (3), (4) or (4A) must not be earlier than the date on which the tenancy could, apart from this Part, be brought to an end by notice to quit given by the landlord on the same date as the notice under this section.

(6) Where a notice under this section is served with respect to a secure tenancy for a term certain, it has effect also with respect to any periodic tenancy arising on the termination of that tenancy by virtue of section 86; and subsections (3) to (5) of this section do not apply to the notice.

(7) Regulations under this section shall be made by statutory instrument and may make different provision with respect to different cases or descriptions of case, including different provision for different areas.

86.—Periodic tenancy arising on termination of fixed term.

(1) Where a secure tenancy ('the first tenancy') is a tenancy for a term certain and comes to an end—

    (a) by effluxion of time, or

    (b) by an order of the court under section 82(3) (termination in pursuance of provision for re-entry or forfeiture),

a periodic tenancy of the same dwelling-house arises by virtue of this section, unless the tenant is granted another secure tenancy of the same dwelling-house (whether a tenancy for a term certain or a periodic tenancy) to begin on the coming to an end of the first tenancy.

(2) Where a periodic tenancy arises by virtue of this section—

(a) the periods of the tenancy are the same as those for which rent was last payable under the first tenancy, and

(b) the parties and the terms of the tenancy are the same as those of the first tenancy at the end of it;

except that the terms are confined to those which are compatible with a periodic tenancy and do not include any provision for re-entry or forfeiture.

91—Assignment in general prohibited.

(1) A secure tenancy which is—

(a) a periodic tenancy, or

(b) a tenancy for a term certain granted on or after 5 November 1982,

is not capable of being assigned except in the cases mentioned in subsection (3).

(2) If a secure tenancy for a term certain granted before 5 November 1982 is assigned, then, except in the cases mentioned in subsection (3), it ceases to be a secure tenancy and cannot subsequently become a secure tenancy.

(3) The exceptions are—

(a) an assignment in accordance with section 92 (assignment by way of exchange);

(b) an assignment in pursuance of an order made under—

(i) section 24 of the Matrimonial Causes Act 1973 (property adjustment orders in connection with matrimonial proceedings),

(ii) section 17(1) of the Matrimonial and Family Proceedings Act 1984 (property adjustment orders after overseas divorce, &c.),

(iii) paragraph 1 of Schedule 1 to the Children Act 1989 (orders for financial relief against parents), or

(iv) Part 2 of Schedule 5, or paragraph 9(2) or (3) of Schedule 7, to the Civil Partnership Act 2004 (property adjustment orders in connection with civil partnership proceedings or after overseas dissolution of civil partnership, etc.);

(c) an assignment to a person who would be qualified to succeed the tenant if the tenant died immediately before the assignment.

92—Assignments by way of exchange.

(1) It is a term of every secure tenancy that the tenant may, with the written consent of the landlord, assign the tenancy to another secure tenant who satisfies the condition in subsection (2) [or to an assured tenant who satisfies the conditions in subsection (2A).

(2) The condition is that the other secure tenant has the written consent of his landlord to an assignment of his tenancy either to the first-mentioned tenant or to another secure tenant who satisfies the condition in this subsection.

(2A) The conditions to be satisfied with respect to an assured tenant are—

    (a) that the landlord under his assured tenancy is [the Regulator of Social Housing, a private registered provider of social housing, a registered social landlord or a housing trust which is a charity; and

    (b) that he intends to assign his assured tenancy to the secure tenant referred to in subsection (1) or to another secure tenant who satisfies the condition in subsection (2).

(3) The consent required by virtue of this section shall not be withheld except on one or more of the grounds set out in Schedule 3, and if withheld otherwise than on one of those grounds shall be treated as given.

(4) The landlord may not rely on any of the grounds set out in Schedule 3 unless he has, within 42 days of the tenant's application for the consent, served on the tenant a notice specifying the ground and giving particulars of it.

(5) Where rent lawfully due from the tenant has not been paid or an obligation of the tenancy has been broken or not performed, the consent required by virtue of this section may be given subject to a condition requiring the tenant to pay the outstanding rent, remedy the breach or perform the obligation.

(6) Except as provided by subsection (5), a consent required by virtue of this section cannot be given subject to a condition, and a condition imposed otherwise than as so provided shall be disregarded.

93—Lodgers and subletting.

(1) It is a term of every secure tenancy that the tenant—

    (a) may allow any persons to reside as lodgers in the dwelling-house, but

    (b) will not, without the written consent of the landlord, sublet or part with possession of part of the dwelling-house.

(2) If the tenant under a secure tenancy parts with the possession of the dwelling-house or sublets the whole of it (or sublets first part of it and then the remainder), the tenancy ceases to be a secure tenancy and cannot subsequently become a secure tenancy.

94—Consent to subletting.

(1) This section applies to the consent required by virtue of section 93(1)(b) (landlord's consent to subletting of part of dwelling-house).

(2) Consent shall not be unreasonably withheld (and if unreasonably withheld shall be treated as given), and if a question arises whether the withholding of consent was unreasonable it is for the landlord to show that it was not.

(3) In determining that question the following matters, if shown by the landlord, are among those to be taken into account—

    (a) that the consent would lead to overcrowding of the dwelling-house within the meaning of Part X (overcrowding);

    (b) that the landlord proposes to carry out works on the dwelling-house, or on the building of which it forms part, and that the proposed works will affect the accommodation likely to be used by the sub-tenant who would reside in the dwelling-house as a result of the consent.

(4) Consent may be validly given notwithstanding that it follows, instead of preceding, the action requiring it.

(5) Consent cannot be given subject to a condition (and if purporting to be given subject to a condition shall be treated as given unconditionally).

(6) Where the tenant has applied in writing for consent, then—

    (a) if the landlord refuses to give consent, it shall give the tenant a written statement of the reasons why consent was refused, and

    (b) if the landlord neither gives nor refuses to give consent within a reasonable time, consent shall be taken to have been withheld.

107D—Recovery of possession on expiry of flexible tenancy

(1) Subject as follows, on or after the coming to an end of a flexible tenancy a court must make an order for possession of the dwelling-house let on the tenancy if it is satisfied that the following conditions are met.

(2) Condition 1 is that the flexible tenancy has come to an end and no further secure tenancy (whether or not a flexible tenancy) is for the time being in existence, other than a secure tenancy that is a periodic tenancy (whether or not arising by virtue of section 86).

(3) Condition 2 is that the landlord has given the tenant not less than six months' notice in writing—

    (a) stating that the landlord does not propose to grant another tenancy on the expiry of the flexible tenancy,

    (b) setting out the landlord's reasons for not proposing to grant another tenancy, and

    (c) informing the tenant of the tenant's right to request a review of the landlord's proposal and of the time within which such a request must be made.

(4) Condition 3 is that the landlord has given the tenant not less than two months' notice in writing stating that the landlord requires possession of the dwelling-house.

(5) A notice under subsection (4) may be given before or on the day on which the tenancy comes to an end.

(6) The court may refuse to grant an order for possession under this section if—

    (a) the tenant has in accordance with section 107E requested a review of the landlord's proposal not to grant another tenancy on the expiry of the flexible tenancy, and

    (b) the court is satisfied that the landlord has failed to carry out the review in accordance with provision made by or under that section or that the decision on the review is otherwise wrong in law.

(7) If a court refuses to grant an order for possession by virtue of subsection (6) it may make such directions as to the holding of a review or further review under section 107E as it thinks fit.

(8) This section has effect notwithstanding that, on the coming to an end of the flexible tenancy, a periodic tenancy arises by virtue of section 86.

(9) Where a court makes an order for possession of a dwelling-house by virtue of this section, any periodic tenancy arising by virtue of section 86 on the coming to an end of the flexible tenancy comes to an end (without further notice and regardless of the period) in accordance with section 82(2).

(10) This section is without prejudice to any right of the landlord under a flexible tenancy to recover possession of the dwelling-house let on the tenancy in accordance with this Part.

3.   HOUSING ACT 1988

1—Assured tenancies.

(1) A tenancy under which a dwelling-house is let as a separate dwelling is for the purposes of this Act an assured tenancy if and so long as—

    (a) the tenant or, as the case may be, each of the joint tenants is an individual; and

    (b) the tenant or, as the case may be, at least one of the joint tenants occupies the dwelling-house as his only or principal home; and

    (c) the tenancy is not one which, by virtue of subsection (2) or subsection (6) below, cannot be an assured tenancy.

(1A) Subsection (1) has effect subject to section 15A (loss of assured tenancy status).

5—Security of tenure.

(1) An assured tenancy cannot be brought to an end by the landlord except by–

    (a) obtaining–

        (i) an order of the court for possession of the dwelling-house under section 7 or 21, and

(ii) the execution of the order,

(b) obtaining an order of the court under section 6A (demotion order),

(c) in the case of a fixed term tenancy which contains power for the landlord to determine the tenancy in certain circumstances, by the exercise of that power, or

(d) in the case of an assured tenancy—

    (i) which is a residential tenancy agreement within the meaning of Chapter 1 of Part 3 of the Immigration Act 2014, and

    (ii) in relation to which the condition in section 33D(2) of that Act is met, giving a notice in accordance with that section,

and, accordingly, the service by the landlord of a notice to quit is of no effect in relation to a periodic assured tenancy.

(1A) Where an order of the court for possession of the dwelling-house is obtained, the tenancy ends when the order is executed.

(2) If an assured tenancy which is a fixed term tenancy comes to an end otherwise than by virtue of—

(a) an order of the court of the kind mentioned in subsection (1)(a) or (b) or any other order of the court,

(b) a surrender or other action on the part of the tenant, or

(c) the giving of a notice under section 33D of the Immigration Act 2014,

then, subject to section 7 and Chapter II below, the tenant shall be entitled to remain in possession of the dwelling-house let under that tenancy and, subject to subsection (4) below, his right to possession shall depend upon a periodic tenancy arising by virtue of this section.

(3) The periodic tenancy referred to in subsection (2) above is one—

(a) taking effect in possession immediately on the coming to an end of the fixed term tenancy;

(b) deemed to have been granted by the person who was the landlord under the fixed term tenancy immediately before it came to an end to the person who was then the tenant under that tenancy;

(c) under which the premises which are let are the same dwelling-house as was let under the fixed term tenancy;

(d) under which the periods of the tenancy are the same as those for which rent was last payable under the fixed term tenancy; and

(e) under which, subject to the following provisions of this Part of this Act, the other terms are the same as those of the fixed term tenancy immediately before it came to an end, except that any term which makes provision for determination by the landlord or the tenant shall not have effect while the tenancy remains an assured tenancy.

(4) The periodic tenancy ref\rt of this Act to a statutory periodic tenancy is a reference to a periodic tenancy arising by virtue of this section.

15—Limited prohibition on assignment etc. without consent.

(1) Subject to subsection (3) below, it shall be an implied term of every assured tenancy which is a periodic tenancy that, except with the consent of the landlord, the tenant shall not—

    (a) assign the tenancy (in whole or in part); or

    (b) sub-let or part with possession of the whole or any part of the dwelling-house let on the tenancy.

(2) Section 19 of the Landlord and Tenant Act 1927 (consents to assign not to be unreasonably withheld etc.) shall not apply to a term which is implied into an assured tenancy by subsection (1) above.

(3) In the case of a periodic tenancy which is not a statutory periodic tenancy [or an assured periodic tenancy arising under Schedule 10 to the Local Government and Housing Act 1989] subsection (1) above does not apply if—

    (a) there is a provision (whether contained in the tenancy or not) under which the tenant is prohibited (whether absolutely or conditionally) from assigning or sub-letting or parting with possession or is permitted (whether absolutely or conditionally) to assign, sub-let or part with possession; or

    (b) a premium is required to be paid on the grant or renewal of the tenancy.

(4) In subsection (3)(b) above *premium* includes—

    (a) any fine or other like sum;

    (b) any other pecuniary consideration in addition to rent; and

    (c) any sum paid by way of deposit, other than one which does not exceed one-sixth of the annual rent payable under the tenancy immediately after the grant or renewal in question.

15A Loss of assured tenancy status

(1) Subsection (2) applies if, in breach of an express or implied term of the tenancy, a tenant of a dwelling-house let under an assured tenancy to which this section applies—

    (a) parts with possession of the dwelling-house, or

    (b) sub-lets the whole of the dwelling-house (or sub-lets first part of it and then the remainder).

(2) The tenancy ceases to be an assured tenancy and cannot subsequently become an assured tenancy.

(3) This section applies to an assured tenancy—

  (a) under which the landlord is a private registered provider of social housing or a registered social landlord, and

  (b) which is not a shared ownership lease.

(4) In this section *registered social landlord* has the same meaning as in Part 1 of the Housing Act 1996.

(5) In this section *shared ownership lease* means a lease of a dwelling house—

  (a) granted on payment of a premium calculated by reference to a percentage of the value of the dwelling-house or of the cost of providing it, or

  (b) under which the lessee (or the lessee's personal representatives) will or may be entitled to a sum calculated by reference, directly or indirectly, to the value of the dwelling-house.

4.   DATA PROTECTION ACT 1998

1—Basic interpretative provisions.

(1) In this Act, unless the context otherwise requires—

data means information which—

  (a) is being processed by means of equipment operating automatically in response to instructions given for that purpose,

  (b) is recorded with the intention that it should be processed by means of such equipment,

  (c) is recorded as part of a relevant filing system or with the intention that it should form part of a relevant filing system,

  (d) does not fall within paragraph (a), (b) or (c) but forms part of an accessible record as defined by section 68; or

  (e) is recorded information held by a public authority and does not fall within any of paragraphs (a) to (d);

data controller means, subject to subsection (4), a person who (either alone or jointly or in common with other persons) determines the purposes for which and the manner in which any personal data are, or are to be, processed;

data processor, in relation to personal data, means any person (other than an employee of the data controller) who processes the data on behalf of the data controller;

data subject means an individual who is the subject of personal data;

personal data means data which relate to a living individual who can be identified—

  (a) from those data, or

  (b) from those data and other information which is in the possession of, or is likely to come into the possession of, the data controller,

and includes any expression of opinion about the individual and any indication of the intentions of the data controller or any other person in respect of the individual;

processing, in relation to information or data, means obtaining, recording or holding the information or data or carrying out any operation or set of operations on the information or data, including—

  (a) organisation, adaptation or alteration of the information or data,

  (b) retrieval, consultation or use of the information or data,

  (c) disclosure of the information or data by transmission, dissemination or otherwise making available, or

  (d) alignment, combination, blocking, erasure or destruction of the information or data;

public authority means a public authority as defined by the Freedom of Information Act 2000 or a Scottish public authority as defined by the Freedom of Information (Scotland) Act 2002;

relevant filing system means any set of information relating to individuals to the extent that, although the information is not processed by means of equipment operating automatically in response to instructions given for that purpose, the set is structured, either by reference to individuals or by reference to criteria relating to individuals, in such a way that specific information relating to a particular individual is readily accessible.

(2) In this Act, unless the context otherwise requires—

  (a) *obtaining* or *recording*, in relation to personal data, includes obtaining or recording the information to be contained in the data, and

  (b) *using* or *disclosing*, in relation to personal data, includes using or disclosing the information contained in the data.

(3) In determining for the purposes of this Act whether any information is recorded with the intention—

  (a) that it should be processed by means of equipment operating automatically in response to instructions given for that purpose, or

  (b) that it should form part of a relevant filing system,

it is immaterial that it is intended to be so processed or to form part of such a system only after being transferred to a country or territory outside the European Economic Area.

(4) Where personal data are processed only for purposes for which they are required by or under any enactment to be processed, the person on whom the obligation to process the data is imposed by or under that enactment is for the purposes of this Act the data controller.

(5) In paragraph (e) of the definition of data in subsection (1), the reference to information held by a public authority shall be construed in accordance with section 3(2) of the Freedom of Information Act 2000 or section 3(2), (4) and (5) of the Freedom of Information (Scotland) Act 2002.

(6) Where

(a) section 7 of the Freedom of Information Act 2000 prevents Parts I to V of that Act or

(b) section 7(1) of the Freedom of Information (Scotland) Act 2002 prevents that Act

from applying to certain information held by a public authority, that information is not to be treated for the purposes of paragraph (e) of the definition of data in subsection (1) as held by a public authority.

2—Sensitive personal data.

In this Act *sensitive personal data* means personal data consisting of information as to—

(a) the racial or ethnic origin of the data subject,

(b) his political opinions,

(c) his religious beliefs or other beliefs of a similar nature,

(d) whether he is a member of a trade union (within the meaning of the Trade Union and Labour Relations (Consolidation) Act 1992),

(e) his physical or mental health or condition,

(f) his sexual life,

(g) the commission or alleged commission by him of any offence, or

(h) any proceedings for any offence committed or alleged to have been committed by him, the disposal of such proceedings or the sentence of any court in such proceedings.

4—The data protection principles.

(1) References in this Act to the data protection principles are to the principles set out in Part I of Schedule 1.

(2) Those principles are to be interpreted in accordance with Part II of Schedule 1.

(3) Schedule 2 (which applies to all personal data) and Schedule 3 (which applies only to sensitive personal data) set out conditions applying for the purposes of the first principle; and Schedule 4 sets out cases in which the eighth principle does not apply.

(4) Subject to section 27(1), it shall be the duty of a data controller to comply with the data protection principles in relation to all personal data with respect to which he is the data controller.

7—Right of access to personal data.

(1) Subject to the following provisions of this section and to sections 8, 9 and 9A, an individual is entitled—

    (a) to be informed by any data controller whether personal data of which that individual is the data subject are being processed by or on behalf of that data controller,

    (b) if that is the case, to be given by the data controller a description of—

        (i)   the personal data of which that individual is the data subject,

        (ii) the purposes for which they are being or are to be processed, and

        (iii) the recipients or classes of recipients to whom they are or may be disclosed,

    (c) to have communicated to him in an intelligible form—

        (i)   the information constituting any personal data of which that individual is the data subject, and

        (ii) any information available to the data controller as to the source of those data, and

    (d) where the processing by automatic means of personal data of which that individual is the data subject for the purpose of evaluating matters relating to him such as, for example, his performance at work, his credit worthiness, his reliability or his conduct, has constituted or is likely to constitute the sole basis for any decision significantly affecting him, to be informed by the data controller of the logic involved in that decision-taking.

(2) A data controller is not obliged to supply any information under subsection (1) unless he has received—

    (a) a request in writing, and

    (b) except in prescribed cases, such fee (not exceeding the prescribed maximum) as he may require.

(3) Where a data controller—

    (a) reasonably requires further information in order to satisfy himself as to the identity of the person making a request under this section and to locate the information which that person seeks, and

    (b) has informed him of that requirement,

the data controller is not obliged to comply with the request unless he is supplied with that further information.

(4) Where a data controller cannot comply with the request without disclosing information relating to another individual who can be identified from that information, he is not obliged to comply with the request unless—

(a) the other individual has consented to the disclosure of the information to the person making the request, or

(b) it is reasonable in all the circumstances to comply with the request without the consent of the other individual.

(5) In subsection (4) the reference to information relating to another individual includes a reference to information identifying that individual as the source of the information sought by the request; and that subsection is not to be construed as excusing a data controller from communicating so much of the information sought by the request as can be communicated without disclosing the identity of the other individual concerned, whether by the omission of names or other identifying particulars or otherwise.

(6) In determining for the purposes of subsection (4)(b) whether it is reasonable in all the circumstances to comply with the request without the consent of the other individual concerned, regard shall be had, in particular, to—

(a) any duty of confidentiality owed to the other individual,

(b) any steps taken by the data controller with a view to seeking the consent of the other individual,

(c) whether the other individual is capable of giving consent, and

(d) any express refusal of consent by the other individual.

(7) An individual making a request under this section may, in such cases as may be prescribed, specify that his request is limited to personal data of any prescribed description.

(8) Subject to subsection (4), a data controller shall comply with a request under this section promptly and in any event before the end of the prescribed period beginning with the relevant day.

(9) If a court is satisfied on the application of any person who has made a request under the foregoing provisions of this section that the data controller in question has failed to comply with the request in contravention of those provisions, the court may order him to comply with the request.

(10) In this section—

prescribed means prescribed by the [Secretary of State] ³ by regulations ;

the prescribed maximum means such amount as may be prescribed;

the prescribed period means forty days or such other period as may be prescribed;

the relevant day, in relation to a request under this section, means the day on which the data controller receives the request or, if later, the first day on which the data controller has both the required fee and the information referred to in subsection (3).

(11) Different amounts or periods may be prescribed under this section in relation to different cases.

29—Crime and taxation.

(1) Personal data processed for any of the following purposes—

    (a) the prevention or detection of crime,

    (b) the apprehension or prosecution of offenders, or

    (c) the assessment or collection of any tax or duty or of any imposition of a similar nature,

are exempt from the first data protection principle (except to the extent to which it requires compliance with the conditions in Schedules 2 and 3) and section 7 in any case to the extent to which the application of those provisions to the data would be likely to prejudice any of the matters mentioned in this subsection.

(2) Personal data which—

    (a) are processed for the purpose of discharging statutory functions, and

    (b) consist of information obtained for such a purpose from a person who had it in his possession for any of the purposes mentioned in subsection (1),

are exempt from the subject information provisions to the same extent as personal data processed for any of the purposes mentioned in that subsection.

(3) Personal data are exempt from the non-disclosure provisions in any case in which—

    (a) the disclosure is for any of the purposes mentioned in subsection (1), and

    (b) the application of those provisions in relation to the disclosure would be likely to prejudice any of the matters mentioned in that subsection.

(4) Personal data in respect of which the data controller is a relevant authority and which—

    (a) consist of a classification applied to the data subject as part of a system of risk assessment which is operated by that authority for either of the following purposes—

        (i) the assessment or collection of any tax or duty or any imposition of a similar nature, or

        (ii) the prevention or detection of crime, or apprehension or prosecution of offenders, where the offence concerned involves any unlawful claim for any payment out of, or any unlawful application of, public funds, and

    (b) are processed for either of those purposes,

are exempt from section 7 to the extent to which the exemption is required in the interests of the operation of the system.

(5) In subsection (4)—

public funds includes funds provided by any [EU] 1 institution ;

relevant authority means—

(a) a government department,

(b) a local authority, or

(c) any other authority administering housing benefit or council tax benefit.

35—Disclosures required by law or made in connection with legal proceedings etc.

(1) Personal data are exempt from the non-disclosure provisions where the disclosure is required by or under any enactment, by any rule of law or by the order of a court.

(2) Personal data are exempt from the non-disclosure provisions where the disclosure is necessary—

(a) for the purpose of, or in connection with, any legal proceedings (including prospective legal proceedings), or

(b) for the purpose of obtaining legal advice,

or is otherwise necessary for the purposes of establishing, exercising or defending legal rights.

SCHEDULE I THE DATA PROTECTION PRINCIPLES – PART I

First Principle

1—(1) In determining for the purposes of the first principle whether personal data are processed fairly, regard is to be had to the method by which they are obtained, including in particular whether any person from whom they are obtained is deceived or misled as to the purpose or purposes for which they are to be processed.

(2) Subject to paragraph 2, for the purposes of the first principle data are to be treated as obtained fairly if they consist of information obtained from a person who—

(a) is authorised by or under any enactment to supply it, or

(b) is required to supply it by or under any enactment or by any convention or other instrument imposing an international obligation on the United Kingdom.

2—(1) Subject to paragraph 3, for the purposes of the first principle personal data are not to be treated as processed fairly unless—

(a) in the case of data obtained from the data subject, the data controller ensures so far as practicable that the data subject has, is provided with, or has made readily available to him, the information specified in sub-paragraph (3), and

(b) in any other case, the data controller ensures so far as practicable that, before the relevant time or as soon as practicable after that time, the data subject has, is provided with, or has made readily available to him, the information specified in sub-paragraph (3).

(2) In sub-paragraph (1)(b) the relevant time means—

(a) the time when the data controller first processes the data, or

(b) in a case where at that time disclosure to a third party within a reasonable period is envisaged—

(i) if the data are in fact disclosed to such a person within that period, the time when the data are first disclosed,

(ii) if within that period the data controller becomes, or ought to become, aware that the data are unlikely to be disclosed to such a person within that period, the time when the data controller does become, or ought to become, so aware, or

(iii) in any other case, the end of that period.

(3) The information referred to in sub-paragraph (1) is as follows, namely—

(a) the identity of the data controller,

(b) if he has nominated a representative for the purposes of this Act, the identity of that representative,

(c) the purpose or purposes for which the data are intended to be processed, and

(d) any further information which is necessary, having regard to the specific circumstances in which the data are or are to be processed, to enable processing in respect of the data subject to be fair.

3—(1) Paragraph 2(1)(b) does not apply where either of the primary conditions in sub-paragraph (2), together with such further conditions as may be prescribed by the [Secretary of State] [1] by order, are met.

(2) The primary conditions referred to in sub-paragraph (1) are—

(a) that the provision of that information would involve a disproportionate effort, or

(b) that the recording of the information to be contained in the data by, or the disclosure of the data by, the data controller is necessary for compliance with any legal obligation to which the data controller is subject, other than an obligation imposed by contract.

4—(1) Personal data which contain a general identifier falling within a description prescribed by the [Secretary of State] [1] by order are not to be treated as processed fairly and lawfully unless they are processed in compliance with any conditions so prescribed in relation to general identifiers of that description.

(2) In sub-paragraph (1) a general identifier means any identifier (such as, for example, a number or code used for identification purposes) which—

(a) relates to an individual, and

(b) forms part of a set of similar identifiers which is of general application.

Second Principle

5. The purpose or purposes for which personal data are obtained may in particular be specified—

(a) in a notice given for the purposes of paragraph 2 by the data controller to the data subject, or

(b) in a notification given to the Commissioner under Part III of this Act.

6. In determining whether any disclosure of personal data is compatible with the purpose or purposes for which the data were obtained, regard is to be had to the purpose or purposes for which the personal data are intended to be processed by any person to whom they are disclosed.

Fourth Principle

7. The fourth principle is not to be regarded as being contravened by reason of any inaccuracy in personal data which accurately record information obtained by the data controller from the data subject or a third party in a case where—

(a) having regard to the purpose or purposes for which the data were obtained and further processed, the data controller has taken reasonable steps to ensure the accuracy of the data, and

(b) if the data subject has notified the data controller of the data subject's view that the data are inaccurate, the data indicate that fact.

Sixth Principle

8. A person is to be regarded as contravening the sixth principle if, but only if—

(a) he contravenes section 7 by failing to supply information in accordance with that section,

(b) he contravenes section 10 by failing to comply with a notice given under subsection (1) of that section to the extent that the notice is justified or by failing to give a notice under subsection (3) of that section,

(c) he contravenes section 11 by failing to comply with a notice given under subsection (1) of that section, or

    (d) he contravenes section 12 by failing to comply with a notice given under subsection (1) or (2)(b) of that section or by failing to give a notification under subsection (2)(a) of that section or a notice under subsection (3) of that section.

Seventh Principle

9. Having regard to the state of technological development and the cost of implementing any measures, the measures must ensure a level of security appropriate to—

    (a) the harm that might result from such unauthorised or unlawful processing or accidental loss, destruction or damage as are mentioned in the seventh principle, and

    (b) the nature of the data to be protected.

10. The data controller must take reasonable steps to ensure the reliability of any employees of his who have access to the personal data.

11. Where processing of personal data is carried out by a data processor on behalf of a data controller, the data controller must in order to comply with the seventh principle—

    (a) choose a data processor providing sufficient guarantees in respect of the technical and organisational security measures governing the processing to be carried out, and

    (b) take reasonable steps to ensure compliance with those measures.

12. Where processing of personal data is carried out by a data processor on behalf of a data controller, the data controller is not to be regarded as complying with the seventh principle unless—

    (a) the processing is carried out under a contract—

        (i) which is made or evidenced in writing, and

        (ii) under which the data processor is to act only on instructions from the data controller, and

    (b) the contract requires the data processor to comply with obligations equivalent to those imposed on a data controller by the seventh principle.

Eighth Principle

13. An adequate level of protection is one which is adequate in all the circumstances of the case, having regard in particular to—

    (a) the nature of the personal data,

    (b) the country or territory of origin of the information contained in the data,

(c) the country or territory of final destination of that information,

(d) the purposes for which and period during which the data are intended to be processed,

(e) the law in force in the country or territory in question,

(f) the international obligations of that country or territory,

(g) any relevant codes of conduct or other rules which are enforceable in that country or territory (whether generally or by arrangement in particular cases), and

(h) any security measures taken in respect of the data in that country or territory.

14 The eighth principle does not apply to a transfer falling within any paragraph of Schedule 4 , except in such circumstances and to such extent as the [Secretary of State] may by order provide.

15—(1) Where—

(a) in any proceedings under this Act any question arises as to whether the requirement of the eighth principle as to an adequate level of protection is met in relation to the transfer of any personal data to a country or territory outside the European Economic Area, and

(b) a Community finding has been made in relation to transfers of the kind in question,

that question is to be determined in accordance with that finding.

(2) In sub-paragraph (1) Community finding means a finding of the European Commission, under the procedure provided for in Article 31(2) of the Data Protection Directive, that a country or territory outside the European Economic Area does, or does not, ensure an adequate level of protection within the meaning of Article 25(2) of the Directive.

SCHEDULE 1:THE DATA PROTECTION PRINCIPLES – PART II INTERPRETATION OF THE PRINCIPLES IN PART I

First Principle

1—(1) In determining for the purposes of the first principle whether personal data are processed fairly, regard is to be had to the method by which they are obtained, including in particular whether any person from whom they are obtained is deceived or misled as to the purpose or purposes for which they are to be processed.

(2) Subject to paragraph 2, for the purposes of the first principle data are to be treated as obtained fairly if they consist of information obtained from a person who—

(a) is authorised by or under any enactment to supply it, or

(b) is required to supply it by or under any enactment or by any convention or other instrument imposing an international obligation on the United Kingdom.

2—(1) Subject to paragraph 3, for the purposes of the first principle personal data are not to be treated as processed fairly unless—

(a) in the case of data obtained from the data subject, the data controller ensures so far as practicable that the data subject has, is provided with, or has made readily available to him, the information specified in sub-paragraph (3), and

(b) in any other case, the data controller ensures so far as practicable that, before the relevant time or as soon as practicable after that time, the data subject has, is provided with, or has made readily available to him, the information specified in sub-paragraph (3).

(2) In sub-paragraph (1)(b) the relevant time means—

(a) the time when the data controller first processes the data, or

(b) in a case where at that time disclosure to a third party within a reasonable period is envisaged—

(i) if the data are in fact disclosed to such a person within that period, the time when the data are first disclosed,

(ii) if within that period the data controller becomes, or ought to become, aware that the data are unlikely to be disclosed to such a person within that period, the time when the data controller does become, or ought to become, so aware, or

(iii) in any other case, the end of that period.

(3) The information referred to in sub-paragraph (1) is as follows, namely—

(a) the identity of the data controller,

(b) if he has nominated a representative for the purposes of this Act, the identity of that representative,

(c) the purpose or purposes for which the data are intended to be processed, and

(d) any further information which is necessary, having regard to the specific circumstances in which the data are or are to be processed, to enable processing in respect of the data subject to be fair.

3—(1) Paragraph 2(1)(b) does not apply where either of the primary conditions in sub-paragraph (2), together with such further conditions as may be prescribed by the Secretary of State by order, are met.

(2) The primary conditions referred to in sub-paragraph (1) are—

(a) that the provision of that information would involve a disproportionate effort, or

(b) that the recording of the information to be contained in the data by, or the disclosure of the data by, the data controller is necessary for compliance with any legal obligation to which the data controller is subject, other than an obligation imposed by contract.

4—(1) Personal data which contain a general identifier falling within a description prescribed by the Secretary of State by order are not to be treated as processed fairly and lawfully unless they are processed in compliance with any conditions so prescribed in relation to general identifiers of that description.

(2) In sub-paragraph (1) a general identifier means any identifier (such as, for example, a number or code used for identification purposes) which—

(a) relates to an individual, and

(b) forms part of a set of similar identifiers which is of general application.

Second Principle

5 The purpose or purposes for which personal data are obtained may in particular be specified—

(a) in a notice given for the purposes of paragraph 2 by the data controller to the data subject, or

(b) in a notification given to the Commissioner under Part III of this Act.

6 In determining whether any disclosure of personal data is compatible with the purpose or purposes for which the data were obtained, regard is to be had to the purpose or purposes for which the personal data are intended to be processed by any person to whom they are disclosed.

Fourth Principle

7 The fourth principle is not to be regarded as being contravened by reason of any inaccuracy in personal data which accurately record information obtained by the data controller from the data subject or a third party in a case where—

(a) having regard to the purpose or purposes for which the data were obtained and further processed, the data controller has taken reasonable steps to ensure the accuracy of the data, and

(b) if the data subject has notified the data controller of the data subject's view that the data are inaccurate, the data indicate that fact.

Sixth Principle

8 A person is to be regarded as contravening the sixth principle if, but only if—

    (a) he contravenes section 7 by failing to supply information in accordance with that section,

    (b) he contravenes section 10 by failing to comply with a notice given under subsection (1) of that section to the extent that the notice is justified or by failing to give a notice under subsection (3) of that section,

    (c) he contravenes section 11 by failing to comply with a notice given under subsection (1) of that section, or

    (d) he contravenes section 12 by failing to comply with a notice given under subsection (1) or (2)(b) of that section or by failing to give a notification under subsection (2)(a) of that section or a notice under subsection (3) of that section.

Seventh Principle

9   Having regard to the state of technological development and the cost of implementing any measures, the measures must ensure a level of security appropriate to—

    (a) the harm that might result from such unauthorised or unlawful processing or accidental loss, destruction or damage as are mentioned in the seventh principle, and

    (b) the nature of the data to be protected.

10 The data controller must take reasonable steps to ensure the reliability of any employees of his who have access to the personal data.

11 Where processing of personal data is carried out by a data processor on behalf of a data controller, the data controller must in order to comply with the seventh principle—

    (a) choose a data processor providing sufficient guarantees in respect of the technical and organisational security measures governing the processing to be carried out, and

    (b) take reasonable steps to ensure compliance with those measures.

12 Where processing of personal data is carried out by a data processor on behalf of a data controller, the data controller is not to be regarded as complying with the seventh principle unless—

    (a) the processing is carried out under a contract—

        (i) which is made or evidenced in writing, and

        (ii) under which the data processor is to act only on instructions from the data controller, and

    (b) the contract requires the data processor to comply with obligations equivalent to those imposed on a data controller by the seventh principle.

Eighth Principle

13 An adequate level of protection is one which is adequate in all the circumstances of the case, having regard in particular to—

(a) the nature of the personal data,

(b) the country or territory of origin of the information contained in the data,

(c) the country or territory of final destination of that information,

(d) the purposes for which and period during which the data are intended to be processed,

(e) the law in force in the country or territory in question,

(f) the international obligations of that country or territory,

(g) any relevant codes of conduct or other rules which are enforceable in that country or territory (whether generally or by arrangement in particular cases), and

(h) any security measures taken in respect of the data in that country or territory.

14 The eighth principle does not apply to a transfer falling within any paragraph of Schedule 4, except in such circumstances and to such extent as the [Secretary of State] [1] may by order provide.

15—(1) Where—

(a) in any proceedings under this Act any question arises as to whether the requirement of the eighth principle as to an adequate level of protection is met in relation to the transfer of any personal data to a country or territory outside the European Economic Area, and

(b) a Community finding has been made in relation to transfers of the kind in question,

that question is to be determined in accordance with that finding.

(2) In sub-paragraph (1) Community finding means a finding of the European Commission, under the procedure provided for in Article 31(2) of the Data Protection Directive, that a country or territory outside the European Economic Area does, or does not, ensure an adequate level of protection within the meaning of Article 25(2) of the Directive.

SCHEDULE 3 CONDITIONS RELEVANT FOR PURPOSES OF THE FIRST PRINCIPLE: PROCESSING OF SENSITIVE PERSONAL DATA

1. The data subject has given his explicit consent to the processing of the personal data.

2—(1) The processing is necessary for the purposes of exercising or performing any right or obligation which is conferred or imposed by law on the data controller in connection with employment.

(2) The Secretary of State may by order—

    (a) exclude the application of sub-paragraph (1) in such cases as may be specified, or

    (b) provide that, in such cases as may be specified, the condition in sub-paragraph (1) is not to be regarded as satisfied unless such further conditions as may be specified in the order are also satisfied.

3.   The processing is necessary—

    (a) in order to protect the vital interests of the data subject or another person, in a case where—

        (i) consent cannot be given by or on behalf of the data subject, or

        (ii) the data controller cannot reasonably be expected to obtain the consent of the data subject, or

    (b) in order to protect the vital interests of another person, in a case where consent by or on behalf of the data subject has been unreasonably withheld.

4.   The processing—

    (a) is carried out in the course of its legitimate activities by any body or association which—

    (i) is not established or conducted for profit, and

    (ii) exists for political, philosophical, religious or trade-union purposes,

    (b) is carried out with appropriate safeguards for the rights and freedoms of data subjects,

    (c) relates only to individuals who either are members of the body or association or have regular contact with it in connection with its purposes, and

    (d) does not involve disclosure of the personal data to a third party without the consent of the data subject.

5   The information contained in the personal data has been made public as a result of steps deliberately taken by the data subject.

6   The processing—

    (a) is necessary for the purpose of, or in connection with, any legal proceedings (including prospective legal proceedings),

    (b) is necessary for the purpose of obtaining legal advice, or

    (c) is otherwise necessary for the purposes of establishing, exercising or defending legal rights.

7—(1) The processing is necessary—

    (a) for the administration of justice,

    (aa) for the exercise of any functions of either House of Parliament,

(b) for the exercise of any functions conferred on any person by or under an enactment, or

(c) for the exercise of any functions of the Crown, a Minister of the Crown or a government department.

(2) The Secretary of State may by order—

(a) exclude the application of sub-paragraph (1) in such cases as may be specified, or

(b) provide that, in such cases as may be specified, the condition in sub-paragraph (1) is not to be regarded as satisfied unless such further conditions as may be specified in the order are also satisfied.

7A—(1) The processing—

(a) is either–

(i) the disclosure of sensitive personal data by a person as a member of an anti-fraud organisation or otherwise in accordance with any arrangements made by such an organisation; or

(ii) any other processing by that person or another person of sensitive personal data so disclosed; and

(b) is necessary for the purposes of preventing fraud or a particular kind of fraud.

(2) In this paragraph *an anti-fraud organisation* means any unincorporated association, body corporate or other person which enables or facilitates any sharing of information to prevent fraud or a particular kind of fraud or which has any of these functions as its purpose or one of its purposes.

7B The processing is necessary for the purposes of making a disclosure in good faith under a power conferred by—

(a) section 21CA of the Terrorism Act 2000 (disclosures between certain entities within regulated sector in relation to suspicion of commission of terrorist financing offence or for purposes of identifying terrorist property), or

(b) section 339ZB of the Proceeds of Crime Act 2002 (disclosures within regulated sector in relation to money laundering suspicion).

8—(1) The processing is necessary for medical purposes and is undertaken by—

(a) a health professional, or

(b) a person who in the circumstances owes a duty of confidentiality which is equivalent to that which would arise if that person were a health professional.

(2) In this paragraph, medical purposes includes the purposes of preventative medicine, medical diagnosis, medical research, the provision of care and treatment and the management of health care services.

163

9—(1) The processing—

    (a) is of sensitive personal data consisting of information as to racial or ethnic origin,

    (b) is necessary for the purpose of identifying or keeping under review the existence or absence of equality of opportunity or treatment between persons of different racial or ethnic origins, with a view to enabling such equality to be promoted or maintained, and

    (c) is carried out with appropriate safeguards for the rights and freedoms of data subjects.

(2) The Secretary of State may by order specify circumstances in which processing falling within sub-paragraph (1)(a) and (b) is, or is not, to be taken for the purposes of sub-paragraph (1)(c) to be carried out with appropriate safeguards for the rights and freedoms of data subjects.

10 The personal data are processed in circumstances specified in an order made by the Secretary of State for the purposes of this paragraph.

5.   FRAUD ACT 2006

1 Fraud

(1) A person is guilty of *fraud* if he is in breach of any of the sections listed in subsection (2) (which provide for different ways of committing the offence).

(2) The sections are–

    (a) section 2 (fraud by false representation),

    (b) section 3 (fraud by failing to disclose information), and

    (c) section 4 (fraud by abuse of position).

(3) A person who is guilty of fraud is liable–

    (a) on summary conviction, to imprisonment for a term not exceeding 12 months or to a fine not exceeding the statutory maximum (or to both);

    (b) on conviction on indictment, to imprisonment for a term not exceeding 10 years or to a fine (or to both).

(4) Subsection (3)(a) applies in relation to Northern Ireland as if the reference to 12 months were a reference to 6 months.

2 Fraud by false representation

(1) A person is in breach of this section if he–

    (a) dishonestly makes a false representation, and

    (b) intends, by making the representation–

        (i) to make a gain for himself or another, or

      (ii) to cause loss to another or to expose another to a risk of loss.

(2) A representation is false if–

    (a) it is untrue or misleading, and

    (b) the person making it knows that it is, or might be, untrue or misleading.

(3) *Representation* means any representation as to fact or law, including a representation as to the state of mind of–

    (a) the person making the representation, or

    (b) any other person.

(4) A representation may be express or implied.

(5) For the purposes of this section a representation may be regarded as made if it (or anything implying it) is submitted in any form to any system or device designed to receive, convey or respond to communications (with or without human intervention).

3 Fraud by failing to disclose information

A person is in breach of this section if he–

    (a) dishonestly fails to disclose to another person information which he is under a legal duty to disclose, and

    (b) intends, by failing to disclose the information–

      (i) to make a gain for himself or another, or

      (ii) to cause loss to another or to expose another to a risk of loss.

4 Fraud by abuse of position

(1) A person is in breach of this section if he–

    (a) occupies a position in which he is expected to safeguard, or not to act against, the financial interests of another person,

    (b) dishonestly abuses that position, and

    (c) intends, by means of the abuse of that position–

      (i) to make a gain for himself or another, or

      (ii) to cause loss to another or to expose another to a risk of loss.

(2) A person may be regarded as having abused his position even though his conduct consisted of an omission rather than an act.

5 Gain and loss

(1) The references to gain and loss in sections 2 to 4 are to be read in accordance with this section.

(2) *Gain* and *loss*–

    (a) extend only to gain or loss in money or other property;

    (b) include any such gain or loss whether temporary or permanent;

and *property* means any property whether real or personal (including things in action and other intangible property).

(3) *Gain* includes a gain by keeping what one has, as well as a gain by getting what one does not have.

(4) *Loss* includes a loss by not getting what one might get, as well as a loss by parting with what one has.

6. PREVENTION OF SOCIAL HOUSING FRAUD ACT 2013

1 Unlawful sub-letting: secure tenancies

(1) A tenant of a dwelling-house let under a secure tenancy commits an offence if—

    (a) in breach of an express or implied term of the tenancy, the tenant sublets or parts with possession of—

        (i) the whole of the dwelling-house, or

        (ii) part of the dwelling-house without the landlord's written consent,

    (b) the tenant ceases to occupy the dwelling-house as the tenant's only or principal home, and

    (c) the tenant knows that the conduct described in paragraph (a) is a breach of a term of the tenancy.

(2) A tenant of a dwelling-house let under a secure tenancy commits an offence if—

    (a) dishonestly and in breach of an express or implied term of the tenancy, the tenant sub-lets or parts with possession of—

        (i) the whole of the dwelling-house, or

        (ii) part of the dwelling-house without the landlord's written consent, and

    (b) the tenant ceases to occupy the dwelling-house as the tenant's only or principal home.

(3) The offence under subsection (1) is not committed where the tenant takes the action described in paragraphs (a) and (b) of that subsection because of violence or threats of violence by a person residing in, or in the locality of, the dwelling-house—

    (a) towards the tenant, or

(b) towards a member of the family of the tenant who was residing with the tenant immediately before the tenant ceased to occupy the dwelling-house.

(4) The offence under subsection (1) is not committed if a person (P) who occupies the dwelling-house as a result of the conduct described in subsection (1)(a) is—

    (a) a person entitled to apply to the court for an order giving P a right to occupy the dwelling-house or to have the tenancy transferred to P, or

    (b) a person in respect of whom an application may be made to have the tenancy transferred to P or to another person to be held for P's benefit.

(5) A person convicted of an offence under subsection (1) is liable on summary conviction to a fine not exceeding level 5 on the standard scale.

(6) A person convicted of an offence under subsection (2) is liable—

    (a) on summary conviction, to imprisonment for a term not exceeding 6 months or a fine not exceeding the statutory maximum (or both);

    (b) on conviction on indictment, to imprisonment for a term not exceeding 2 years or a fine (or both).

2 Unlawful sub-letting: assured tenancies

(1) A tenant of a dwelling-house let under an assured tenancy to which this section applies commits an offence if—

    (a) in breach of an express or implied term of the tenancy, the tenant sublets or parts with possession of the whole or part of the dwelling-house,

    (b) the tenant ceases to occupy the dwelling-house as the tenant's only or principal home, and

    (c) the tenant knows that the conduct described in paragraph (a) is a breach of a term of the tenancy.

(2) A tenant of a dwelling-house let under an assured tenancy to which this section applies commits an offence if—

    (a) dishonestly and in breach of an express or implied term of the tenancy, the tenant sub-lets or parts with possession of the whole or part of the dwelling-house, and

    (b) the tenant ceases to occupy the dwelling-house as the tenant's only or principal home.

(3) This section applies to an assured tenancy—

    (a) under which the landlord is a private registered provider of social housing or a registered social landlord, and

    (b) which is not a shared ownership lease.

(4) The offence under subsection (1) is not committed where the tenant takes the action described in paragraphs (a) and (b) of that subsection because of

violence or threats of violence by a person residing in, or in the locality of, the dwelling-house—

    (a) towards the tenant, or

    (b) towards a member of the family of the tenant who was residing with the tenant immediately before the tenant ceased to occupy the dwelling-house.

(5) The offence under subsection (1) is not committed if a person (P) who occupies the dwelling-house as a result of the conduct described in subsection (1)(a) is—

    (a) a person entitled to apply to the court for an order giving P a right to occupy the dwelling-house or to have the tenancy transferred to P, or

    (b) a person in respect of whom an application may be made to have the tenancy transferred to P or to another person to be held for P's benefit.

(6) A person convicted of an offence under subsection (1) is liable on summary conviction to a fine not exceeding level 5 on the standard scale.

(7) A person convicted of an offence under subsection (2) is liable—

    (a) on summary conviction, to imprisonment for a term not exceeding 6 months or a fine not exceeding the statutory maximum (or both);

    (b) on conviction on indictment, to imprisonment for a term not exceeding 2 years or a fine (or both).

3 Prosecution of offences

(1) Proceedings for an offence under section 1(1) or 2(1) may be brought within the period of 6 months beginning with the date on which evidence sufficient in the opinion of the prosecutor to warrant the proceedings came to the prosecutor's knowledge.

(2) But no such proceedings may be brought more than three years—

    (a) after the commission of the offence, or

    (b) in the case of continuous contravention, after the last date on which the offence was committed.

(3) A certificate signed by the prosecutor and stating the date on which such evidence came to the prosecutor's knowledge is conclusive evidence of that fact; and a certificate to that effect and purporting to be so signed is to be treated as being so signed unless the contrary is proved.

(4) Subsections (1) to (3) also apply in relation to an associated offence which is a summary offence (to the extent that they would not otherwise apply to that offence).

(5) A local authority may prosecute an offence under section 1 or 2 in relation to a dwelling-house—

    (a) whether or not the dwelling-house is or was let under a tenancy under which the local authority is or was the landlord, and

(b) whether or not the dwelling-house is located in the local authority's area.

(6) Subsection (5) also applies in relation to an associated offence (to the extent that it would not otherwise apply to that offence).

4 Unlawful profit orders: criminal proceedings

(1) This section applies if a person (the offender) is convicted of—

(a) an offence under section 1 or 2, or

(b) an associated offence in relation to an offence under section 1 or 2.

(2) The court by or before which the offender is convicted—

(a) must, on application or otherwise, decide whether to make an unlawful profit order, and

(b) may, if it considers it appropriate to do so, make such an order, instead of or in addition to dealing with the offender in any other way.

(3) An *unlawful profit order* is an order requiring the offender to pay the landlord an amount representing the profit made by the offender as a result of the conduct constituting the offence.

(4) If the court decides not to make an unlawful profit order, it must give reasons for that decision on passing sentence on the offender.

(5) The amount payable under an unlawful profit order must be such amount as the court considers appropriate, having regard to any evidence and to any representations that are made by or on behalf of the offender or the prosecutor, but subject to subsections (6) and (7).

(6) The maximum amount payable under an unlawful profit order is calculated as follows—

Step 1

Determine the total amount the offender received as a result of the conduct constituting the offence (or the best estimate of that amount).

Step 2

Deduct from the amount determined under step 1 the total amount, if any, paid by the offender as rent to the landlord (including service charges) over the period during which the offence was committed.

(7) Where an unlawful profit order has been made against the offender under section 5, an order under this section may only provide for the landlord to recover an amount equal to the aggregate of the following—

(a) any amount by which the amount of the offender's profit found under this section exceeds the amount payable under the order made under section 5, and

(b) a sum equal to any portion of the amount payable under the order made under section 5 that the landlord fails to recover,

169

and the landlord may not enforce the order under this section, so far as it relates to a sum mentioned in paragraph (b), without the leave of the court.

(8) Subsection (9) applies where the court considers—

    (a) that, as well as being appropriate to make an unlawful profit order, it would be appropriate to impose a fine, and

    (b) that the offender has insufficient means to pay both—

        (i) an appropriate sum under an unlawful profit order, and

        (ii) an appropriate sum under a fine.

(9) The court must give preference to making an unlawful profit order (though it may impose a fine as well).

(10) If the amount required to be paid by a person under an unlawful profit order is not paid when it is required to be paid, that person must pay interest on the amount for the period for which it remains unpaid.

(11) The rate of interest is the same rate as that for the time being specified in section 17 of the Judgments Act 1838 (interest on civil judgment debts).

(12) Sections 131 to 133 of the Powers of Criminal Courts (Sentencing) Act 2000 (supplementary provisions about compensation orders) apply to unlawful profit orders as if—

    (a) references to a compensation order were to an unlawful profit order (subject to paragraph (d)),

    (b) references to the compensation to be paid under a compensation order were to the amount to be paid under an unlawful profit order,

    (c) section 133(3)(a) and (b) were omitted, and

    (d) the reference in section 133(3)(c)(ii) to an unlawful profit order under section 4 were to a compensation order under section 130 of the Powers of Criminal Courts (Sentencing) Act 2000.

(13) In this section *the landlord* means the landlord under the tenancy in respect of which the offence was committed.

5 Unlawful profit orders: civil proceedings

(1) The court may, on the application of the landlord of a dwelling-house let under a secure or an assured tenancy, make an unlawful profit order if—

    (a) in the case of a secure tenancy, the conditions in subsection (3) are met, and

    (b) in the case of an assured tenancy, the conditions in subsection (4) are met.

(2) An *unlawful profit order* is an order requiring the tenant against whom it is made to pay the landlord an amount representing the profit made by the tenant from the conduct described in subsection (3)(a) or (4)(c).

(3) The conditions in the case of a secure tenancy are that a tenant under the tenancy—

   (a) in breach of an express or implied term of the tenancy, has sub-let or parted with possession of—

      (i) the whole of the dwelling-house, or

      (ii) part of the dwelling-house without the landlord's written consent,

   (b) has ceased to occupy the dwelling-house as the tenant's only or principal home, and

   (c) has received money as a result of the conduct described in paragraph (a).

(4) The conditions in the case of an assured tenancy are that—

   (a) the landlord is a private registered provider of social housing or a registered social landlord,

   (b) the tenancy is not a shared ownership lease,

   (c) in breach of an express or implied term of the tenancy, a tenant under the tenancy has sub-let or parted with possession of the whole or part of the dwelling-house,

   (d) the tenant has ceased to occupy the dwelling-house as the tenant's only or principal home, and

   (e) the tenant has received money as a result of the conduct described in paragraph (c).

(5) The amount payable under an unlawful profit order must be such amount as the court considers appropriate, having regard to any evidence and to any representations that are made by or on behalf of the landlord or the tenant, but subject to subsections (6) and (7).

(6) The maximum amount payable under an unlawful profit order is calculated as follows—

Step 1

Determine the total amount the tenant received as a result of the conduct described in subsection (3)(a) or (4)(c) (or the best estimate of that amount).

Step 2

Deduct from the amount determined under step 1 the total amount, if any, paid by the tenant as rent to the landlord (including service charges) over the period during which the conduct described in subsection (3)(a) or (4)(c) took place.

(7) Where an unlawful profit order has been made against the tenant under section 4, an order under this section may only provide for the landlord to recover an amount equal to the aggregate of the following—

   (a) any amount by which the amount of the tenant's profit found under this section exceeds the amount payable under the order made under section 4, and

(b) a sum equal to any portion of the amount payable under the order made under section 4 that the landlord fails to recover,

and the landlord may not enforce the order under this section, so far as it relates to a sum mentioned in paragraph (b), without the leave of the court.

(8) For the purposes of this section *the court* means the High Court or the county court.

(9) Section 110(3) of the Housing Act 1985 (by which the claimant in proceedings relating to a secure tenancy may not recover the claimant's costs if the proceedings are taken in the High Court) does not apply to proceedings under this section.

6 Loss of assured tenancy status

After section 15 of the Housing Act 1988 insert—

15A Loss of assured tenancy status

(1) Subsection (2) applies if, in breach of an express or implied term of the tenancy, a tenant of a dwelling-house let under an assured tenancy to which this section applies—

(a) parts with possession of the dwelling-house, or

(b) sub-lets the whole of the dwelling-house (or sub-lets first part of it and then the remainder).

(2) The tenancy ceases to be an assured tenancy and cannot subsequently become an assured tenancy.

(3) This section applies to an assured tenancy—

(a) under which the landlord is a private registered provider of social housing or a registered social landlord, and

(b) which is not a shared ownership lease.

(4) In this section *registered social landlord* has the same meaning as in Part 1 of the Housing Act 1996.

(5) In this section *shared ownership lease* means a lease of a dwelling house—

(a) granted on payment of a premium calculated by reference to a percentage of the value of the dwelling-house or of the cost of providing it, or

(b) under which the lessee (or the lessee's personal representatives) will or may be entitled to a sum calculated by reference, directly or indirectly, to the value of the dwelling-house.

7 Regulations about powers to require information

(1) The appropriate authority may by regulations provide for the exercise, for prescribed housing fraud investigation purposes, of powers to require the provision of information.

172

(2) The appropriate authority may by regulations—

    (a) make provision about the persons by whom powers conferred by regulations under this section may be exercised;

    (b) in particular, make provision for the authorisation by local authorities of persons to exercise those powers.

(3) The provision that may be made by regulations under this section includes, in particular, provision equivalent to—

    (a) provision made by a relevant enactment, or

    (b) provision that is capable of being made under a relevant enactment,

with such modifications as the appropriate authority thinks fit.

(4) For the purposes of subsection (3), each of the following enactments is a relevant enactment—

    (a) section 109B of the Social Security Administration Act 1992 (powers to require information);

    (b) section 110A of that Act (authorisations by local authorities to exercise powers of investigation);

    (c) section 121DA(2) and (3) of that Act (interpretation of Part 6 of that Act).

(5) After the repeal of section 110A of the Social Security Administration Act 1992 by Part 1 of Schedule 14 to the Welfare Reform Act 2012, the reference to that section in subsection (4) is to that section as it had effect immediately before it was repealed.

(6) A person exercising powers conferred by regulations under this section must have regard to guidance issued or approved by the appropriate authority.

(7) In this section *housing fraud investigation purposes* means purposes relating to the prevention, detection or securing of evidence for a conviction of—

    (a) an offence under this Act;

    (b) an offence under the Fraud Act 2006 relating to the unlawful sub-letting or parting with possession of the whole or part of a dwelling-house let by a local authority, a private registered provider of social housing or a registered social landlord,

    (c) an offence under the Fraud Act 2006 relating to an application for an allocation of housing accommodation under Part 6 of the Housing Act 1996,

    (d) an offence under the Fraud Act 2006 relating to an application for accommodation, or for assistance in obtaining accommodation, under Part 7 of the Housing Act 1996 or under Part 2 of the Housing (Wales) Act 2014,

    (e) an offence under the Fraud Act 2006 relating to—

(i) a claim to exercise the right to buy under Part 5 of the Housing Act 1985,

(ii) a claim to exercise the right to acquire under section 16 of the Housing Act 1996, or

(iii) a claim to exercise the right to acquire under section 180 of the Housing and Regeneration Act 2008, or

(f) an associated offence in relation to an offence mentioned in any of paragraphs (a) to (e).

(8) In this section *prescribed* means prescribed by regulations under this section.

8 Regulations about related offence

(1) The appropriate authority may by regulations provide for the creation of an offence that may be committed by a person by refusing or failing to provide any information or document when required to do so by or under regulations under section 7.

(2) Regulations under this section—

(a) must provide for an offence under the regulations to be triable only summarily;

(b) may not provide for such an offence to be punishable with a fine exceeding level 3 on the standard scale.

(3) Regulations under this section—

(a) may provide, in a case where a person is convicted of an offence under the regulations and the act or omission constituting the offence continues after the conviction, for the person to be guilty of a further offence and liable on summary conviction to a daily fine;

(b) may not provide for the daily fine to exceed £40.

(4) The appropriate authority may by regulations make provision—

(a) about defences to an offence under regulations under this section;

(b) about the commission by a body corporate of such an offence;

(c) about the conduct of proceedings for such an offence;

(d) about the time limits for bringing such proceedings;

(e) about the determination of issues arising in such proceedings;

(f) about other matters of procedure and evidence in relation to such an offence.

9 Regulations: supplementary

(1) In sections 7 and 8 *the appropriate authority* means—

(a) the Secretary of State, in relation to England, and

(b) the Welsh Ministers, in relation to Wales.

(2) Regulations under section 7 or 8—

    (a) are to be made by statutory instrument,

    (b) may make different provision for different cases or circumstances, and

    (c) may contain incidental, supplementary, consequential, transitional, transitory or saving provision.

(3) A statutory instrument containing regulations made by the Secretary of State under section 7 or 8 may not be made unless a draft of the instrument has been laid before and approved by a resolution of each House of Parliament.

(4) A statutory instrument containing regulations made by the Welsh Ministers under section 7 or 8 may not be made unless a draft of the instrument has been laid before and approved by a resolution of the National Assembly for Wales.

10 Consequential amendments

The Schedule (consequential amendments) has effect.

11 Interpretation

(1) In this Act—

    (a) *secure tenancy* has the meaning given by section 79 of the Housing Act 1985, and

    (b) *assured tenancy* has the same meaning as in Part 1 of the Housing Act 1988.

(2) In the application of this Act in relation to a secure tenancy, the following expressions have the same meaning as in the Housing Act 1985 — dwelling-house (see section 112 of that Act); landlord (see section 621 of that Act); tenancy (see section 621 of that Act); tenant (see section 621 of that Act).

(3) In the application of this Act in relation to an assured tenancy, the following expressions have the same meaning as in the Housing Act 1988— dwelling-house (see section 45(1) of that Act); landlord (see section 45(1) and (3) of that Act); tenancy (see section 45(1) of that Act); tenant (see section 45(1) and (3) of that Act).

(4) References in this Act to a member of the tenant's family (in relation to a secure or an assured tenancy) are to be construed in accordance with section 113 of the Housing Act 1985.

(5) In this Act *shared ownership lease* means a lease of a dwelling-house—

    (a) granted on payment of a premium calculated by reference to a percentage of the value of the dwelling-house or of the cost of providing it, or

(b) under which the lessee (or the lessee's personal representatives) will or may be entitled to a sum calculated by reference, directly or indirectly, to the value of the dwelling-house.

(6) References in this Act to the landlord under a secure or an assured tenancy include—

(a) in a case where the tenancy has ended, a person who was the landlord under the tenancy, and

(b) in a case where the tenancy has ceased to be a secure or an assured tenancy, the person who was the landlord under the tenancy when it was a secure or an assured tenancy.

(7) References in this Act to the tenant under a secure or an assured tenancy include—

(a) in a case where the tenancy has ended, a person who was the tenant under the tenancy, and

(b) in a case where the tenancy has ceased to be a secure or an assured tenancy, a person who was the tenant under the tenancy when it was a secure or an assured tenancy.

(8) In this Act *local authority* means a county council, a county borough council, a district council, a London borough council, the Common Council of the City of London or the Council of the Isles of Scilly.

(9) In this Act *registered social landlord* has the same meaning as in Part 1 of the Housing Act 1996.

(10) In this Act *associated offence*, in relation to an offence, means—

(a) an offence of aiding, abetting, counselling or procuring the commission of that offence,

(b) an offence of attempting or conspiring to commit that offence, or

(c) an offence under Part 2 of the Serious Crime Act 2007 (encouraging or assisting crime) in relation to that offence.

12 Extent, commencement and short title

(1) This Act extends to England and Wales only, subject to subsection (2).

(2) An amendment of an Act made by this Act has the same extent as the provision to which it relates.

(3) The provisions of this Act, apart from this section, come into force—

(a) in relation to England, on such day as the Secretary of State may by order appoint;

(b) in relation to Wales, on such day as the Welsh Ministers may by order appoint.

(4) An order under subsection (3) is to be made by statutory instrument.

(5) An order under subsection (3) may—

   (a) appoint different days for different purposes, and

   (b) make transitional, transitory or saving provision.

(6) This Act may be cited as the Prevention of Social Housing Fraud Act 2013.

APPENDIX B

Secondary legislation

I. NOTICES TO QUIT ETC. (PRESCRIBED INFORMATION) REGULATIONS 1988/2201 – REGULATION 2, SCH. I

Prevention of Social Housing Fraud (Power to Require Information) (England) Regulations 2014/899 – regulations 3 to 7

1. Notices to Quit etc. (Prescribed Information) Regulations 1988/2201

2. Where, on or after the date these Regulations come into force, a landlord gives a notice to quit any premises let as a dwelling, or a licensor gives a notice to determine a periodic licence to occupy premises as a dwelling (and the premises are not let or occupied as specified in section 5(1B) of the Protection from Eviction Act 1977), the information prescribed for the purposes of section 5 of the Protection from Eviction Act 1977 shall be that in the Schedule to these Regulations.

Schedule 1

1. If the tenant or licensee does not leave the dwelling, the landlord or licensor must get an order for possession from the court before the tenant or licensee can lawfully be evicted. The landlord or licensor cannot apply for such an order before the notice to quit or notice to determine has run out.

2. A tenant or licensee who does not know if he has any right to remain in possession after a notice to quit or a notice to determine runs out can obtain advice from a solicitor. Help with all or part of the cost of legal advice and assistance may be available under the Legal Aid Scheme. He should also be able to obtain information from a Citizens' Advice Bureau, a Housing Aid Centre or a rent officer.

2. PREVENTION OF SOCIAL HOUSING FRAUD (POWER TO REQUIRE INFORMATION) (ENGLAND) REGULATIONS 2014/899
3.— Authorisations by local authorities

(1) Subject to paragraphs (2) and (3), a local authority may grant an authorisation to an individual to exercise the powers conferred on an authorised officer under regulation 4.

(2) A local authority may only grant authorisation to an individual if that person is—

  (a) an individual employed by that authority;

  (b) an individual employed by another local authority or joint committee that carries out functions relating to housing fraud investigation purposes on behalf of that authority.

(3) An authorisation granted to an individual for the purposes of these Regulations—

  (a) must be in writing and provided to that individual as evidence of that individual's entitlement to exercise powers conferred by these Regulations;

  (b) may contain provision as to the period for which the authorisation is to have effect; and,

  (c) may restrict the powers exercisable by virtue of the authorisation so as to prohibit their exercise except for particular purposes or in particular circumstances.

(4) An authorisation may be withdrawn at any time in writing by the local authority that granted it.

(5) The written authorisation or withdrawal of an authorisation by any local authority must be issued under the hand of either—

  (a) the officer designated under section 4 of the Local Government and Housing Act 1989 as the head of the authority's paid service; or

  (b) the officer who is the authority's chief finance officer (within the meaning of section 5 of that Act).

(6) A local authority may grant an authorisation for housing fraud investigation purposes in relation to offences in the area of another local authority, as well as in relation to offences in the area of the authority granting the authorisation.

4.— Power to require information

(1) An authorised officer may exercise the powers conferred by this regulation for any of the housing fraud investigation purposes (but not for any other purpose).

(2) An authorised officer who has reasonable grounds for suspecting that a person—

  (a) is a person falling within paragraph (3) below, and

  (b) has or may have possession of or access to any information about any matter that is relevant to housing fraud investigation purposes,

  may, by written notice, require that person to provide all such information described in the notice of which that person has possession, or to which that person has access, and which it is reasonable for the authorised officer to require for the purpose so mentioned.

(3) The persons who fall within this paragraph are—

   (a) any bank;

   (b) any person carrying on a business the whole or a significant part of which consists in the provision of credit (whether secured or unsecured) to members of the public;

   (c) any water undertaker or sewerage undertaker;

   (d) any person who—

    (i) is the holder of a licence under section 7 of the Gas Act 1986 to convey gas through pipes; or,

    (ii) is the holder of a licence under section 7A of that Act to supply gas through pipes;

   (e) any person who (within the meaning of the Electricity Act 1989) distributes or supplies electricity;

   (f) any person who provides a telecommunications service;

   (g) any servant or agent of any person mentioned in sub-paragraphs (a) to (f).

(4) Subject to the following provisions of this regulation, the powers conferred by this regulation on an authorised officer to require information from any person by virtue of that person falling within paragraph (3) shall be exercisable for the purpose only of obtaining information relating to a particular person identified (by name or description) by the officer.

(5) An authorised officer shall not, in exercise of those powers, require any information from any person by virtue of that person falling within paragraph (3) unless it appears to that officer that there are reasonable grounds for believing that the person to whom it relates is—

   (a) a person who has committed, is committing or intends to commit an offence listed in section 7(7) of the Prevention of Social Housing Fraud Act 2013; or

   (b) a person who is a member of the family of a person falling within sub-paragraph (a).

(6) The powers conferred by this regulation shall not be exercisable for obtaining from any person providing a telecommunications service any information other than information which (within the meaning of section 21 of the Regulation of Investigatory Powers Act 2000) is communications data but not traffic data.

(7) An authorised person may exercise the powers conferred by this regulation to require, from a person who provides a telecommunications service, information about the identity and postal address of a person identified by the authorised officer solely by reference to a telephone number or electronic address used in connection with the provision of such a service.

(8) The obligation of a person to provide information in accordance with a notice under this regulation shall be discharged only by the provision of that

information, at such reasonable time and in such form as may be specified in the notice, to the authorised officer who—

(a) is identified by or in accordance with the terms of the notice; or

(b) has been identified, since the giving of the notice, by a further written notice given by the authorised officer who imposed the original requirement or another authorised officer.

(9) The power of an authorised officer under this regulation to require the provision of information shall include a power to require the production and delivery up and (if necessary) creation of any such documents containing the information as may be specified or described in the notice imposing the requirement, or the creation of copies of or extracts from any such documents.

(10) No person shall be required under this regulation to provide—

(a) any information that tends to incriminate either that person or, in the case of a person who is married or is a civil partner, that person's spouse or civil partner; or

(b) any information in respect of which a claim to legal professional privilege would be successful in any proceedings;

and for the purposes of this paragraph it is immaterial whether the information is in documentary form or not.

(11) In this regulation—

Bank means—

(a) a person who has permission under Part 4A of the Financial Services and Markets Act 2000 4 to accept deposits;

(b) an EEA firm of the kind mentioned in paragraph 5(b) of Schedule 3 to that Act 5 which has permission under paragraph 15 of that Schedule (as a result of qualifying for authorisation under paragraph 12 of that Schedule) to accept deposits or other repayable funds from the public; or

(c) a person who does not require permission under that Act to accept deposits in the course of that person's business in the United Kingdom;

Credit includes a cash loan or any form of financial accommodation, including the cashing of a cheque;

Family is to be construed in accordance with section 113 of the Housing Act 1985;

Telecommunications service has the same meaning as in section 2(1) Regulation of Investigatory Powers Act 2000.

(12) The definition of *bank* in paragraph (11) must be read in accordance with—

(a) section 22 of the Financial Services and Marketing Act 2000;

(b) any relevant order under that section; and

(c) Schedule 2 to that Act.

5—Delay, obstruction etc of an authorised officer

(1) If a person (P) —

    (a) intentionally delays or obstructs an authorised officer in the exercise of any power under regulation 4; or

    (b) refuses or fails, without reasonable excuse, to provide any information or to provide any document when required to do so under regulation 4,

P shall be guilty of an offence and liable on summary conviction to a fine not exceeding level 3 on the standard scale.

(2) Where P is convicted of an offence under paragraph (1)(b) and the refusal or failure is continued by P after P's conviction, P shall be guilty of a further offence and liable on summary conviction to a fine not exceeding £40 for each day on which it is continued.

6—Liability of directors etc.

(1) Where an offence under regulation 5 which has been committed by a body corporate is proved to have been committed with the consent or connivance of, or to be attributable to any neglect on the part of, a director, manager, secretary or other similar officer of the body corporate, or any person who was purporting to act in any such capacity, that person, as well as the body corporate, shall be guilty of that offence and be liable to be proceeded against accordingly.

(2) Where the affairs of a body corporate are managed by its members, paragraph (1) applies in relation to the acts and defaults of a member in connection with that member's functions of management as if that member were a director of the body corporate.

7—Legal proceedings

(1) Proceedings for an offence under regulation 5 may be brought within the period of 6 months beginning with the date on which evidence sufficient in the opinion of the prosecutor to warrant the proceedings came to the prosecutor's knowledge.

(2) But no such proceedings may be brought more than three years —

    (a) after the commission of the offence, or

    (b) in the case of a continuous contravention, after the last date on which the offence was committed.

(3) A certificate signed by the prosecutor and stating the date on which such evidence came to the prosecutor's knowledge is conclusive evidence of that fact; and a certificate to that effect and purporting to be signed is to be treated as being so signed unless the contrary is proved.

Civil Procedure Rules

PART 18 – FURTHER INFORMATION

OBTAINING FURTHER INFORMATION

18.1

(1) The court may at any time order a party to –

  (a) clarify any matter which is in dispute in the proceedings; or

  (b) give additional information in relation to any such matter,

  whether or not the matter is contained or referred to in a statement of case.

(2) Paragraph (1) is subject to any rule of law to the contrary.

(3) Where the court makes an order under paragraph (1), the party against whom it is made must –

  (a) file his response; and

  (b) serve it on the other parties,

  within the time specified by the court.

(Part 22 requires a response to be verified by a statement of truth.)

PRELIMINARY REQUEST FOR FURTHER INFORMATION OR CLARIFICATION

1.1 Before making an application to the court for an order under Part 18, the party seeking clarification or information (the first party) should first serve on the party from whom it is sought (the second party) a written request for that clarification or information (a Request) stating a date by which the response to the Request should be served. The date must allow the second party a reasonable time to respond.

1.2 A Request should be concise and strictly confined to matters which are reasonably necessary and proportionate to enable the first party to prepare his own case or to understand the case he has to meet.

1.3 Requests must be made as far as possible in a single comprehensive document and not piecemeal.

1.4 A Request may be made by letter if the text of the Request is brief and the reply is likely to be brief; otherwise the Request should be made in a separate document.

1.5 If a Request is made in a letter, the letter should, in order to distinguish it from any other that might routinely be written in the course of a case,

(1) state that it contains a Request made under Part 18, and

(2) deal with no matters other than the Request.

1.6

(1) A Request (whether made by letter or in a separate document) must –

 (a) be headed with the name of the court and the title and number of the claim,

 (b) in its heading state that it is a Request made under Part 18, identify the first party and the second party and state the date on which it is made,

 (c) set out in a separate numbered paragraph each request for information or clarification,

 (d) where a Request relates to a document, identify that document and (if relevant) the paragraph or words to which it relates,

 (e) state the date by which the first party expects a response to the Request.

(2) (a) A Request which is not in the form of a letter may, if convenient, be prepared in such a way that the response may be given on the same document.

 (b) To do this the numbered paragraphs of the Request should appear on the left hand half of each sheet so that the paragraphs of the response may then appear on the right.

 (c) Where a Request is prepared in this form an extra copy should be served for the use of the second party.

1.7 Subject to the provisions of rule 6.23(5) and (6) and paragraphs 4.1 to 4.3 of Practice Direction 6A, a request should be served by e-mail if reasonably practicable.

DISCLOSURE BEFORE PROCEEDINGS START

31.16

(1) This rule applies where an application is made to the court under any Act for disclosure before proceedings have started.[1]

(2) The application must be supported by evidence.

(3) The court may make an order under this rule only where–

    (a) the respondent is likely to be a party to subsequent proceedings;

    (b) the applicant is also likely to be a party to those proceedings;

    (c) if proceedings had started, the respondent's duty by way of standard disclosure, set out in rule 31.6, would extend to the documents or classes of documents of which the applicant seeks disclosure; and

    (d) disclosure before proceedings have started is desirable in order to –

        (i)   dispose fairly of the anticipated proceedings;

        (ii) assist the dispute to be resolved without proceedings; or

        (iii) save costs.

(4) An order under this rule must–

    (a) specify the documents or the classes of documents which the respondent must disclose; and

    (b) require him, when making disclosure, to specify any of those documents–

        (i)   which are no longer in his control; or

        (ii) in respect of which he claims a right or duty to withhold inspection.

(5) Such an order may–

    (a) require the respondent to indicate what has happened to any documents which are no longer in his control; and

    (b) specify the time and place for disclosure and inspection.

ORDERS FOR DISCLOSURE AGAINST A PERSON NOT A PARTY

31.17

(1) This rule applies where an application is made to the court under any Act for disclosure by a person who is not a party to the proceedings.[2]

(2) The application must be supported by evidence.

(3) The court may make an order under this rule only where–

    (a) the documents of which disclosure is sought are likely to support the case of the applicant or adversely affect the case of one of the other parties to the proceedings; and

    (b) disclosure is necessary in order to dispose fairly of the claim or to save costs.

(4) An order under this rule must–

    (a) specify the documents or the classes of documents which the respondent must disclose; and

    (b) require the respondent, when making disclosure, to specify any of those documents –

        (i) which are no longer in his control; or

        (ii) in respect of which he claims a right or duty to withhold inspection.

(5) Such an order may–

    (a) require the respondent to indicate what has happened to any documents which are no longer in his control; and

    (b) specify the time and place for disclosure and inspection.

Rule 78.26 contains rules in relation to the disclosure and inspection of evidence arising out of mediation of certain cross-border disputes.

POWER TO CALL WITNESS FOR CROSS-EXAMINATION ON HEARSAY EVIDENCE

33.4

(1) Where a party –

    (a) proposes to rely on hearsay evidence; and

    (b) does not propose to call the person who made the original statement to give oral evidence,

the court may, on the application of any other party, permit that party to call the maker of the statement to be cross-examined on the contents of the statement.

(2) An application for permission to cross-examine under this rule must be made not more than 14 days after the day on which a notice of intention to rely on the hearsay evidence was served on the applicant.

Landlord checklist

- Prepare/update social housing fraud policy.

- Establish data sharing agreements with other relevant organisations/ departments: consider the Information Commissioner's Data Sharing Code of Practice.

- Undertake regular tenancy audits: seek documentary evidence of residence and identity.

- Obtain credit reference reports and electoral information where misuse of premises suspected.

- Speak to neighbours and contractors visiting subject premises.

- Obtain statements from any sub-tenants, and collate relevant documentary evidence (eg tenancy agreement with sub-tenant).

- Seek local authority assistance in obtaining bank, utility, etc. information: refer to Prevention of Social Housing Fraud (Power to Require Information) (England) Regulations 2013.

- Where appropriate seek information from the police on criminal behaviour and incidents concerning the tenant(s) and household, and addresses used by them.

- Interview prospective defendant(s) – request information and consider caution process.

- Check utility usage in only or principal home cases.

- After issuing civil proceedings consider use of Part 18 Request for Information, witness summonses and/or applications for specific (and/or third-party) disclosure.

Index